**50 years of the
replica shirt**

Admiral — 50 years of the replica shirt

Introduction *Adam Bushby and Rob MacDonald*	4
The player pioneer — Peter Shilton interview	10
Admiral and the aesthetic merit of design *Professor Andrew Groves*	12
The advent of the replica shirt market *Professor Jean Williams*	18
Football, fanwear and fashion *Jacqui McAssey*	24
The early years *Adam Bushby*	30

Decade overview: 1970s *Rob MacDonald* — 34

Leeds United '73–'76 *Rob Bagchi*	42
Don built a formidable team – Eddie Gray interview	54
Luton Town '74–'76 *Rob MacDonald*	56
England '74–'80 *Adam Bushby and Rob MacDonald*	60
Unbeaten at Wembley in an Admiral shirt — Gerry Francis interview	66
Making history in Admiral — Viv Anderson interview	68
Manchester United '75–'80 *Rob MacDonald*	70
Bright colours, bright football — Lou Macari interview	76
The Admiral FA Cup Final '76 *Rob MacDonald*	78
Wales '76–'79 *Andi Thomas*	84
Leicester City '76–'79 *Rob MacDonald*	92
The importance of shirts — Gary Lineker interview	96
Dundee '76–'80 *Rob MacDonald*	98
Norwich City '76–'81 *Andrew Lawn*	100
Servette '76–'79 *Adam Bushby*	104
Saudi Arabia '76–'78 *Adam Bushby*	106
West Ham United '76–'80 *Jacob Steinberg*	110
Without doubt, my favourite shirt — Mick Clifford, Collector	118
Simply iconic — Alvin Martin interview	120
Orient '77–'80 *Rob MacDonald*	122
Tottenham Hotspur '77–'80 *Ian King*	124
Crystal Palace '77–'80 *Adam Bushby and Rob MacDonald*	134
Malmö FF '78–'79 *Adam Bushby*	136
Coventry City '78–'80 *Adam Bushby*	140
Like bars of chocolate — Tommy Hutchison interview	148
Admiral and the NASL *Ian Plenderleith*	150

Decade overview: 1980s *Adam Bushby*	**160**
Grimsby Town '80–'81 *Rob MacDonald*	168
FC Dordrecht '80–'81 *Adam Bushby*	170
England '80–'83 *Harry Pearson*	172
Belgium '82 *Adam Bushby*	188
Hull City '82–'86 *Rob MacDonald*	192
Leicester City '83–'88 *Rob MacDonald*	196
Derby County '84–'85 *Phil Lowe*	202
Swansea City '86–'87 *Pete Jones*	206
Decade overview: 1990s *Adam Bushby*	**210**
Rangers '90–'92 *Alasdair McKillop*	218
Its simplicity is iconic — Mark Hateley interview	223
Motherwell '90–'91 *Adam Bushby*	224
Admiral and the Premier League *Daniel Gray*	228
Remembering those first shirts — Alan Shearer interview	238
Heart of Midlothian '92–'93 *Grant Young and Adam Bushby*	240
San Marino '92–'93 *Adam Bushby*	244
Birmingham City '95–'96 *Rob MacDonald*	250
York City '95–'97 *Adam Bushby*	252
Decade overview: 2000– *Rob MacDonald*	**256**
Bristol City '01–'02 *Mark and Paul Watson*	264
Wolverhampton Wanderers '02–'04 *James Bird*	268
Leeds United Women '05–'06 *Maisie Adam*	272
A bittersweet shirt — Sue Smith interview	278
Tampa Bay Rowdies '13 *Adam Bushby*	280
Gibraltar '13–'14 *Adam Bushby*	282
AFC Wimbledon '14–'16 *Andi Thomas*	284
Queen's Park '20–'22 *Rob MacDonald*	288
Admiral x The Square Ball *Daniel Chapman*	292
Admiral and music *James Brown*	296
Walthamstow '23–'25 *Andi Thomas*	302
Shirt directory	**310**
Acknowledgements	330

Introduction:
Adam Bushby and Rob MacDonald

As John Griffin set off for home down the M1, he could scarcely have imagined the astonishing effect a chance meeting with a First Division football manager would have on both their industries. It helped, of course, that the manager in question was Don Revie and that his team, Leeds United, were the best in the country.

They hadn't been in each other's diaries — Griffin had travelled north in the hope of selling a diverse new product range to Kays, a Leeds-based mail-order company. His employers, a knitwear firm called Cook & Hurst, were trading under a new name and moving into athletics and leisurewear. Griffin presented rugby and football jersey samples and introduced his unwitting client to a name that would become synonymous with some of the most iconic kits ever seen — Admiral.

Half an hour later, Griffin and his sales rep were back outside and back to square one. But things took a transformational turn as Griffin happened upon a Leeds training session next door to where he was having a consolation breakfast. The morning would end with him making a finger-in-the-air offer to Revie over tea in the manager's office. Implausibly, the day would end with the way football and football fans looked, felt and presented themselves, changed forever.

The early Admiral Headquarters.

Admiral's entry into the kit manufacturing market might seem slightly haphazard, but Bert Patrick, Griffin's partner at Admiral, was anything but. There was more in play than simple good fortune — in fact, the specific fertile conditions for the replica shirt market to blossom had been signed into law five years earlier. The 1968 Copyright Act was to be Admiral's passport to the big time as they now owned the design they had committed to replica. No more cheap knock-offs or reproductions meant that Admiral no longer needed to be satisfied with a mere slice of the market; they now had access to the whole pie.

A reputation for innovation was only enhanced with the collaboration with England's World Cup-winning goalkeeper Gordon Banks, who had a special fitting ahead of the tournament to make sure his sleeves were an inch and a half longer than a regulation jersey, enabling the sprightliest of keepers to feel that bit more agile. Examples of that flair for breaking with tradition characterise the spirit of the shirts filling this book, as you will see. A marker was being laid and the speed of revolution was soon to be dizzying.

Peter Shilton puts across his ideas to Bert (left) and John (right).

Peter Shilton, another pioneer, had dabbled with various improvements to his jerseys, thwarted by the Football League until he became Admiral's first-ever player ambassador. But no one had really spotted the gap in the market to exclusively clothe an entire club, until Bert, John and Admiral filled it.

The Leeds United shirt, set in train by that chance meeting with Revie and released for sale just in time for Christmas 1973, was the shirt that started the revolution. Designs pre-1973 were essentially limited in their ambition and execution to a plain, striped or hooped cotton jersey with a badge sown on. That was your lot. Your granny could buy a red shirt from the market, sit down with her sewing needle, thread and a club badge. There was nothing unique about a football shirt that could be accessorised at home to then bear a mere passing resemblance to the ones worn by George Best or Kevin Keegan.

The Admiral warehouse, with boxed replica shirts.

Bert chats with Kevin Keegan and Peter Shilton at an England/Admiral photoshoot.

Admiral's influence on the English game was undeniable — by the 1977-1978 season, 84 of the 92 English football league clubs were wearing a manufacturer's logo on their shirts. But sales of replicas were limited to children — there was no market as such, among match-going adults anyway, for kits; even Patrick had only really expected the appeal of 'dress like your heroes' to apply to younger customers, who would then badger their parents. It was only in the 1980s that a shirt was released in an adult size — Admiral's iconic England design — and only really in the '90s that it became an item of clothing you would wear to a game.

Not everyone was smitten with England's new-look Admiral strip, launched in May 1980 at Wembley v Argentina, with Brian Clough quipping: "The wraps are off England's new kit — and I'm saying now I don't like it. It has the looks of one of my mother's old pinnies!" Commentating on the game, the legendary Barry Davies mused on the merits (or in this case, otherwise) of incorporating the colours of the Union Jack.

Still, the shirt sold in its droves. It was available to buy at men's fashion chain Burton Menswear, crucially placing the football shirt as a legitimate item of general-purpose adult male leisurewear and easily accessible at a popular high-street chain.

Now, the football shirt is an object of cultural currency in the modern world, be it a sign of unwavering loyalty to your club or merely a fashion statement. Since Ralph Lauren helped design Admiral's New York Cosmos jersey in 1979 — a collaboration way ahead of its time — football and fashion link ups have been in the ascendance: Yohji Yamamoto and Real Madrid, Drôle de Monsieur and Monaco, Palace and Juventus, Nemen and AC Milan, Diesel and Vicenza, Daily Paper and Ajax, Marcelo Burlon and Napoli, ARTE and Anderlecht, Wales Bonner and Jamaica ... the list is endless. Balenciaga, Louis Vuitton and Dolce & Gabbana have come up with their own takes on the humble football shirt, as it trades the terrace for the catwalk. And in 2016, the US edition of GQ, there was even an article entitled 'How to Wear a Soccer Jersey (If You Don't Know Anything About Soccer)', leading with a picture of Drake sporting a Juventus shirt. "In terms of pure wearability they might even be the best of any pro athlete uniform," gushes writer Jake Woolf.

As the great Arrigo Sacchi once said: "Football is the most important of the least important things in life." For most fans that's true enough, for others it doesn't go anywhere near far enough. Players and managers come and go, owners are temporary custodians, stadiums can be rebuilt or even moved. So all that is left, really, is the abstract concept of a football club or national team, made tangible by the shirt. Colour acts as an easy distinguisher of what is 'us' and what is 'them'. Some colours become sacrosanct, others are shunned. All the while, the football shirt is the tie that binds. Football demands emotional attachment and the ready-made portal that shirts offer to a goal, a game, a season, a year, makes them an easy canvas for our own personal history; memories made solid.

These shirts in particular sit at the confluence of a number of factors: nostalgia, innovation, genuinely beautiful design and genuinely incredible stories. Their social importance; their role as time machines, is hard to overstate. And so as well as being a book that records and celebrates great designs with beautiful pictures, this is also a book that explains why these shirts *mean* something. Why wearing a vintage design in club or national colours offers authenticity, and perhaps as importantly, identity, to fans as the pace of change in the game and society accelerates around them. It celebrates the true pioneering nature and convention-defying approach of some great designers. Above all, it provides a document of how the world learned to love the football shirt and the very special place Admiral has in that process.

The football shirt is an object of cultural currency in the modern world, be it a sign of unwavering loyalty to your club or merely a fashion statement.

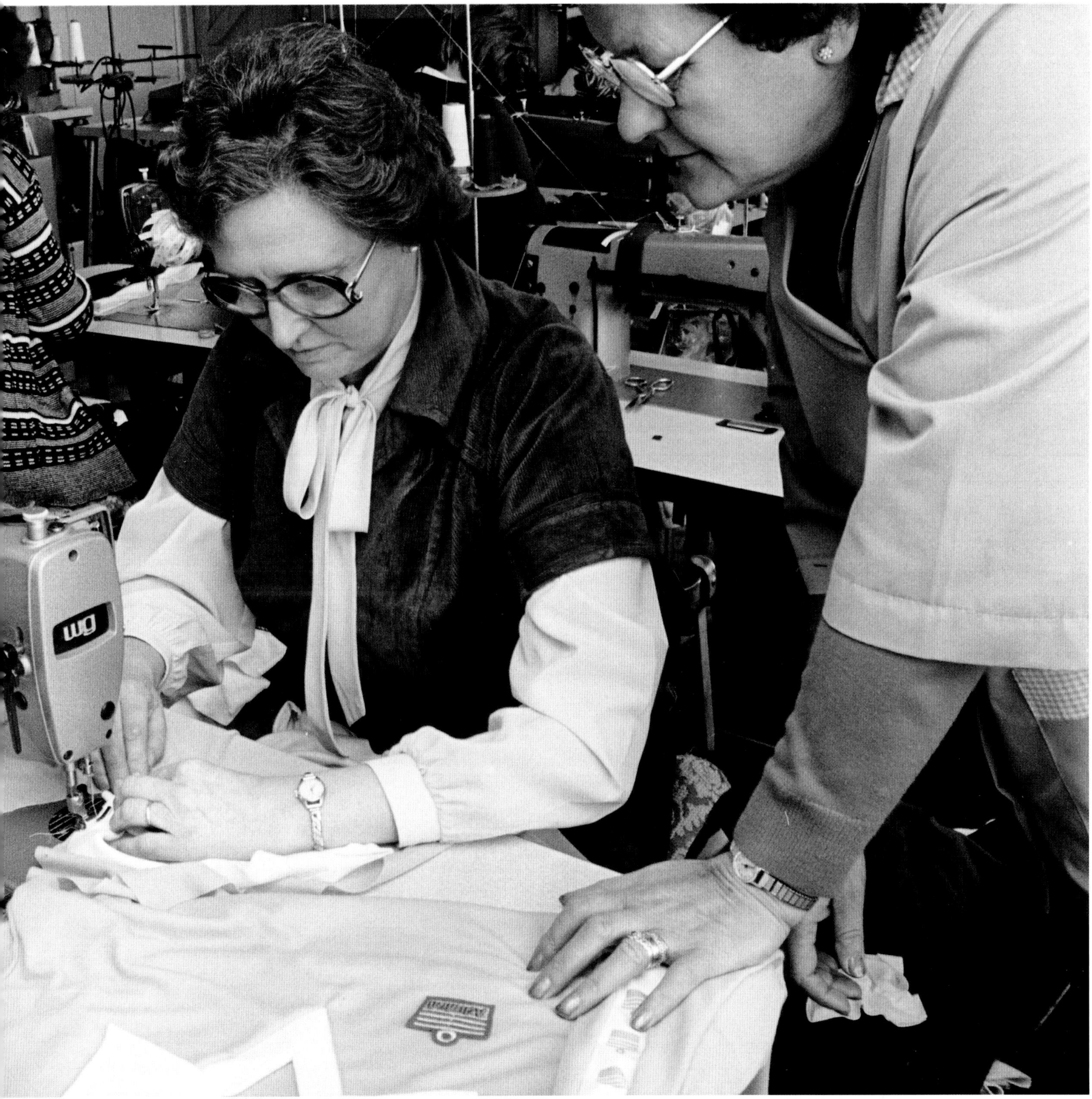

The player pioneer — Peter Shilton

Admiral's first ever brand ambassador in 1973 was the perfect fit — a pioneer in his own right who'd already had multiple kit innovations blocked by the Football League. A meeting with Admiral opened the door to the original personally-branded football shirt.

Peter poses with the Admiral kit machinists.

"I was coming up with some original ideas, in terms of design, on a goalkeeper's jersey — I wanted to add a zip to a collar, but the Football League said it was too dangerous. I also designed a plain jersey, but it had two stripes going under the arm and down the side, so when you dived, it really looked distinctive. And then that wasn't allowed by the Football League, because it was a different colour. I'd even created a logo, a P with an S going through it, and that was what would have been on the original jerseys. Len Shipman, who was my chairman at Leicester City, was also chairman of the Football League, and so was instrumental in getting my jerseys banned and I thought 'oh thanks very much!'

"That was when we went to Admiral. It came about because when I first got into the team at Leicester, Jon [Holmes, Shilton's manager] was working for a company in the city and I the club went to them and said Peter needs some help with his management, that's how it originated. And I had a meeting with them, and they obviously got in touch with Admiral because they were a local firm. We met the two bosses, about me getting involved with them and of course then, this kit idea came up.

"I'd looked at Real Madrid, who were one of my favourite teams at the time, there were a couple of great sides when I was growing up, and obviously they looked fantastic in all-white, and I thought 'well why can't a goalkeeper wear that sort of kit?'. So they made me an all-white kit with a roll-up collar to replace the zip that had been banned. It was fantastic — it had the PS logo on it along with Admiral's.

'Shilts' appeared across Admiral advertising as their first-ever brand ambassador.

"After that, we made the socks, shirts and jersey in a pack and there weren't restrictions on different colours anymore, so it was sold in a number of different types [red, blue, and black and amber shirts with white shorts and socks].

"It was sold in kids sizes first, it wasn't like today when grown men are buying full kits, it was pretty much all for children in the newspaper ads — 'Play like Shilts' was an advertising strapline.

"As a Leicester player it was exciting to start with a Leicester-based company and get involved with them and then to see them take off. Leicester and textiles were quite synonymous with each other, certainly in those days, and that's why I originally thought I could get involved in manufacturing my own kit — and I often sit and think if I'd have actually gone for that — making jerseys and socks and that sort of thing, who knows where it could have led.

"I remember going to their offices quite a few times in Wigston. Admiral suddenly rose very quickly in football, getting kits out there. They came from nowhere really, and it was so exciting to be involved with them because they were pioneers in terms of getting clubs signed up." ●

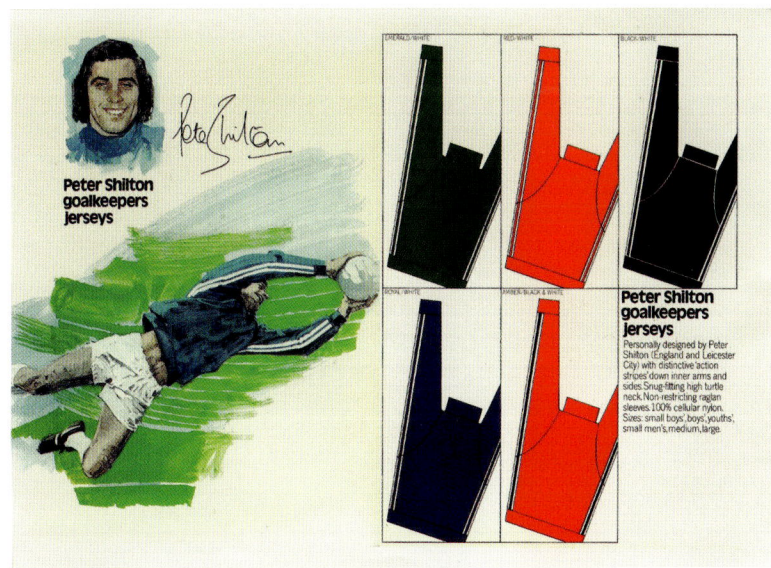

Admiral and the aesthetic merit of design

Words: Professor Andrew Groves

For someone who grew up in the 1970s, walking into Admiral's archive is to be immediately transported back to your childhood. It conjures up a time which has perhaps unfairly been described as the decade that taste forgot. In part, this may be due to the fact that so much of what was produced during that decade was excessive, contradictory or disruptive. Admiral sat amidst that visual overload: Slade, Evel Knievel, Bay City Rollers, Ziggy Stardust, the Sex Pistols; all thrilling, exciting and unique. Yet all of these cultural iconoclasts had one thing in common – they used dress to reject the past, subvert the norm and promise a more exciting future.

To understand the extent to which Admiral revolutionised the sportswear industry, it's important to first understand what had come before. The predominant kit manufacturing business model was to sell directly to sports outfitters and club chairmen, rather than to individuals. As a result, kits were sold on their value for money and their robust functionality – the quality of the materials and construction, colour fast dyes, reinforced seams and chill-resistant cotton among the prized assets.

Any thoughts that may have been harboured relating to the design of the football kit remained largely unexpressed and shirts were almost completely immune from the whims of fashion, going relatively unchanged from season to season, and from club to club.

However, change was on the way and it was England's success in the 1966 World Cup that would spark it. Umbro's growth in the football kit market of the time meant they had to outsource work to other manufacturers, including Cook & Hurst, who owned the Admiral brand in Leicester. Predominantly a knitted underwear manufacturer, the company had already started providing special football shirts for Leicester City's Gordon Banks, ensuring that the sleeves were long enough for him. And, while it is commonly stated that England wore Umbro for the 1966 FIFA World Cup, this was only for the outfield players, as Banks wore shirts provided by Admiral throughout the tournament. It demonstrated the potential space for another brand in the market; however, Admiral recognised that they could not compete on volume and price, and that in order to be successful they would need to find another way to differentiate their products from their competitors.

As it turned out, a timely and fortuitous change in legislation provided the answer. The introduction of the Design Copyright Bill 1968, which amended Section 10 of the 1956 Act, ensured that unregistered designs received automatic copyright protection upon creation, rather than having to go through an expensive and time-consuming registration process. Furthermore, while previous copyright legislation was concerned with what were described as 'artistic works', implying some form of artistic merit, the new legislation gave protection for design with no requirements as to their artistic merit.

In effect, while the previous costs associated with registering an individual design may have discouraged companies from taking creative risks, the new legislation allowed industry to capitalise on creativity without fear of their designs being copied by a competitor. Admiral recognised that differentiation through design was critical to claiming copyright on each new kit, prompting their designer Lindsay Jelley to devise ever-more elaborate ways of incorporating design features into their kits through new materials, pattern cutting, embroidery, print, embellishment, branding, applique and jacquard weaves. Within the fashion industry, *haute couture* is normally regarded as the only area in which a designer can experiment and be creative without regard for budget or buyers. And while Admiral in the 1970s was almost the polar opposite in terms of market and price, it excelled creatively in ways that only a couture house would have allowed.

Differentiation through design — Lindsay Jelley's sketches and pattern cutting templates.

Designer Lindsay Jelley looked to devise ever-more elaborate ways of incorporating design into their kits through new materials, pattern cutting and more.

Not only had the designs changed, but so too had the fabrics. Throughout the early 20th century, innovation in the production of synthetic fibres such as nylon (1931), acrylic (1950) and polyester (1953) led to their manufacturers, including DuPont, trying to find new markets for these materials that aligned with their unique properties. While surprisingly little research has been conducted into how synthetic fibres and materials were first incorporated into football kits, we do know from various sports outfitters' catalogues that nylon has been used for football socks since at least 1953, and by the mid-1960s, some shorts were being produced from Terylene, with the first nylon football shirt mentioned in 1965.

However, there is little mention of polyester until the 1970s. Polyester, which was lightweight, breathable and hydrophobic, allowed moisture to be drawn away from the skin and onto the outer surface of the garment where it would evaporate, making it a natural choice for sportswear. It quickly became the material of choice for football shirts because it was inexpensive, stain and crease resistant, and allowed for the creation of the most complex and intensely coloured designs through the use of sublimation printing.

The West Ham shirt displayed new levels of invention.

This is evident when looking through the Admiral archive, where the brand's sheer inventiveness is visible in almost every single garment. Admiral's West Ham kit from the 1975-76 European Cup Winners' Cup Final is perhaps the most extreme example. The upper chest of the shirt is made of blue jersey with four claret stripes woven into it, while the main body is made of claret jersey. The upper section has been darted to shape the stripes into an oblique chevron that extends up to the V-neck collar, which is bound with jersey and has an oversized, rounded penny collar. A large Admiral logo has been printed on either side wide of the collar, and the blue jersey sleeves are bound in claret rib. Finally, the West Ham crest of a castle with cross irons has been embroidered in the centre of the shirt, helping to conceal where the shirt is darted for fit. The shirt would have been far more technically challenging to manufacture than a standard shirt, and thus far more expensive to produce.

But this approach to design was Admiral's competitive advantage; it not only allowed them to claim copyright over their kits, making them financially rewarding for both the company and their clubs, but it also allowed them to rapidly change how football actually *looked* in less than five years, going from designing for three teams in 1973 to 24 by 1978. This had a snowball effect, and with more and more clubs requesting their maximalist, fashion-led approach, the more Admiral had to push design innovation for each new strip. In essence, as the number of clubs they designed for rose at a rapid rate, the more their excessive aesthetic became the dominant one in English football.

Admiral would have been the first overtly branded clothing that most children growing up in the 1970s would have worn.

Central to understanding Admiral's design approach was that although theoretically, they were meant to be designing the kit for an adult football team, their designs were actually focused on appealing to young children, who were their primary consumers. And the world in which children were growing up had become increasingly focused on them as consumers, be it for toys, television shows, pop music, sports or fashion. In particular, as colour television became more popular in the 1970s, children's shows began emphasising the use of colour as part of their aesthetic, such as ITV's *Rainbow*, which began in 1972, *Tiswas* in 1974, and *Multi-Coloured Swap Shop* in 1976 on BBC1. A key component of *Swap Shop* was the top-10 board, which featured items that young viewers wanted to swap for more desirable goods. Unusually for the BBC, which aimed to avoid advertising, it frequently featured branded products, contributing to the fertile conditions in which more exclusive sportswear could thrive.

However, while Admiral's success was due to their ability to create a distinct, fashion-led look aimed at children, the whims of fashion eventually contributed to their demise by the 1980s. Admiral would have been the first overtly branded clothing that most children growing up in the 1970s would have worn. Though ostensibly intended to visually signal which team you supported, in reality it was being worn as much for its aesthetic and its ability to signal to others that you could afford expensive sportwear, rather than the generic versions found in shopping catalogues.

As these predominantly working-class children became teenagers, their semiotic use of brands became increasingly complex, as did their adoption of clothing from other British sportswear companies, as well as continental brands from Italy and France. The appropriation of sportswear designed for a specific purpose, into the medium through which notions of style and taste could be mediated, can be seen as a direct result of Admiral's repositioning of sportswear from a functional garment into an aesthetic one.

In pioneering this approach, Admiral played a significant role in the emergence of the casual subculture in the late 1970s, but, more importantly, in branded sportswear becoming the predominant style of dress for a large section of the population some 50 years later. ●

The advent of the replica shirt market

Words: Professor Jean Williams

The importance of the replica shirt to football fans is a relatively new phenomenon in the grand scheme of things, developing from the late 1950s onwards initially as a full strip (shirt, shorts, socks) sold boxed as a children's toy. Over 100 years of codified football preceded these developments, as the Football Association formed under the Laws of the Game in 1863. As the most visible totem of a football club's colours, the design of the football kit, in particular, the shirt colour and pattern, had been the primary means of representing the team. The visual impact of the football strip evoked simple nicknames such as 'Reds', or 'Blues' and provided a palette for homemade merchandise, including rattles, scarves and rosettes for men, women, boys and girls. In that sense, memorabilia was androgynous, multi-use and generic.

The shoe uniform was delineated to theses inaugural laws, but this didn't apply to the football strip: Rule 13 read: 'No player shall wear projecting nails, iron plates, or gutta percha on the soles or heels of his boots.' Shirts only slowly changed from flannelette and woollen garments to synthetic fibres, such as nylon, during the first 100 years of the game.

Prior to the late 1950s, amateur and youth football clubs purchased shirts in club colours like major teams, but without specific endorsement. Having distinctive clothing for sport was expensive and beyond most young men at the turn of the 20th century — we know this because soldiers stationed abroad in the First World War often wrote home asking for kit, and also wrote to professional clubs asking for second-hand boots, and balls. Many were sent just a packet of cigarettes or a chocolate bar instead.

Post-Second World War, wages began to rise, leading Prime Minister Harold Macmillan to declare at a Conservative rally in Bedford in 1957: "We've never had it so good." Children and young people began to dress less like their parents and more like one another. Products aimed at commercialising youth abounded, like the new 45 rpm records, jukeboxes and teen magazines. Football goods manufacturers followed suit, targeting youths aged five to 12, in a 'wear the shirt, play like your hero' strategy. This had been successful with boots since the 1930s — Herbert Chapman-endorsed footwear while Arsenal manager. But there was no copyright and, alas, zero exclusivity.

An advert for the Admiral replica shirt range from the late 1970s.

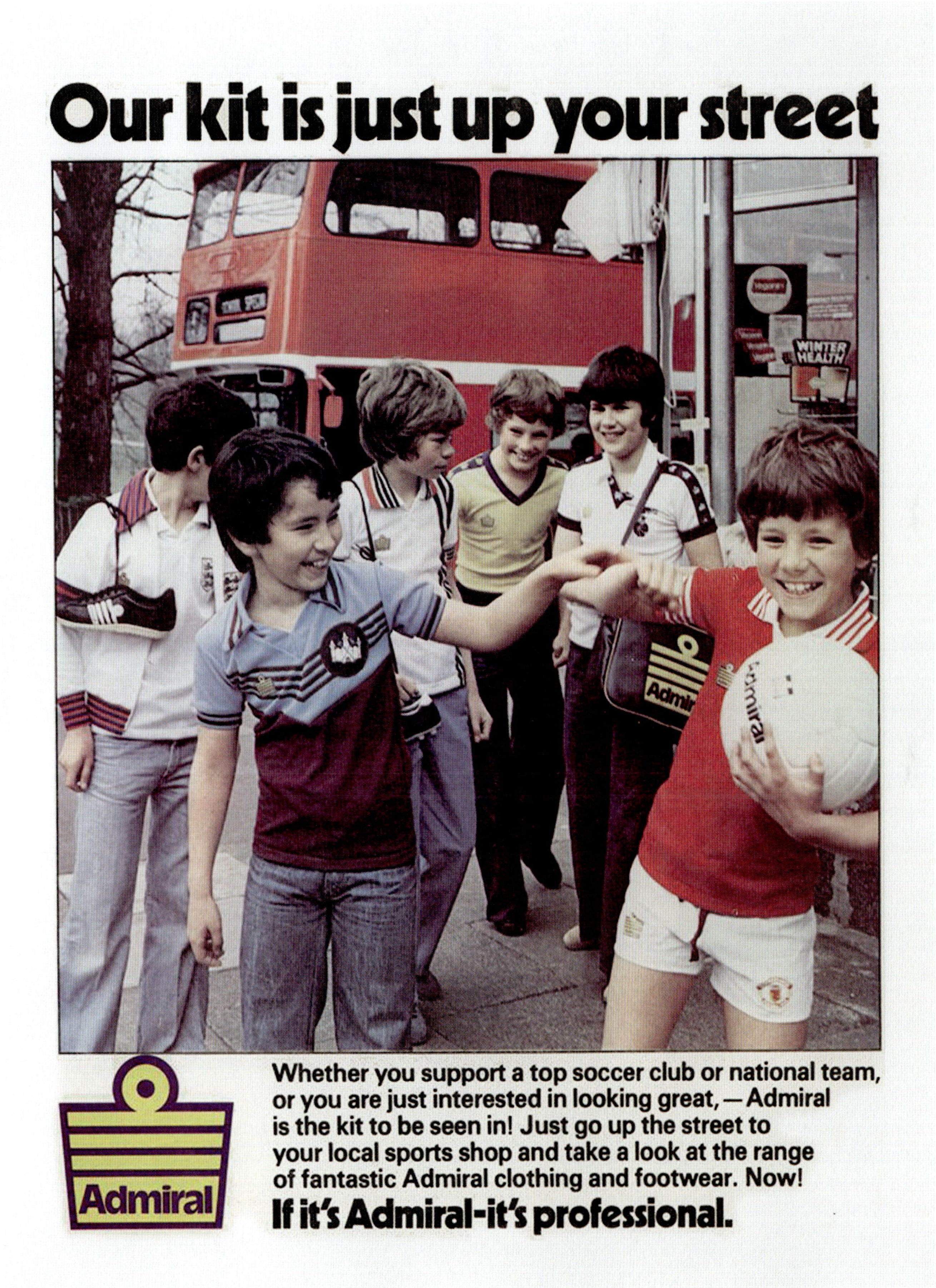

Our kit is just up your street

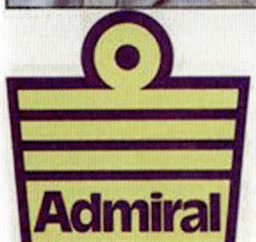

Whether you support a top soccer club or national team, or you are just interested in looking great,—Admiral is the kit to be seen in! Just go up the street to your local sports shop and take a look at the range of fantastic Admiral clothing and footwear. Now!

If it's Admiral-it's professional.

When Leicester-based Admiral produced its first child replicas in 1972, rival manufacturers also produced similar unbadged red shirts with white infill collar and cuffs for, say, young Manchester United fans. Worse still, several clubs used essentially the same designs — with no specific visual features, Admiral's 1973 advert used plain white shirts and navy shorts to represent Spurs, Derby and England.

The same year, realising its own problem with a lack of authenticity, Admiral was the first company to link up with a football club to become the sole producer of a copyrighted kit. Owner Bert Partrick realised that Admiral could establish a licensing arrangement with Leeds United, one of the dominant forces in English football and, under dynamic manager Don Revie, a club consciously looking to modernise. Admiral reimagined the away kit at the start of the 1973-74 season, subsequently copyrighting the design and becoming the sole legal supplier to both the club and retailers.

This exclusivity came at a cost, however — Admiral paid Leeds an initial fee of £10,000, offset against a 5% commission on sales of both shirts and other leisurewear. They took over production of the home kit midway through the 1973-74 season.

Within just five years, the industry as a whole had completely revolutionised. Foreign manufacturers who had concentrated up until this point on either clothing or footwear saw the potential to produce head-to-toe branded strips licensed to specific clubs, gaining a direct line to their fanbases as a result.

In 1976, just as colour TVs first outsold black and white, Bert Patrick targeted clubs like Southampton and West Ham with new designs ahead of big televised games. Colour on shirts could be played with like never before. Copyrighting helped to reimagine shirt design, as each had to be distinctive and authentic to only one club, while television and new glossy football publications fed these designs to potential consumers, such as *Shoot!* magazine aimed exclusively at young football fans.

Television and new glossy football publications mediated designs to potential consumers.

Front cover of Shoot! magazine, featuring an Admiral-clad Coventry City team.

In design terms, club badges were an easy way of providing a stamp of the originality of a shirt. Collar and cuff designs were another visual cue, assisted by new printing and manufacturing capabilities that introduced new patterns and motifs. Leicester City's 1976 shirt included epaulettes on the shoulders, for instance, suggestive of militaria. Initially an added extra, kit manufacturers' logos gradually joined the visual lexicon as sponsors realised they were missing exposure for the price of a few pence.

But even in the early 1980s, the majority of adults at FA Cup Finals were not wearing replica shirts. Instead, a homemade culture of carnivalesque prevailed; just look at the crowd pictures of West Ham's win in 1980 for evidence. The generational difference of some young fans wearing replica shirts is also apparent. By the time Manchester United's beat Crystal Palace to win the FA Cup Final in 1990, shirt-wearing had become a fan monoculture — not so much an authentication of an item of clothing as part of the identity of an authentic fan.

The advent of the Premier League in 1992 and the enhanced manufacturing capabilities that could now add trims, flashes, micro patterning and accent colours added nuance to shirt design. It also meant that redesigns became ever more frequent and, inevitably, prices rose. In response to this financial exploitation of fans' interest, long-standing supporters who may have witnessed this revolution in style began to reject the new designs in favour of their retro jerseys, perhaps from historic matches. Clubs and designers realised the market was developing, self-consciously embracing retro design features, such as favouring crew necks, lace-up collars and chevrons. A nostalgic, retrospective turn drew upon club history to celebrate key seasons, anniversaries and players. As such, they are heritage clothing brands, as well as sporting clubs and pillars of communities.

Promoting Leicester City's new kit (top) and a new Wimbledon strip, fit for the Premier League era (right).

Old replicas, such as Admiral reissues, are increasingly being used to further reinforce football fans' identities as genuine, deep and longstanding.

This market segmentation has accelerated in the athleisure market, where retro-replica manufacturers produced both shirts and broader leisurewear from 1990s onwards. Here, Admiral led the way again, reproducing its 1970s and 1980s kit designs, as part of branded leisurewear. It was the starter gun to a race that all the big sporting manufacturers wanted to run.

Over the 50 years since replica shirts were introduced, the value of innovation has changed. Shirts have become both extremely accessible and frequently changed, perhaps giving rise to a fandom that critics say is purchased rather than deeply felt, especially given the ease with which it can be obtained due to the extent and range of merchandise in club shops. Academics commonly refer to the 'tradium', rather than the stadium, because fans are encouraged to consume food, beverages, and experiences in the grounds themselves.

The academic John Bale used the term 'topophilia', meaning a love of place, to describe how many fans feel in the stadium, and clubs rely upon that affection in many ways, not least their commercial strategies. It informs the wider museumification of the clubs' branding, in which visitor attraction techniques are used to sell food and beverage, experiences like tours, and the history of the team. A pint of beer named after a fantastic season, a 150th anniversary club tour, a shirt release named after a famous player. Each acts to teach the fan more about the club history, while validating their identification with the brand.

Selling nostalgic experiences is not limited to the wearing of shirts. Globally, the Premier League has encouraged overseas fan groups who will never set foot in the stadium itself. Beyond consumption, there is now a form of nostalgic sophistication in which old replicas, or ones which refer to the past, such as Admiral reissues, are increasingly being used to further reinforce football fans' identities as genuine, deep and longstanding; the legacy fan if you will.

Given the gallows humour of fans, this may even extend to 'BIRFing', which stands for Basking In (the) Reflected Failure', be it a relegation, cup final defeat or any other unsuccessful spell. This is part of the celebrated history of their club, and their club alone. Conversely, they may also favour a shirt from before they were born as a way of critiquing the present, and invoking a totemic past, such as Derby's 1984 Centenary Admiral kit, sponsored by BASS.

As such, the wearing of shirts is ambiguous, shifting and deeply personal, even as the demographic continues to expand. The photographer Jacqui McAssey has captured women's clothing strategies as shirt-wearing fans, including one who tied her handbag to her branded sweatshirt, to prevent rival fans from knocking the bag from her arm. Diverse fans, therefore, connect individually with the shirt as part of their wider identity.

The football shirt has moved from sportswear to leisurewear to the catwalk. A uniform of consumerism, displaying fandom to rivals and colleagues, the shirt is both a symbol of individualism, and a celebration of being part of the crowd. Its power extends far beyond the fabric it is made from. ●

The classic Leeds United 1992 shirt reissue. Credit: James Pearson-Howes

Football, fanwear and fashion

Words: Jacqui McAssey

Fifty years on from Admiral's production of the first replica shirt, football fanwear is currently very much 'in fashion'. The viral trend for wearing football jerseys, or to give it its correct term, 'Blokecore', has spread exponentially across social media platforms, where digital creators invite viewers to 'Get Dressed With Me' (#GDWM) as they translate one football shirt into five separate looks. Often oversized and worn with baggy jeans, along with the ubiquitous pair of trainers, football shirts have become a global, gender-neutral uniform for younger fans of football and fashion (or in many cases, just fashion). This old-but-new aesthetic is an amalgamation of how a match-going supporter would dress in the 1980s and 1990s, but the trend has a global reach.

Be it a rare shirt, or one designed for a grassroots women's team, no kit is seemingly off-limits. With a 50-plus-year archive of pre-loved shirts to explore, anyone looking to buy into the trend can easily find one on resale sites, or hunt for a second-hand bargain.

Increasingly, more experimental or upcycled garments are emerging, the football shirt capturing the imagination of a new wave of young designers, as well as the mega-brands wanting to collaborate with them to help decode the Gen-Z fashion scene. Designer Sophie Hird's Dolly Parton-esque Bury FC shirt springs to mind, commissioned for Zoe Hitchen's 'We Are Bury' exhibition in 2019 after the expulsion of the club from the English Football League. Replica shirts laid the foundations of this trend, but what happened in between?

Admiral's replica shirt for children, launched in time for Christmas 1973, was only the start of a broader shift in lifestyle changes that shaped how people dressed for leisure activities. A boom in jogging (a slower running style) crossed from the USA to the UK, and the recreational athlete began to take on the uniform of real athletes. Admiral's Training Suit of the early '70s was also originally produced for children, but the iconic two-piece, worn by martial arts film star Bruce Lee and singer Bob Marley, became a firm off-field look.

The Bob Marley x Mundial x Admiral collaboration.

An array of fanwear, from club shirts (left and below) to England '82-inspired jumpers (bottom).

The influence of celebrities, coupled with advances in audio visual technology, instigated further fitness trends. Families could jog outdoors, women could 'feel the burn' with Jane Fonda's aerobic at-home workouts played on Video Home System (VHS) machines. Children could cruise around their neighbourhoods on BMX bikes or wearing pastel-coloured roller boots. Personal exercise was becoming more commercialised, which only stimulated the demand for new styles of leisurewear further.

Technological advances in fabric also changed the feel of leisurewear in this decade. The addition of Lycra, (by DuPont) meant that the relationship between sport, fitness and fashion took on a closer, figure-hugging relationship. This fabric was designed to enhance the look of toned bodies.

The story of leisurewear continued to develop until celebrity and athlete-led trends gave way to a counter-cultural movement, defined by sports fans themselves. This era marked a new chapter in the history of football and fashion.

Although leisurewear was beginning to flourish, the replica football shirt was not a staple of the football crowd. Another trend, but this time in football violence, increased from the 1970s to the 1980s and wearing obvious team colours only made fan groups more easily identifiable. Territories were fought for along transport routes, in pubs, outside grounds or inside the stadium itself by male football fans, who would actively look for, encounters with opposing supporters, none more so than between fans of teams in the North and South or at derby games or matches against bitter rivals. For that reason, the football shirt was out.

Admiral x Represent collaboration — tramline tracksuit, woolly hat and gloves.

A new appetite for football-led fashion has been amplified by clubs, brands and the players themselves.

'Casual' culture, widely documented as a significant moment in the history of football fashion, originated because of the success of top-flight English football teams in Europe. With each visit to the continent, contemporary sportswear with slick silhouettes and fabrications was brought back by fans to be worn in their home stadiums. This was especially so for Liverpool supporters, whose continental travels in the late 1970s and early 1980s had ensured exposure to leisurewear brands in France, Italy and Germany. Known as 'Scallies' in Liverpool and 'Perry Boys' in Manchester and Salford, (their fierce rivals) as European campaigns progressed from city to city, new clothing styles were introduced back home on football terraces. It was a smart look, but with swagger, its roots in Mod culture aligning perfectly with the elegance of continental brands.

Football casual culture fell out of fashion in the late '80s when another youth-centric movement, rave, bounced onto the scene. Expensive jackets and knitwear served no purpose for the 24-hour party people perspiring across the dancefloors of the clubs, or fields, of the UK.

Soon after, small football club souvenir shops gave way to more commercialised business, as clubs designed their own fanwear collections, buoyed by the new global market created by the Premier League. Mail order catalogues, full of football-crested fashion (and bedding, jewellery, crystal whisky glasses, etc.) meant you could achieve a sense of belonging without ever visiting the stadium of your favourite team.

The viral football fashion trend of football shirt plus 'Scally' or 'Perry Boy' flair has successfully broken through the digital noise and a new appetite for football-led fashion has been amplified by the clubs, brands and the players themselves; 'training day fits' are a particular source of current fashion inspiration on social media. The success of women's football, banned by the FA from 1921-1971, and the response to the Lionesses' Euros win in 2022, has also driven a demand for women's football fanwear, as well as women-run brands. This new market will evolve and define its own fashion culture as the women's game and fanbase matures. Wearing football fashion, with its explicit sense of community and self-expression, will ensure that the 'ins and outs' of sportswear are universally discussed for another 50 years at least. ●

The early years

Words: Adam Bushby

It all began with knickers. Nuns' knickers to be precise. From holy but humble beginnings, Admiral changed the very fabric of the beautiful game forever from a factory on Long Street, in the textile town of Wigston, Leicestershire.

During its industrial heyday, Leicester was a textile behemoth, proudly peddling the motto: "Leicester clothes the world". It was no idle boast — the city had exploded into one of the manufacturing centres of Europe, as well as one of its richest cities, its prosperity reflected in the elegant brick buildings lining broad paved streets and genteel residences housing the *nouveau riche*.

Before Admiral became Admiral, in 1903 it was a hosiery manufacturer, becoming Cook & Hurst five years later. Founders Christopher Cook and Harold Hurst assembled a small team of skilled workers as a fulcrum, manning the eight machines used to fashion high-quality woollen underwear.

Within a decade, the outbreak of the First World War in 1914 propelled an expansion of manufacturing operations — there were millions of military men to provide underwear for. The underwear range included long wool pants and a short- or long-sleeved button-front vest for men to wear in winter, and interlock sleeveless vests and trunks for the summertime, a precursor to today's base layer garments.

The Royal Navy, delighted with Admiral's end product and a reputation synonymous with superior British manufacturing, signed the firm up to a contract to provide sportswear and exercise garments, which would have historic implications for football. A phlegmatic Admiral's head was chosen to launch the Admiral brand in 1914 and the name was trademarked eight years later.

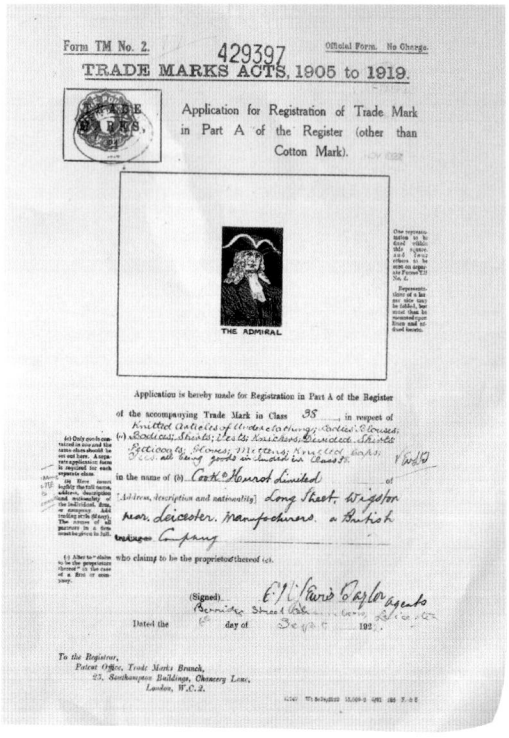

The original trademark document for Admiral, dated September 1922 (above).

An original 1940s rugby shirt, made by Admiral (right).

Early unbranded Admiral shirts for Birmingham City and Derby County.

The outbreak of war again in 1939 saw Admiral rally once more, the company's Wigston factory operating night and day to supply British and American forces with garments in support of the war effort. The first Admiral sports catalogue dates back to 1935, including a special line of cream interlock sportswear. Interlock textiles were used for their thicker and more stable properties, while also being stretchier and more durable than jersey textiles.

Once there was a cessation in hostilities, Admiral's penchant for high-quality garments meant the naval connection continued, with every sailor issued with a white and a navy-coloured shirt made by Admiral for use in sporting activities. In fact, in its 50 years in Wigston, Admiral supplied garments to most branches of the British services during two world wars and in the years afterwards.

Entrepreneur and former journalist Bert Patrick swept onto the scene in 1956 and quickly understood that Admiral needed to prioritise sportswear over underwear. Initially, Admiral dipped its toe in this new market by selling its expertise to Cheshire-based sportswear firms Umbro and Bukta, helping them fulfil orders of shirts, its name occasionally appearing on a back label. At this point, there was no replica shirt market to speak of. Jerseys were plain, with badges and numbers sold separately.

Patrick would have eyes for a picture far larger than this, though he wouldn't yet know it. He commissioned Paul Oakley of Oakley Young Associates to create the now legendary Admiral stripe-laden insignia and the brand we recognise today emerged, though not hitherto fully formed.

Gordon Banks wearing his famous yellow keeper shirt, made by Admiral, in the 1966 World Cup final.

Banks chose the jersey for its performance rather than sponsorship.

A significant development would take place in 1966, coinciding with England's finest footballing hour. The challenge ahead of the forthcoming World Cup on English soil was to design a new style of lightweight interlock football jersey. The neck and cuffs were elasticated, freedom of movement that appealed to goalkeeper Gordon Banks. The local Leicester lad would wear an unbranded but distinctive yellow Admiral shirt throughout the '65-'66 season for his club, retaining it for the entirety of that magical World Cup-winning campaign. Banks chose the jersey for its performance rather than sponsorship.

This was only the beginning of Admiral's journey to the pinnacle of the football shirt world. And what a wild ride it would be. ●

1970

Introduction:
Rob MacDonald

1970s

The revolution was televised — in fact, the revolution was television.

England fans bring the colour (and the sombreros) to the Estadio León, at Mexico '70.

Everything changed, but really, everything was already different. Once Geoff Hurst had scored Schrödinger's Goal, before adding England's fourth, once Bobby Moore had hoisted Jules Rimet above his head, once Nobby had danced, football never looked back.

What's more, the revolution was televised — in fact, the revolution was television. The World Cup final of 1966 had been broadcast live, but for those who could afford it, the 1970 edition was beamed into living rooms in the UK drenched in colour. It was as if someone had emptied bottles of thick, oil-based paints into the top of the set and they had run, vivid and primary, down the screen and all over the action. That Brazil happened to wear a kit that was made all the more in-your-face by early colour TVs' inability to regulate contrast — and that the canary yellow shirt and blue shorts were set against the luminous green grass of a football pitch — made the whole thing even more intoxicating.

The 1970 World Cup even contains one of England's most famous matches, against the vibrant Brazil, which is — in that rarest of English-football-supporting reactions — celebrated as much for moments and for simply happening than for the result. It was a performance worthy of defending champions in the sweltering heat. Banks's save. Moore's tackles on Jairzinho, and just about everyone else. Jeff Astle screwing wide from 10 yards. Alan Ball, possibly more at risk of melting in the conditions than any other Englishman, hitting the bar. Moore's shirt swap with Pelé.

The tournament as a whole is similarly feted — a "parade of innovations," ESPN has described it since. Here were substitutes, introduced for the first time. Likewise, yellow and red cards. An official World Cup ball — the ubiquitous Telstar, of which although only 20 were supplied to the tournament, 600,000 were sold after it, according to FIFA. The first ever Panini World Cup sticker book. The last outing for old Jules as Brazil won a third title and took him home with them forever. A Hurst goal against West Germany that *was* ruled out. Truly a new era was being ushered in, with England playing a part.

1970s

What happened next rather depends on your perspective. In cold, hard football terms, England's decade had already peaked. The feeling around the national team rapidly changed from the buoyancy of the World Cup to a sagging negativity as one uninspiring performance followed another. That's possibly generous, too — I say, 'uninspiring performance', you say, 'national humiliation'. They didn't qualify for another tournament in the 1970s (see: Tomaszewski, Jan) and had to wait until a new generation finally made it to the Euros in 1980, then returned to the World Cup in 1982. More on them — and their shirts — elsewhere in this book.

That national complacency seemed endemic. Though it felt in 1970 that the post-war boom years would just carry on, with the fillip of a World Cup victory ensuring the '60s kept swinging, the rest of the decade was a struggle for many, blighted by economic and political turmoil.

It was a perfect storm, if by 'perfect', we actually mean 'really bad'. Ted Heath's Conservative government unexpectedly came to power in June 1970 with a 30-seat majority and enjoyed a reasonable honeymoon period, with the economy strong and unemployment relatively low. But it wouldn't last, torpedoed in late 1973 by a combination of rising inflation, the consequent industrial action by miners and railway workers over pay and, further afield, the OAPEC embargo and resulting oil crisis. The notorious three-day week, introduced to curb electricity consumption in light of the shortages, came at a time when the economy slumped into recession.

The feeling around the national team rapidly changed from the buoyancy of the World Cup to a sagging negativity as one uninspiring performance followed another.

Ron Greenwood and Kevin Keegan deep in discussion at an England training session.

And despite a change in Government — Harold Wilson returned as Labour Prime Minister at the second time of asking in 1974 — inflation continued to rise towards 30% and the country even required a $4 billion bailout, the largest ever requested from the IMF, to resolve its issues, which had been further exacerbated by a currency crisis in 1976.

British industry was in disarray or decline wherever you looked, but nowhere more so than in manufacturing. Unrest in the unions was one thing, but the UK had fallen behind in so many areas that, as new global competition emerged, its output was limited, inefficient and outdated — yet expensive — by comparison. As British workers laboured in poor conditions and with little recourse to pay increases, they did so on pre-war machines. Where salaries did increase, they had to be funded by price increases on finished products, making British goods even less attractive.

For some reason, modernisation didn't seem to have occurred to anyone, and the advantages that the country had enjoyed post-war, while much of Europe was in ruins, were obliterated when factories on both the continent and notably in Japan were rebuilt with modern, automated tools installed. Even joining the EEC, which on the face of it appeared to provide a ready-made market for British goods, was borderline pointless when they couldn't be competitive. Jeff Astle hadn't been the only one to take his eye off the ball.

1970s

There was a knock-on effect on design, too, as manufacturers became far less willing to take risks on new styles. The hugely confident and experimental approach that existed in the booming post-war period of expression was stifled, and the prevailing uncertainty meant that reworking classical themes and motifs became the go-to look and feel across a variety of products.

That could be the reason that some of the most notorious art and design of the decade was commissioned and born in college classrooms, rather than on factory floors. One such classroom, at the Royal College of Art, produced both the famed 'Dark Side of the Moon' album artwork for Pink Floyd, and the all-time great Rolling Stones lips and tongue artwork (later featured on an Admiral collaboration shirt), commissioned from John Pasche by Mick Jagger in 1971, having seen Pasche's work at his final degree show in 1970.

Though some creativity was extinguished, there were plenty of flickers of innovation elsewhere. The day after Jimi Hendrix had died in a London hotel, a small performing arts festival took place for the first time in Glastonbury, Somerset, featuring both The Kinks and free milk from the farm for all 1,500 attendees. The follow-up version in 1971 saw Hawkwind and David Bowie play to 12,000 people on a new 'main' stage, constructed from scaffolding and covered with plastic sheeting to create the shape of a pyramid. Bowie, particularly, is a remarkable yardstick for innovation, driving a variety of androgynous glam rock-type fashions, including oversized collars, drainpipe trousers, flares and platform shoes. Colour TV plus Ziggy Stardust certainly blew more than a few minds.

The hastily constructed new main stage at Glastonbury in 1971.

Later in the decade, disco style (i.e. coloured three-piece suits) enjoyed a brief flash in the pan, while sportswear, jeans and trainers were the emerging trends that ultimately had the greater longevity. Mods and punks bookended the decade. Hippies continued to represent ongoing anti-war ideals. If it seems a little hard to pin down, that's because the main feature of fashion in the 1970s was choice — cheaper, mass produced synthetic clothing flooded Western markets from the Far East and the sheer amount meant that culture and counterculture evolved rapidly throughout the decade.

And, in a similar spirit of reinvention, albeit in a very different field, something was stirring at a small clothing company in Leicester. The city was buzzing in the late '60s as the heart of the knitted textile industry, exporting garments all over the world. Admiral had perceptively started making football jerseys in the run up to World Cup in 1966, able to convert the machines that up until that point had made cotton interlock knitted fabrics into working with polyester sportswear fabrics. It began with orders for local football clubs and schools. It ended with a revolution that would give fans all over the world the chance to recreate the looks of their heroes, though it would also ultimately drive football clubs, players and fans into the arms of clothing manufacturers for ever-greater sums.

Business boomed for Admiral in the late '70s, but for the UK as a whole, the decade ended in further acrimony. The 'Winter of Discontent' gripped the country from November 1978 until February the following year, as pay disputes and frequent bad weather made for a miserable period that spelled the end for Labour in power, under the leadership of James Callaghan.

It was, therefore, a contrary and inconsistent decade. But for all its dystopian realities, there were green shoots of something different. On the pitch, mavericks emerged — Worthington, George, Friday, Bowles, Marsh — welcome relief for those with a disdain for authority and convention. In this climate of innovation, Admiral matched the swagger on the pitch with a flair for design. A new era of individualism was coming. ●

On the pitch, mavericks emerged — Worthington, George, Friday, Bowles and Marsh. Admiral matched the swagger on the pitch with a flair for design.

Stan Bowles poses in the Admiral England kit, which first appeared in 1974.

1970s

Leeds United '73–'76

Words: Rob Bagchi

As spring crawled towards summer in 1973, Leeds United were finished. At Second Division Sunderland's homecoming after beating Don Revie's side in the FA Cup final, six of their supporters carried a coffin on to the Roker Park pitch with 'Leeds died 1973' crowingly daubed on the side. The remains of Europe's most consistently strong side over the past nine years were laid to rest in the centre-circle. A few days later Leeds were swizzed out of the Cup Winners' Cup by a refereeing performance of such baroque partiality in the final against AC Milan that it seemed to symbolise the nadir of all the lousy luck they had endured over the preceding decade. Worse still, on the eve of that travesty in Salonika, Revie, manager since 1961, had confessed to a delegation of his players led by Johnny Giles and Norman Hunter that the rumours were true: partly for financial reasons, partly because of a sentimental aversion to dismantling a team he had so assiduously assembled, nurtured and championed, he would be leaving them for an eight-year contract with Everton. A signing on fee of £50,000 and a salary of £25,000, a 66 per cent hike to his wages at Elland Road, would be balm for his break-up heartache. The obituaries were written. All it needed was the last rites.

And yet if the outlook was bleak, as at all deathbed scenes, no team was better equipped with mental fortitude to rage, rage against the dying of the light. They would fork lightning one last time. Sunderland could snark, the world could write them off and Revie, who knew them best, could underestimate them, too. But there would be no sweet surrender to eternal rest. The players still believed in each other. Leeds United would smash open the crypt and chillingly invade their enemies' illusions.

Dennis Skinner was an unwitting ally for Revie's Leeds United family. When the 'Beast of Bolsover', then a 41-year-old serving his first term as a member of parliament, learned of Everton's offer, he demanded that the Secretary of State for Employment in the Heath government submit the case to the Pay Board set up by the Counter-Inflation Act. Its purpose was to review executive salaries to ensure new hires were not paid more than the people they were replacing and the £25,000 pa on the table, 1,200% more than the UK average wage and almost double the deal Harry Catterick had been on, was a flagrant provocation to act.

1970s

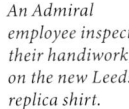
An Admiral employee inspects their handiwork on the new Leeds replica shirt.

Sir John Moores, the Everton chairman, wary of government censure and Leeds' objections to the tapping up of their manager, backed off, leaving Revie to flirt with an even better offer from Panathinaikos. Back home in Alwoodley from his holiday as a guest on the yacht owned by the Olympiakos owner, who had tried to persuade him to take over the Greece national side rather than his great Athens rivals, Revie finally announced he would stay. If, ultimately, he could not give up on them and fashion a new team, he would foster a new team fashion.

In the 85th year of professional football in England, even the biggest teams continued to buy their own kit. You only have to look at photographs of training sessions in the late 1960s and early 1970s to see the consequences of that. Thrift dictated that players would work in cast-offs and hand-me-downs, an odd assortment of Omo-blanched, obsolete strips, rugby-style shirts, slate grey trawlermen's ganseys and scrawny, faded drill tops and bottoms pummelled tissue-thin by the mangle.

On matchdays, Leeds would wear the shirts, shorts and what the manufacturers still referred to as 'hose' or 'stockings' they had purchased from James Frew Sports Outfitters at Harehills Corner in the north-east of the city. The shop, owned by United's former left-back, Jimmy Frew, would arrange the embroidery of the owl badge and, from 1971, the cursive LUFC script on the left, for an additional fee and would sell the numbers for the club's laundry staff to sew on. In 1972, looking for a cheaper option, they switched to Bukta for a handful of games but while the flapping wing collars were suitably *à la mode*, the material was a throwback to the rough and scratchy twill of two decades before and the club quickly changed their order.

For years, the only external logo was printed by the right hip, all but invisible, as intended, on players who tucked their shirts in, as almost all still did. By the time of that 1973 FA Cup final, the FA had rescinded its blanket ban on promotion, if not on sponsorship. There were team shirts on sale before 1973, but only in the sense that you could buy a rough approximation from a variety of sources, not including Jack Charlton's stall on Elland Road and the club's Sports and Souvenir Shop, which was opened in 1972 but stuck to rosettes, button badges, hats, scarves, photographs and programmes.

The Subbuteo team catalogue from that year is instructive: the standard blue shirt-white shorts-blue socks combo stood for Everton, Leicester, Ipswich, Portsmouth, Cardiff, Peterborough, Carlisle, Chesterfield, Gillingham and Rochdale. Team colours in the form of shirts, largely for kids, were readily available but there was nothing exclusive about the product. Even Leeds, which seemed pretty distinctive after Revie replaced the old municipal blue and gold with the all-white of Real Madrid in 1961-62 both as a visualisation aid and a statement of aspiration, had to share with the heirs of Di Stéfano and, more prosaically, Swansea, Tranmere and Torquay. Allowing teams to wear the maker's logo changed the game and not just in Subbuteo.

1970s

Within weeks of taking the job, Don Revie had ditched more than 40 years of tradition to change the colour of the kit, had riffled through club crests and was now sending his team out with the modernist, egg yolk 'smiley badge'.

Manufacturers could now move on from the generic, to package both exclusivity and authenticity. Soon enough, and I write from bitter experience, any self-respecting six-year-old running round in his lilywhite, bobbly, bri-nylon, market-stall, pride and joy with Peter Lorimer's No.7 stitched on painstakingly by his browbeaten granny, would be rendered a 'saddo' by someone sporting the real thing.

Bert Patrick, who had bought the Leicester sportswear company Admiral in 1958, and John Griffin, his managing director, were sharpest at identifying this new opportunity and grasping what it meant. Yet they told the documentary *Get Shirty* that their meeting with Don Revie in October 1973 was pure happenstance. The company, which had made the scarlet British and Irish Lions jerseys for their tour of New Zealand in 1971, had been attempting to get their range into Kays' catalogue and had driven to its Holbeck HQ for an early morning meeting. The mail order giant rejected their pitch in less than an hour and they went to console themselves in Sheila's Café on Elland Road before heading home. As they ate in the venerable establishment named for and run by Terry Yorath's mother-in-law, the Leeds United squad, who had started the season with seven successive victories and were still undefeated at the top of the table in autumn, climbed the concrete steps from the West Stand car park through the wire and on to Fullerton Park for a training session. Griffin, intrigued, went over to watch and approached Revie afterwards to introduce himself.

If it was a fluke, he could not have picked a more amenable top-flight manager than Revie. Within weeks of taking the job, Don had ditched more than 40 years of tradition to change the colour of the kit, had riffled through club crests and was now sending his team out with the modernist, egg yolk 'smiley badge', occasionally, the eagle-eyed noted, attached upside-down. In 1972, he had not only listened to the ideas of the maverick illustrator Paul Trevillion on novel ways to bypass the hostile London press and promote Leeds United beyond the West Riding, he had actually implemented them.

It involved marketing ploys, such as the Mileta Indentitabs — aka numbered, tasselled sock tags — which the players were supposed to hand out to children after the game, vigorous pre-match choreographed callisthenics designed to whip the crowd into a frenzy, plastic 'Johnny Giles Target' footballs that were booted into the stands as souvenirs, and saluting with one arm raised as the players pirouetted through 360 degrees on the halfway line before kick-off while wearing tracksuits with their names in iron-on lettering on the back. Little wonder, then, that Revie was receptive to Griffin's off-the-cuff proposal to make Leeds a new strip and actually pay them to wear it. Revie told him the home kit was sacrosanct, but Admiral could do what it liked with the away strip and tracksuits and Griffin shook hands on a £7,000 fee for the club. He knew his company could copyright the new design and become the sole legal source of replica kits. Naturally parents, induced by its exclusiveness and their children's desire for the genuine article, would strive to purchase the legitimate one and trade up from the standard version of the past. No longer would kids who wanted to emulate their heroes at the Vetch, Prenton Park or Elland Road wake up on Christmas morning and open essentially the same present. Admiral had cottoned on to the appeal of individuality.

1970s

Because Leeds had no existing contract with anyone, changing suppliers was straightforward and happened midway through October, shortly after that first meeting over tea in Don Revie's office. There had been nothing uniform about the design before: they had purchased V-neck versions, ones in Aertex with crew necks and others with flapping collars. Sometimes, depending on preference and weather, a match could start with Peter Lorimer in a round neck, Billy Bremner in the V and Jack Charlton with wings. Unlike Arsenal, whose captain dictated whether all the team should wear short or long sleeves, Revie's men were given free rein. Allan Clarke almost always went for long sleeves, gripping the ends in clenched fists like Denis Law.

The first Admiral kits were in the same colours as the ones they replaced: plain white for home and yellow for away, the stiffer nylon of the change-strip shorts a more vibrant custard shade than the lemon of the shirts. The latter were first worn for a 2-2 draw with Leicester City at Filbert Street in Admiral's home town on 13 October, giving the company barely a month to manufacture stock to launch their official replica kits into the shops in time for Christmas. This was a product not aimed at all generations, though. Adult lust for wearing the shirt as a symbol and proclamation of tribal identity really only took off in the 1990s. It was unthinkable in 1973 to envisage anyone above what the size-guide termed 'large youth' wanting a shirt for everyday wear. The age was more formal than people remember. Of course, there was a burgeoning culture of cults and gangs — glam kids, the many mutations of mod into skin and beyond, a few vicious Teds, alas, survived in Leeds, 'heads' morphing into proggers. But in not one of those scenes would a replica shirt pass muster. Admiral knew the market and their kit range was available solely in juvenile sizes.

An early ad for Admiral, promoting their deal with the league champions (right).

Paul Reaney, Johnny Giles, Norman Hunter and Frank Gray lead the team out, bedecked in pristine tracksuits, albeit with the 'smiley' logo stitched upside down (below).

Rarely has a garment been more coveted than the Leeds United tracksuit top, the first item by Admiral's chief designer, Lindsay Jelley.

By 22 December, when Leeds had stretched their unbeaten run to 21 matches by beating Norwich 1-0, Admiral's top brass were guests in the directors' box at Elland Road and their shirts, with the logo based on the Royal Navy gold braid insignia, were flying off the shelves. And not just in West Yorkshire but throughout the country. If your child wanted a shirt 'just like the players wore', the runaway Division One leaders were the only choice.

There was also a roaring trade for the tracksuit tops, which were made in adult sizes, and retailed at £8 a pop when the average weekly UK wage was £35. This was the first item on which Admiral's chief designer, Lindsay Jelley, could show her chops. The players had worn plain white tracksuit tops with 'Leeds United' stitched on the back as early as the 1965 FA Cup final and by the Centenary Cup final seven years later they were walking out of the tunnel in white tops with blue hem, collar and cuffs with their own names on the back. Jelley changed the trim to yellow for her first design but introduced the Admiral bands at biceps level, two hoops of primrose serving as the filling in a double-decker sandwich of royal blue. These sleeve garters, this extra splash of colour, were the touch that gave it a modern twist, pushing it away from mere function and towards style. Taking inspiration from America's collegiate patterns, Admiral went bold by plastering its name across the chest, ADM on the right side of the zip and, asymmetrically, IRAL on the left. Rarely has a garment been more coveted, but at that price most of us had to wait for Arkwright's retro-boom of the late 1980s to finally get our hands on a copy.

Leeds and Admiral may have embraced the economy of mass production, but human error still intervened occasionally to demonstrate the many hands in the process from raw cloth to pitch. The famous picture of Leeds United's players saluting the Gelderd End in 1974 is framed and on many fans' walls but it jars with one's inner pedant as Gordon McQueen, crowned league champion for the only time in his career, greets the fans with 'Gordon McQeen' emblazoned on his back. In another photo that year Joe Jordan comes out as 'Joe Jordon'. Sometimes I like to imagine it was those two impostors, Jordon and McQeen, rather than our fearsome and inseparable Scottish centre-forward and centre-half, who had headed off to Manchester United four years later.

1970s

Marching

on together

At the start of the season, Revie had rallied his players to summon their defiance. "You lads are good enough to ram the criticism back down the throats of all those who have denied you the respect you deserve," he told them. "You must go out to show them all what you can do, what good footballers you are. I want the title. I think you're more than good enough to do that. I also think you could go through the season without losing." This quest for an invincible year did not last, but they set a record of 29 games unbeaten until Stoke fought back from 2-0 down against an injury-ravaged side to win 3-2 on 23 February. Terry Cooper managed only two games all season, Eddie Gray eight, top-scorer Mick Jones was limited to 28 starts by the chronic knee injury that would end his career before his 30th birthday the following year, and Johnny Giles, Revie's 'Brains', missed five months of action. The defeat sparked a wobble that allowed Liverpool to eat into their nine-point lead.

On 30 March, Giles was finally back for the trip to West Ham and, although Leeds lost 3-1, their third consecutive defeat, the match stands out for the first appearance of Admiral's classic away kit. For the first few weeks of their deal, preoccupied naturally by Christmas, they had stuck to basic, primary colours. Now, with three months to work on the project, Admiral produced a yellow kit with blue and white stripes down the sleeves, the sides of the shorts and hooped around the tops of the socks. At last, something truly unique. *The Daily Telegraph* would sneer about 'hot piping, redolent of Ruritanian bandsmen', but it was a huge hit in the replica market and Admiral sold tens of thousands over the seven years they maintained the core elements of its design. Indeed it provided the template for the England shirt they would produce from 1975 when Revie had moved to the national side, as well as multiple other club strips that their initial £7,000 investment with Leeds United rapidly yielded.

The Leeds squad pose for an 'interesting' pre-season photo (left).

Mick Bates and Paul Madeley run out of the tunnel vs Stoke, 1974 (below right).

That defeat at Upton Park, Leeds' fourth of the season, was their last and their home victories over Derby, Sheffield United and Ipswich Town proved too much for Liverpool to match. Leeds won the title sitting at home, with a match to spare, when Arsenal won at Anfield on 24 April, the same night Revie's *This Is Your Life* was broadcast on ITV. "I feel as though someone has come along and lifted six tons of coal off my back," the manager said.

Leeds had never been hip and to their critics' eyes never would be. Revie, with his mohair suits, side-parting, sideburns creeping towards his earlobes and what Arthur Hopcraft memorably called his 'outdoors face as if he lives permanently in a keen wind', was forced to grow up far too young on the loss of his mother to cancer when he was 12. It made him cautious and conservative about appearance and etiquette. In his last few winters at Leeds, he liked a sheepskin coat but before that it had been crombies and macs. For men born in the 1920s and who had been children in the North through the Depression, middle-age struck early, but with Revie it never calcified his innovative streak. In his link-up with Admiral, once again he proved himself a pioneer with an enterprising sense as keen as the company's. Leeds United were the first of the modern, truly commercial English football clubs. Written off in the summer, they finished the following spring more stylish and formidable than ever. Dead and buried? Yesterday's men? They settled instead for 'the greatest in the land'.

Written off in the summer, they finished the following spring more stylish and formidable than ever.

1970s

Don built a formidable team — Eddie Gray

Eddie Gray was a cultured winger and one-club man, playing 454 games for Leeds United and scoring 52 goals. He made his debut three weeks shy of his 18th birthday and became an integral part of the legendary Leeds United side of the late '60s and '70s under manager Don Revie. He was never booked.

"I could've gone to Celtic but I picked Leeds only because I liked the manager, Don Revie. The scout John Barr invited me down and I'd been to a few clubs — I used to train at Celtic Park — and Don was waiting for me at the station himself when I was 15. The next day he took me training with the first team. When you're 15, that impresses you.

"Even though I was only 15, I realised how many good players were in that squad, even though they were just coming through the ranks then. There was no doubt they were gonna be successful. There was a great manager at the helm, who knew the game inside out, who knew players. So, when I got back to Glasgow, I just said to my dad, who was a big Celtic fan, that I was going to Leeds and that was that.

Eddie Gray goes on a mazy dribble against QPR.

"I was fortunate that I got in the team at an early age, when I was 17, and played there all my career. I think that's the thing about football — people talk about footballers now and money and all that but footballers want to play. All footballers want to play. That's what you're in the game for.

"Don built a team that was pretty formidable. A team that he could see playing together for 10 years and that's a long period of time in any footballer's career. I presume that's why so many of the players stayed around the Leeds area. A lot of the players stayed at Leeds … Norman [Hunter], Peter Lorimer, Terry [Yorath].

"Peter's the best striker of a ball I've seen. Not just a shot, he was just a clean striker of the ball. Peter's great asset was that he didn't need any back-lift. The ball would be nearly under Peter's feet and he could still hit it as hard as anyone could with a 20-yard run up.

"We had 14, 15 players … you get people like Terry, Mick Bates who was a terrific player … Mick stayed around all his career. He should probably have moved on. If Mick would've moved on, he'd probably have played for England. He decided to stay at Leeds but it was very hard to get into the team in the midfield area. I mean, I was a central midfield player but I was fortunate, I could play out wide so that didn't bother me. But Mick couldn't have played wide, his position was in the middle of the park so then you're up against Bremner and Giles, two of the greatest players that played. Funnily enough, Mick played about 200 games for Leeds. He was my mate, a good lad, terrific player … I always said to him: "You should have left and then you would have played with England." But he was so happy at Leeds.

"He just liked the whole atmosphere. I think that's what Don built. He built that atmosphere around the club, everybody would pull for one another and when you went there, you felt you were part of Don's family.

"When I first came down, I used to love to listen to Don telling me stories about [Tom] Finney and [Stanley] Matthews, about how good they were. I mean, great players could play in any era.

"The standards were very high and you realised that if you wanted to get in the team, you had to keep working hard. Training sessions were frightening at times. We used to play England against Scotland games and Don had to stop them because they were so competitive.

"I've got a few shirts lying about but I don't know where they are! My wife stores them somewhere. I've still got the tracksuit. In those days, when you're a player you don't really think about strips, you just think about whether you're gonna play or not. It's just when you get a little bit older and you look at the strip and you think: Oh I like that strip!.

"Funnily enough, somebody has done a painting of me but it looks like a photograph. It's quite big and I'm wearing the Admiral strip on it. It's a good picture." ●

1970s

Luton Town '74–'76

Words: Rob MacDonald

For 53 years, it had been black and white. But this was an era of colour, and it was time to stand out. Enter Eric Morecambe.

"Eric wanted something more striking on the pitch", says Roger Wash, Hatters' Heritage chairman. "Floodlights were far less powerful than they are today and he suggested orange, probably because Blackpool were one of his local League clubs when he was growing up and he was taken with their tangerine".

Morecambe had been attending games at Kenilworth Road since moving to Harpenden in 1969, relinquishing the chairmanship at his hometown club Morecambe FC as he did so. His love of football was genuine and shared by his family. His father and brother both played, and Eric and teenage son Gary began to watch Luton for their weekend fixes. In next to no time he was elected to the club's board — the story goes that Luton club secretary had put them in seats next to the director's box — and would be a director for more than five years. It was a position he'd take seriously throughout, quite apart from the boisterous spirit of the *Morecambe & Wise Show*.

Completely overhauling the club's colours, however, did speak slightly more to the latter. An orange, as reminiscent of the Dutch masters as much as it was of the Seasiders, dominated, with a nod to the white retained as a thick vertical stripe running the full length of the shirt, from left shoulder to the hem at the waist, accented either side by slimmer navy trims. Collars and cuffs, depending on the year or perhaps even the month, were either black or navy, though this settled into navy as standard when Admiral took over the manufacturing of the shirt in 1974.

It wasn't just a sartorial step up. Luton had just won promotion to Division One and the first Admiral kit incorporated a brand new club crest, also with orange at its centre. Although designed a year earlier, it was first displayed on the already-popular stripe when Luton played Liverpool, wearing Admiral, in August 1974. On-pitch success was hard to come by that season and ultimately Luton were relegated by a single point, but the orange shirt became a firm staple of their look and Admiral produced the kit until 1979. It was one of their most dramatic shirts and one of the most fondly recalled.

1970s

Eric Morecambe at the heart of the Luton Town team photo, 1974.

1970s

Luton Town FC may not have been the most fashionable — Eric was asked by a boy in a 1973 Valerie Singleton interview why, with so many superior clubs to choose from, he didn't support "a good team like Arsenal". But the answer, after describing in detail exactly where the enquirer's black eye would appear (it was a different time), was an actually quite profound "I support Luton because I like Luton". Perhaps the simplicity appealed — the one place where Eric could be a spectator.

Nevertheless, Luton were catapulted into popular culture by their celebrity fan, who made regular references to the club on his prime-time TV show throughout the decade. Slightly less expected was the 1974 single featuring the squad called 'Hatters Hatters', by the Barron Knights, a 'humorous pop rock group'. It was a collaboration that could have gone either way, but in the end, eschewed the potential for the daft. They decided to play it as heartfelt as the great man's attachment to both his football clubs, who now play for the Eric Morecambe Trophy on the occasions they meet, just one small part of a colossal — and colourful — legacy. ●

England '74–'80

Words: Adam Bushby and Rob MacDonald

If the lustre of England's World Cup victory was fading by the time they let a 2-0 lead slip to West Germany in the 1970 quarter-finals, it had completely dissipated as Alf Ramsey's men trooped off the Wembley turf having failed to qualify for the 1974 tournament, undone by the goalkeeping heroics of Jan Tomaszewski, a man Brian Clough had disparaged as a "clown".

Ramsey, knighted in 1967 for delivering the Jules Rimet trophy the previous summer, was dismissed in May 1974, and despite Joe Mercer becoming a candidate after relative success in a caretaker role, the FA were set on his replacement. Enter Don Revie, whose Leeds side had just scythed through the First Division to the 1973-74 title, already one of football's great modernisers and the very man to take England forward.

Arriving at Lancaster Gate, Revie sought to shake up everything, from — optimistically, it turned out — introducing 'Land of Hope and Glory' as a go-to England anthem and, in an unprecedented and controversial break with tradition, changing the kit.

Although renowned for not being the most progressive bunch of suits in the world, the FA were making efforts to modernise and Revie did have at least one forward-looking ally among the executive — Secretary (effectively Chief Executive) Ted Croker. A former Charlton Athletic defender, Croker's career had been curtailed by injuries sustained while a pilot in the RAF, which he had joined in 1942. By the early 1950s, he had established a heavy machinery company and through the '60s had become a successful entrepreneur, ultimately selling Liner-Croker Ltd in 1973.

Companies looking to pitch for a slice of the FA's commercial pie viewed his appointment as a statement of intent, Croker says in his autobiography: "A number of companies, believing that I would be more receptive to their proposals than my predecessors, wrote asking if they could bid for the exclusive contract for supplying the England kit … I advised the international committee that we should accept the most advantageous offer but it would mean redesigning the England strip. They agreed …".

1970s

Away shirt (left), third shirt (below) and walk-out jacket (bottom).

Admiral's experience in the market and their relationship with Revie from his time at Leeds meant they were invited to present to the FA, who voted through their designs and the first-ever England commercial agreement. It would see Admiral paying £15,000 a year, or a 10% royalty, whichever was greater, to exclusively manufacture the kits but also replicate and market them to boys.

"I was enthusiastic about the idea," Croker wrote, "because it would give boys the chance to identify with the national side, a chance that had been denied them when the England shirt was no different from an ordinary t-shirt. It also meant that parents could buy their sons a present which would be used often and not be discarded when the novelty wore off, as happens with so many presents given to children."

And the new England shirts were novel indeed. The design was like nothing the national team had worn before: white, with a V-neck and winged collar (the first time in 20 years an England jersey had a collar) now featuring a red and royal blue stripe at the edge. The same bold red and blue lines ran down the sleeves to the cuffs, edged just like the collar, with the England badge embroidered on a white patch on the left breast and — most controversially of all — the Admiral logo, ironed on in yellow or white, on the right.

1970s

The reaction to the new kits, first worn in October 1974, ranged from smitten (every child in every playground) to appalled (traditionalists everywhere … former England forward Jimmy Greaves stated that the new stripes made the kit look like pyjamas). The shirts weren't the only thing to bear the now-iconic Admiral logo — it, and the company name, was generously applied to walk-out jackets, warm-up gear and even the physio's bags, which when naturally placed alongside an injured player gave the company the greatest billboard imaginable, as pictures were beamed into houses all over the country. Along with those watching at home, a crowd of 83,000 inside Wembley saw Revie's new-look England beat Czechoslovakia 3-0. It was the best possible start.

Variations in kit style were commonplace during the '70s and the eagle-eyed among the Wembley crowd could spot yellow vinyl Admiral logos alongside white ones on the shirts of the England players during the same game. Against Scotland, in May 1975, there were no logos at all. For the first game in Bratislava against Czechoslovakia in October of the same year, abandoned by heavy fog after 17 minutes, and for the hastily rearranged fixture the next day, more than half the side wore shirts with no emblem on the left breast — Colin Bell, Mick Channon, Allan Clarke, Gerry Francis, Kevin Keegan and Malcolm Macdonald were the logo-less ones. Uniformity was not, it seems, a concern for said uniforms in those early days.

The company name was generously applied to walk-out jackets, warm-up gear and even the physio's bags.

The lesser-spotted yellow logos also made a rare appearance against Team America during the Bicentennial Cup, held in the US in 1976 to mark America's 200th year of independence. Essentially an NASL selection, England's opponents fielded Pelé, Giorgio Chinaglia and, bizarrely, Bobby Moore and Tommy Smith. England ran out 3-1 winners with a brace from Keegan and one from captain Gerry Francis. The shirt chosen was a lightweight number as a means for the team to cope with the US heat.

There appears to have been great difficulty attaching both the Admiral logo and the three lions badge to the new lightweight versions of the England shirts introduced in 1975, with the emblem placement haphazard at best, but then that's all part of the charm, surely? Before the shirt market went through the stratosphere, we have the endearing spectacle of a different version of the kit every game, with badges embroidered on by hand and placement something of a lottery.

It's also easy to take a disparaging view of England under Revie, but perhaps their record bears a closer look too. A 0-0 draw with Portugal was their undoing in a Euro 1976 qualifying group won by Czechoslovakia, who would go on to be champions. And agonisingly, in the 1978 World Cup qualifiers, they swapped 2-0 victories with Italy, only to miss out on goal difference having scored three goals fewer. If history has taught us one thing though, it's that you really don't want to be referred to as a 'golden generation' among press for whom a World Cup win is still a living memory, and the facts were incontrovertible — a supremely talented group of players missed out on a series of major finals, and Revie had to go. He resigned in 1977.

Admiral's five-year deal meant that the kit, remaining unchanged throughout that time, did eventually see some success, England qualifying undefeated from their 1980 group. Although in the finals themselves, the team would don a new, arguably even more iconic Admiral design.

1970s

Unbeaten at Wembley in an Admiral shirt — Gerry Francis

Gerry Francis made his England debut in the same game as Admiral, a home qualifier vs Czechoslovakia in 1974. Due to injuries he would only make 12 appearances for England between 1974 and 1976, but was captain for eight of those games, scoring three goals.

"When Don Revie took over, there was real hope and great expectation for the England team, due to Don's brilliant club record with Leeds United. The media coverage was massive, including the new Admiral kit. I remember walking out onto the Wembley pitch for my debut, a European Championship Group Qualifier against Czechoslovakia (the eventual winners of Euro '76) to a packed stadium and brilliant atmosphere. We eventually won that game 3-0 against a very good side and the stadium towards the end was electric.

"As it was my debut, I don't recall how big a departure it was from the old kit, but in that summer it seemed everybody was wearing an England Admiral shirt. In May 1976, I had just captained QPR to runners-up in the First Division and had been made captain of England (a fantastic honour) at 23 years of age. On the 13 June, I captained England in a World Cup Qualifier in Helsinki against Finland that we won 4-1 — that was the last time I played for my country. I was 24 years old.

"For the next three seasons I was plagued by injuries to my back and my knee in particular. I was devastated that I missed so much football in my prime, and still wonder what might have been. I was still struggling injury-wise when the World Cup came round in 1978, you reminisce that if you hadn't been injured, would we have qualified?

Gerry Francis leads the England team out as captain for the first time (left).

In the company of greats — Francis is flanked by Moore and Pelé (right).

"I joined Crystal Palace and Terry Venables in June 1979 for £465,000, and got back to my best there, with 40,000-plus gates most weeks, and topped the First Division for a while. The Palace Admiral shirt was loved by everyone and became iconic. I also got back into the England squad being picked by Ron Greenwood, but had to pull out because of a kidney stone can you believe, and wasn't picked again.

"The picture of myself and Bobby Moore and Pelé (below), is also iconic for me personally. Two of the world's greatest ever players. The photo was taken in Philadelphia at the Bicentennial Tournament 1976, when England, Brazil, Italy and Team America played. I still have my Admiral shirt from the Team America game that we won 3-1 (another goal for yours truly), along with Rivellino's shirt from the Brazil game, which alongside with my England Admiral shirt against Scotland, when I scored twice, and many more are very special to me — I also never lost at Wembley playing for England in an Admiral shirt."

1970s

Making history in Admiral — Viv Anderson

In November 1978, Viv Anderson became the first black player to represent England, when he made his debut against Czechoslovakia. He won 30 international caps, scoring twice, and played for Brian Clough's Nottingham Forest for 10 years from 1974-1984, winning back-to-back European Cups, a First Division and League Cup double, and the 1979 European Super Cup. He also represented Arsenal, Manchester United and Sheffield Wednesday.

Viv Anderson makes his debut for England vs Czechoslovakia, 1978.

"If you'd said to me all those years ago that as a skinny lad from Nottingham, I'd play 30 times for my country and win this, that and the other, I'd have said you were mad. To put on your first shirt in a full international — well, I had the same feeling that a fan would have. It's just fantastic. And in those days too, the Wembley tunnel wasn't in the middle of the stand, it was at one end, so you'd come out behind the goal, and you'd listen to the roar getting louder and louder and louder till you got to the middle of the pitch.

"I was very lucky that it happened to be me on that night. There was a lot of speculation before that game that either Lawrie Cunningham, who's sadly not with us anymore, was going to be the first [black player to play for England] or myself. Prior to that game, we'd played in Sofia, in Bulgaria, and we shared a room, so we were thinking and talking about upcoming games, who'd be the first, or not be the first. But there wasn't much we could do, of course, eventually we ended up talking about cars — and ended up buying a car for Lawrie instead!

"Playing for England is a completely different environment, a completely different mindset, but I tried to focus on the basic things that got me in the England squad to start with. My focus — other than 'don't make a fool of yourself please' — was on getting a tackle in, getting a header in, passing to a team mate ... so I just had to do that, and try not to think too much about the fact I was doing it playing for England! I managed to get myself into professional mode and was really focused on getting the result, first and foremost, and ignoring everything on the periphery.

"It was a unique time, and it was a day I'll never forget. Admiral was a big part of all that, it was England's kit selection and they were everywhere at the time, synonymous with football kits, and they were the go-to sports brand. But my personal favourite was obviously my debut, it was in an Admiral shirt and I've still got it to this day. It's my favourite shirt and always will be." ●

1970s

Manchester United '75–'80

Words: Rob MacDonald

These shirts, like many in this book, are time machines. These ones in particular will take you to Manchester United's consecutive Wembley appearances in the late '70s, when the FA Cup was the biggest show in town. Success in the second final in 1977 was massive, not least because it stopped Liverpool, then in pursuit of an historic treble, in their tracks. What more perfect coincidence could there be for a United fan?

Those days are a far cry from the most recent iterations of the club, certainly the Ferguson years and whatever you might call the years that have followed since. They're not at all the relentlessly successful decades of the '90s and '00s, with league titles aplenty, but nor are they the subsequent festival of change, which has put so much distance between us and that age of relative innocence. I sometimes wonder what today's younger fans will be nostalgic about in 30, 40, 50 years' time — remember how your old dad was a fan *without* any non-fungible tokens and *didn't* post on YouTube demanding we buy a striker?

It's no coincidence a Mancunian's choice is between primary colours, red or blue. Football is a basic building block of life.

There's a good chance though, even when the replica shirt's 100th anniversary rolls around, that they will still find something in these shirts. And so they should — because they're some of the few reminders of how things looked, how things felt, how things *were*. Especially in this city, as football-obsessed as they come, the shirt is the ultimate identity — like their Liverpudlian cousins, it's no coincidence a Mancunian's choice is between primary colours, red or blue. Football is a basic building block of life.

1970s

The white away strip was said to have been revved up a little to reflect Docherty's adventurous style of play.

At the time they were worn in anger though, United were a club trying hard to reclaim such significance. The Matt Busby hangover was one that rivals the post-Ferguson era, with the great man still a part of the club, first as general manager, then director, for 11 years, after stepping away from the manager's job. Their 1974 relegation to Division Two is symbolically represented by Denis Law, released on a free transfer by new United manager Tommy Docherty (whom Law recommended for the job), backheeling in a goal for Manchester City to send United down on the last day of the season. Although, let's be fair to poor Denis — even now I can see the devastation on his face … I mean, who concedes from a backheel? — results on the day meant United would have gone down anyway. But George Best, too, departed Old Trafford in 1974 aged only 27, as the club attempted to move into a new era. At least their stay in the Second Division lasted just a season, the likes of Stuart Pearson, Lou Macari and Sammy McIlroy the new stars.

With them for their First Division return in the 1975-76 season were Admiral, who, in something of a coup given the proximity of the existing suppliers, Cheshire-based Umbro, to Old Trafford, had managed to nip in and secure a five-year package off the back of their success with Leeds and England. It was perceptive, again, from Admiral's founder Bert Patrick as the club were clearly on an upward curve under Docherty and, unlike England, United played matches year-round in an awful lot of potential shirt markets — the mammoth 1975 tour was Phileas Fogg-worthy, covering pre-revolution Iran, Hong Kong, Jakarta, Perth, Sydney, Melbourne, Auckland and Los Angeles in 38 days.

It helped Admiral's cause of course that the shirts were treated with the utmost respect. Busby had been in attendance for Patrick's presentation of a new England kit to the FA in 1974, and invited Admiral's managing director to Old Trafford to see what could be done for the club. Like Leeds, the home strip remained largely untouched, unlikely to have gained the approval of either Busby, the Edwards family, or indeed the fans had it been trifled with.

The white away strip was altogether more adventurous and said to have been revved up a little — with the addition of three racing stripes from shoulder to hem — to reflect Docherty's adventurous style of play. It was certainly strikingly progressive on a white shirt; it looked gorgeous on a tracksuit top. Warm-up gear in home colours wasn't excluded either and the full red United tracksuit from 1978, with stripes from Admiral's classic tramlines template that were intended to line up from torso down the legs, looking absolutely wild (if not, the players thought, slightly skeletal) against both its predecessors and competitors.

All that was missing from this bright and forward-looking melting pot of style and substance was success on the pitch. It duly followed, in the form of a third-place finish in the top division and an FA Cup final, although to comply with FA rules the Admiral logo did not appear. Not on the shirt at least; it was pretty hard to miss emblazoned on the back of both United's and Southampton's tracksuits. The United jersey underneath was a classic affair, with a trophy and 'Wembley 1976' embroidered under the club badge.

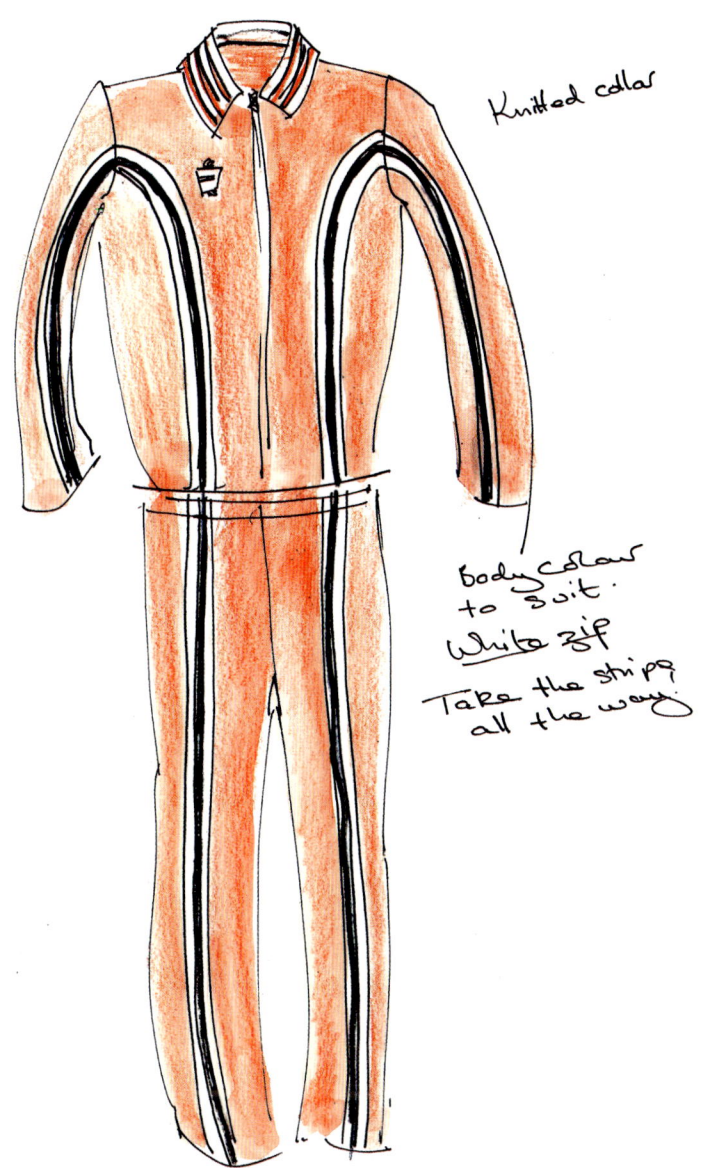

1970s

Admiral's shirt designer Lindsay Jelley's sketch, detailing the United tramline tracksuit.

Personalised walk-out jackets, hoodies and bomber jackets spoilt the United players (right).

Following a shock defeat to Southampton, the trophy remained elusive for another 12 months, but in 1977 United were back, in a slightly less lavish black tracksuit top, but still in a classic Admiral red v-neck jersey, with three narrow red stripes on the white trim, beating Liverpool to lift the cup. It was the perfect way to see in the club's centenary in 1978 and for the '78-'79 season, Admiral also produced a commemorative embroidered crest. Notably, and extremely unusually, Admiral had modified the previous club crest upon taking over the contract in 1975, stitching the ship in the badge in red, when previously it had been gold.

Despite not setting the league on fire over the next two seasons, and following the departure of Docherty, United enjoyed progress in the FA Cup again in '78-'79 and reached a third final in four years under Dave Sexton, where they met Arsenal. It was a classic — the 'five-minute-final' — with a mini-revival from 2-0 down between the 86th and 88th minute having the wind well and truly taken out of its sails by a sucker-punch winner from the Gunners' Alan Sunderland in the 89th. "That's when you're at your most vulnerable, when suddenly you've got it all back," opined the immortal Brian Moore. How right he was.

Manchester United's mini-revival in the '70s coincided with the Admiral boom, a perfect storm in which the Leicester firm had gone straight to the top, signing up Leeds, England and United in their first 18 months of replica kit-making. But even by '79 it was becoming a crowded and competitive marketplace, never more evident than when the United deal came up for renewal in 1980 — despite wanting to continue with Admiral, it was the club that came to the table with the proposed annual fee, which had increased from £15,000 to £100,000. Adidas duly muscled in.

It was a sign of things to come, but what an impression Admiral had left behind. Routinely declared a fan favourite, the fact that the shirt deal spanned five seasons meant these kits, by this brand, did become associated with a team of an era, not just a season, and, perhaps as importantly, an identity and a way of playing under Docherty that the club had been searching for since Busby. Sun-drenched days at Wembley help; a kit for the ages does too.

1970s

Bright colours, bright football — Lou Macari

A member of Celtic's renowned 'Quality Street Gang', Lou Macari was an heir to Celtic's Lisbon Lions and scored 26 goals in 58 games upon breaking into the first team. He moved to Old Trafford in 1973 and spent 11 years at Manchester United, winning a Second Division title and an FA Cup across 329 appearances.

Lou Macari dictates the play vs Norwich City, 1979.

"I had no hesitation. Once I knew Manchester United were interested, I was going there.

"Unfortunately, in my first season we were relegated, but the manager, Tommy Doc, had a great belief that not only would we be back in the next season, that we'd be back and be better. It was a bit of a bold statement, and I'm not so sure many of us believed it ... just because you've gone down and you want to go back to the top league, it just doesn't happen just because you want it to.

"We set about and unbeknown to us, we became a team that people quite liked watching. We got forward when we had the opportunity and we tried to score goals. So we tended to be a team under Tommy Doc that was talked about, because of the attacking style and the fact that we didn't sit back and we had no fear of anybody either.

"So we were back and got ourselves to a Cup Final. I think we lost that one because everyone expected us to win, because of the two names, Manchester United vs Southampton. But anybody that looks back at that Southampton team, they'll see a lot of good players. A strong team, a big team. And on the day, as can happen in Cup Finals, you can not play that well and the opposition get a bit of a break. And the winning goal was the 84th minute ... we didn't really have a chance to get back in the game.

"But I remember getting in the dressing room and Tommy Doc, to lift us all (and we just thought he was saying it just to lift us, not that he believed it), said, "Well, don't worry, lads, we'll be back the following year and we'll win it the next time."

"Well, of course, we *were* back the following year. We didn't expect to win it because it was Liverpool. But pressure was off. We felt like we were a bit like Southampton the year before, there was no pressure on us because they were going for the treble and everybody was tipping them to beat us. I don't think we would have focused on stopping them winning it for any other reason except we wanted to win it, and we wanted to make up for the season before where we didn't play as well as we could have done and as a result, lost it. And of course, we got a break or two on the day.

"There wasn't a great deal back then made of strips, but it was just starting to catch on, it was just changing a little bit. I think previous to that year, maybe every club in the country was what you would expect it be, and there was very little difference.

"Then along started to come a little bit of a new brand of kit, led by Admiral. I think most people liked it ... well, actually you can take it from me that all of my teammates did like the gear, otherwise they — and the club — would have voiced an opinion. They would have said: "This is not Man United, this is not us".

"I think it's fair to say that the Admiral strip did suit us because it was something different. And certainly those years, in bright colours, the team was playing bright football. I've kept a few of mine; I've got my Cup Final ones up the stairs." ●

1970s

The Admiral Cup Final '76

Words: Rob MacDonald

If there was any doubt that Admiral's bosses were shrewd operators when it came to football and its burgeoning television coverage, it was removed by the time of the 1976 FA Cup final. The nation's showpiece sporting event was day-long appointment viewing on the BBC — *Cup Final Grandstand* began at 11.15am at the team hotels. It included coverage from various supporters' buses, a *Cup Final It's A Knockout*, the team's pitch inspections, highlights, profiles, manager interviews, the lot. The only break from Cup Final content all day was 10 minutes of horse racing from Ascot and a package featuring Muhammad Ali's heavyweight title win on points over Jimmy Young in Maryland. In short, it was a day of spectacle that commanded viewing figures in the millions.

Despite Admiral being well into their second year of providing club kits, multiple colours and progressive design was still quite a novel sight on both playing and non-playing staff.

And perhaps burned by the prime marketing television had afforded Admiral upon the launch of the new England kit in 1974, in which the physio bags carried the manufacturer's logo and were visible on screen for minutes on end in the event of an injury, the BBC told Admiral boss Bert Patrick in no uncertain terms that walk-out jackets were not to feature 'ADMIRAL' splashed across the front, as England's new kit had done. Undeterred, Patrick put the company name on the back of the now-famed jackets instead, and was rewarded with an Admiral procession as the cameras, as was tradition, followed the players from behind as they made their way out of the tunnel and onto the pitch.

Tommy Docherty and Lawrie McMenemy lead the teams out at a packed Wembley.

1970s

The walk-out jackets alone were the epitome of Admiral swagger, trailblazing for both sides.

In reality, the kits were probably distinctive enough without company wording. The walk-out jackets alone were the epitome of Admiral swagger, trailblazing for both sides. United's evoked their new away kit, worn for the first time that season, in all white with the now-iconic black stripes down the left hand side, the Admiral logo sitting on top. The manufacturer's first Southampton assignment modelled another innovation, the chevron design, red on white, across the chest, but with the logo-manufacturer badges reversed so Admiral sat on the right, with the Southampton badge on a black background on the left.

Southampton were significant underdogs. They'd even lost the toss for choice of kits, meaning that while United donned their red home jerseys, Lawrie McMenemy's men were wearing yellow shirts with blue shorts underneath the more traditional colours on their jackets. The yellow kit was another classic, mind you, Admiral taking advantage of most clubs' acceptance of more radical changes to away shirts by including taping in blue, sweeping down the arms, and blue trim on the V-neck and cuffs of the sleeves. What's more — if Southampton were looking for any foreshadowing on a day where the bookmakers had them as long as 7-1 for the cup — the Queen, in attendance to watch the game and present the trophy, was wearing the same colours, albeit in the form of a large blue coat rather than a full replica kit.

Peter Osgood and Lou Macari battle for the ball (right).

Gordon Hill (United) shoots at goal past Nicky Holmes (below right).

United had bounced back from the Second Division at the first time of asking and were set fair to finish third in the top-flight upon their return. An FA Cup against a side from the league below was expected to be a routine coronation for Tommy Docherty's team as they looked to make it back to the top of English football. But Southampton had only been relegated alongside United in 1974 because the league had adopted a 'three teams down' rule for the first time — they had actually finished four points better off than Docherty's side. McMenemy had replaced Ted Bates at the end of that campaign, had been allowed to rebuild in the second tier and Southampton were challenging at the right end of the table. They finished sixth, but had endured a colossal fixture pile-up before the final, playing eight times in April, so it was hard to argue with the bookies' assessment of their chances.

1970s

"Bobby Stokes ... hit well ...

In the event, it was to be the Saints' most famous day. Surviving early pressure from United, they grew into the game and had chances of their own in the second half. A late Bobby Stokes goal, struck so early from outside the box that Alex Stepney in the United goal couldn't adjust in time, bounced one, two, three, four times on its way into the far corner. Delirium took hold of the Saints fans in the stands as United claimed Stokes was offside.

In the aftermath, chaos ensued in the best possible way, as only chaos in the aftermath of a giant-killing or shock result can. Southampton partied in London before heading off down the motorway for an open-top bus parade back home, starting at the Dell. Scheduled for 45 minutes, the parade took more than four hours as the whole city seemingly lined the streets. Goalscorer Stokes won a car for scoring the opener in the final, but couldn't drive. He was presented with the Ford Granada on the pitch at the Dell before Mick Channon's testimonial two days later, but couldn't have moved it — presumably someone else did before the game started.

And United didn't suffer for too long — they picked up their runners-up medals and were back, in red and in Admiral, 12 months later for the 1977 final, defeating arch-rivals Liverpool and dashing any hopes of a treble, which they'd probably have preferred anyway. McMenemy would ultimately lead Southampton back to the First Division in 1978, his legendary status secured. And the '76–'77 season saw Admiral sign up more clubs including Leicester City, Norwich City, West Ham United and Sheffield United as they continued to change the sartorial face of football. ●

Bobby Stokes celebrates his winning goal (above).

The Southampton squad line up with the FA Cup pride of place (right).

Oh, it's there!"

1970s

Wales '76–'79

Words: Andi Thomas

In the beginning, the football kit was without form, and void. Practically a rugby shirt, in fact, if you can imagine such indignity. And nowadays? Well, they don't hang around for long at all and there's not just second but third kits too, and sponsors and manufacturers and more colours than you would have thought possible to distinguish one group of 11 players from another.

But between those two points, between the before times and the now times, there was a sweet spot. A couple of decades in which everybody got it right at least once. It's probably not controversial to suggest that almost every fanbase, if pushed, would identify their side's greatest ever shirt as arriving somewhere between the mid-70s, when things started to get interesting, and the late '90s, when things started to get out of hand. And it's pretty much a given that for any Wales fan, unless they're particularly attached to Billy Meredith's lace-up collars, it'll be Admiral '76.

The boys of '58 are the best of Wales, for they had the best players and they had the best story. John Charles, the greatest player in the world, injured for the quarter-final. Pelé, 17, about to take the first step on the journey to becoming Pelé. A case can be made that Wales would have won that game with a fit Charles up front, and as such a case can be made that Wales would have won the World Cup, Pelé notwithstanding. It is not, if we're being honest, an open and shut case; it is conjecture, and hopeful, starry-eyed, possibly deluded conjecture at that. But it is a case. (Buy me a couple of drinks and you can hear me talk myself into it.)

Then there's Gareth Bale and company, who made it to three major tournaments out of four and made Belgium look pretty silly along the way. Indeed, much of the praise they received ahead of Euro 2016 was connected to 1958: these were the drought breakers, bringing the sweet wet kiss of major tournament football back to a parched and thirsty land. Twice, by some bizarre twist of fate, Wales' men's team had found themselves in possession of one of the best players in the world. Twice he'd had a pretty decent supporting cast. Twice that had made the difference between there and not there.

1970s

As for the boys of '76, they did not make it to the finals of the Euros. We can only speculate that somewhere in Wrexham, a young boy truly believed that Arfon Griffiths was the greatest player in the world. Still, they remain the only Wales team ever to top a qualifying group. Bale and co. got to the Euros twice as runners-up, and needed the playoffs to make Qatar 2022, while the path to 1958 was a meandering thing that involved getting knocked out of the European zone, then getting thrown into a playoff against Israel, who had advanced through their qualifiers without playing a game, as opponent after opponent withdrew against the backdrop of the Suez crisis and the Arab League boycott. Technically, Wales went to Sweden as the representatives of Asia and Africa.

And it's not Terry Yorath's fault that the finals of the 1976 European Championships contained exactly four teams. Wales got to the last eight! They got to the quarters! Doesn't count as a major tournament? Only if you're powerfully stingy about where you draw that line. Imagine starting at the semi-finals. How are you supposed to get hyped up for a week? Not so much a sticker album as a sticker pamphlet.

It is one of the quieter iniquities of football: the finest kits don't always clothe the finest football, and the worst don't always get lumbered with the worst. England's Admiral shirt of the early 1980s never got the England triumph it deserved. On the flipside, Fulham completely owned the First Division 2000-01, ending the campaign with a frankly daft 101 points, but an aesthetically just universe would have seen them demoted 99 points for doing so in a plain black and white kit, with only a sponsors' logo in the middle of their shirt adding any pizazz whatsoever. Lovely football, lots of goals, ignominious relegation. Rules is rules.

Alan Curtis turning out for Wales vs England, 1979.

"I think it was the shock of it at first, the design I mean. Some of the older players were like whoa! (laughs). Then you'd pull it on and try and get the stripes on the shirt to align with the ones on the shorts, which wasn't always easy."

– Alan Curtis, Wales International

1970s

There stands Berry, beautiful, short shorts with yellow stripes, track top with plunging yellow chevrons, hair limned with light: Afro as halo.

But while great kits may not always get the performances they deserve, they do acquire resonance in other ways. They gather up stories. Particularly back then, back in the day, when kits were allowed to hang around for season after season, and so came to be associated not just with one campaign but with generational cycles, with teams as they shifted and fans as they grew. This is the Wales kit of that George Berry photo. And this is the Wales kit of perhaps the greatest of the celebrity-in-kit stories. Keep your Drake. The rumour, the myth, the legend has it that Bob Marley wore the Admiral '76 tracksuit top on television.

Nobody seems to be able to find the actual clip, but that's a modest inconvenience. Kit myths evade the scientific method and speak straight to the heart. Marley wore a (navy blue) tracksuit when he was playing in Battersea Park; Admiral head honcho Bert Patrick once claimed that reggae fans were buying the Wales range because it was red, green and yellow … you can see how and why it 'happened', even if it never actually happened. And in any case, the absence of photographic evidence doesn't matter. There weren't many people wearing football tat better than Bob Marley in the '70s, but one of them was George Berry.

You know the photograph. You certainly do if you're a Wales fan with even a passing interest in the excitingly mediocre old days. There stands Berry, beautiful, short shorts with yellow stripes, track top with plunging yellow chevrons, hair limned with light: Afro as halo. His arms are tucked behind his back, his eyes directed off to his right. There are times I look at this picture and see the very image of athletic relaxation, a professional fully in control of his emotions, a man entirely in the zone. But more often I see vulnerability, a hint of apprehension; are those lips puckered, fretting? Is that brow furrowed? Berry was about to make his debut, after all, and West Germany were a pretty decent team. And he was a black man, at the time believed to be Wales' first black international, playing the game at a time that was not kind to black players. If he was a little worried, if he was rocking back on his heels just a touch at the pressure on those shoulders, it would be hard to blame him.

George Berry resplendent in his Wales walk-out jacket, 1979.

1970s

Terry Yorath beats Graeme Souness to the ball at Ninian Park in the Home Nations Championship, 1979.

> "As red as the dragon with daffodil yellow and leek green stripes. It couldn't have screamed more Taff if it had a picture of Richard Burton on the back. I loved it. There is a great photo of kids in Merthyr Tydfil at a summer football school in the '70s. I'd say at least half had that great Wales Admiral kit. It was the absolute required top of its era."
>
> – Jonny Owen, producer, actor and writer

This is a shirt of multiple failures. Berry made his debut in 1979. He and his teammates lost 2-0 to West Germany and ultimately missed out on Euro 1980, which had been expanded to eight teams. The Admiral kit had also failed to qualify for the 1978 World Cup in Argentina: Wales finished bottom of Group 7 after the suits made the dreadful decision to play their last home qualifier, a must-win game against Scotland, at Anfield. The Scottish fans poured down in their thousands, Joe Jordan handled the ball and got a penalty for it, misery and woe abounded.

And then there was '76. Call it another failure on technical grounds, or call it an overlooked and underappreciated success, the general consensus seems to be that Yugoslavia were the better team over two legs and deserved to progress to the finals in … huh, Yugoslavia. Yorath later blamed himself for missing a penalty in the second leg in Cardiff, a 1-1 draw, but most of the rest of the country blamed the referee. Nobody enjoyed the penalty he gave Yugoslavia, nor the Wales goals he ruled out. Indeed, the crowd liked it so little that Wales ended up banned from playing in their own capital.

But look up the footage now and it's the kits that really pop out. Yugoslavia are wearing a strong, sensible blue, with three stripes running down long sleeves. They look precisely as they should. Wales, though. Big lapels. Tight shirts. Short sleeves. Those yellow streaks arcing up from the legs and flashing outwards, accentuating the shoulders, making the big hair bigger. The winning team are anchored firmly in the present; the losing team are losing, yes, but they are bringing through a delirious and uncertain future. This Admiral kit contains all that is to come in kit design, for good and for ill: it will unfold into every triumph and every failure, every misstep, every hubristic adventure into colours that aren't real and shapes that shouldn't be. Squint and you can see the '80s forming, pulsing, ominous. Squint harder and you can see the '90s, in all its psychedelic terror. Squint even harder and you'll pass out, yellow and red and green dancing behind your twitching eyes. ●

Leicester City '76–'79

Words: Rob MacDonald

It was probably inevitable that Leicester's most famous manufacturer would end up clothing its football heroes. The club already enjoyed an indirect relationship with Admiral via Peter Shilton, whose personalised shirts and tracksuit had kickstarted the branding of professional football attire a few years earlier. Nevertheless, when Leicester City took to the field for the 1976-77 First Division season, they were sporting a shirt which, although cotton like its predecessors, was quite unlike them in almost every other way. It was also completely unique for a completely unique reason.

An Admiral advert in *Shoot!* magazine at the time let readers in on an unexpected creative conception: "Manager Jimmy Bloomfield wanted a completely different identity and designed the kit himself". Bloomfield had been appointed Foxes manager upon their promotion back to the First Division in 1971, and by most accounts had been searching for a different identity ever since. This included, as Don Revie had at Leeds, aping Real Madrid and changing Leicester's home kit to all white in 1972, although the change lasted a season and failed to inspire — despite putting out an entertaining team featuring the likes of Frank Worthington, they finished 16th.

This shirt bordered on the space age compared with its predecessors.

It took four years for Bloomfield to try again, but what a eureka moment he must have had. Moving the logo to the centre of the chest was small fry — anyone could do that. The really extraordinary detail was the Admiral logo taping around the arms and armpits, which looked almost like it was designed to enable a sleeveless version, should temperatures rocket uncontrollably in the East Midlands. A confetti of royal blue Admiral logo epaulettes followed the line of the taping, a trick repeated in an even more angular manner on the trim of the V-neck. A white polo neck collar and cuffs, both with blue trim, completed the look that bordered on the space age compared with its predecessors.

1970s

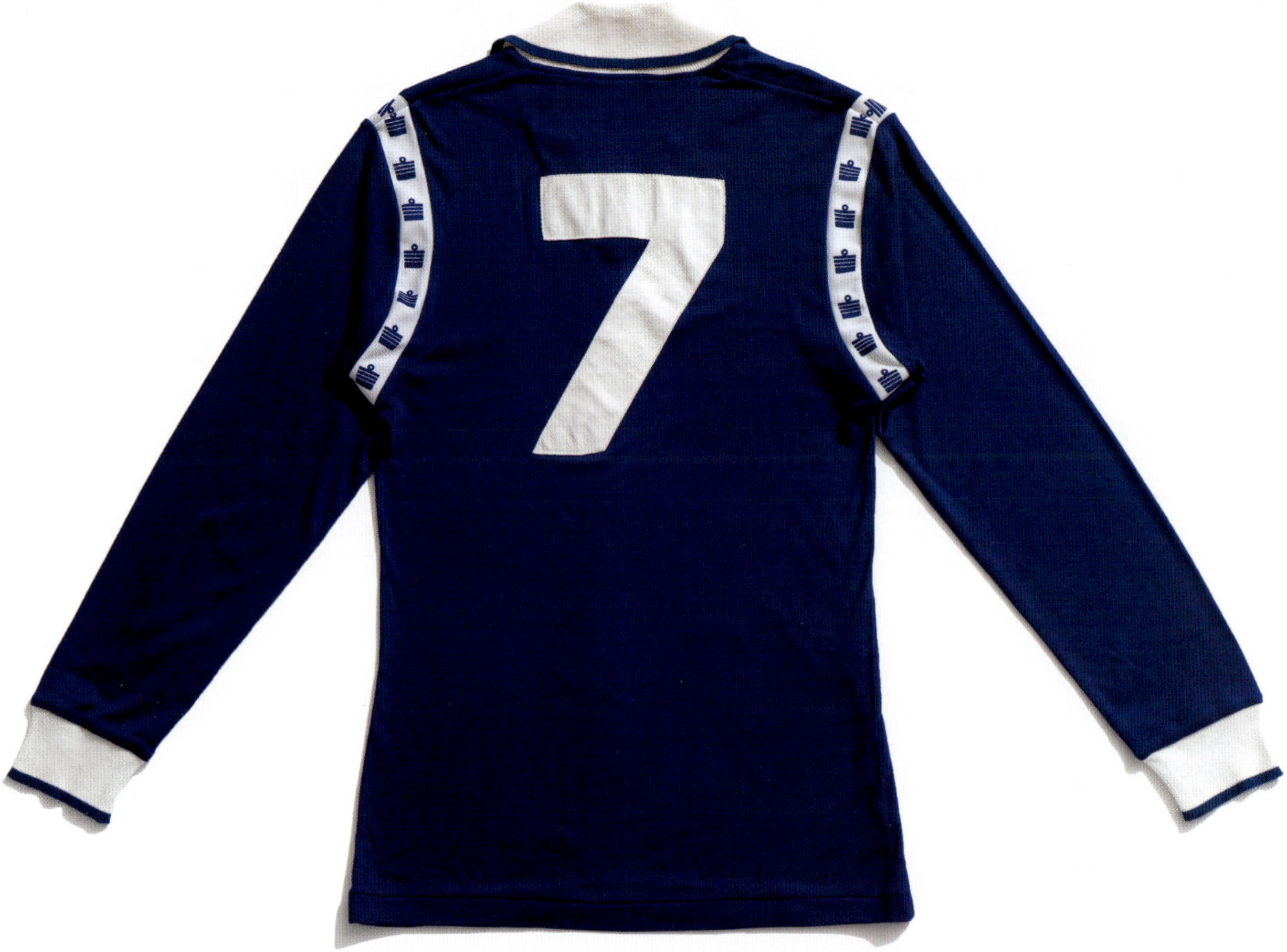
7

Admiral
MENS 101cm
TO FIT CHEST 40in

LEICESTER CITY
FOOTBALL CLUB

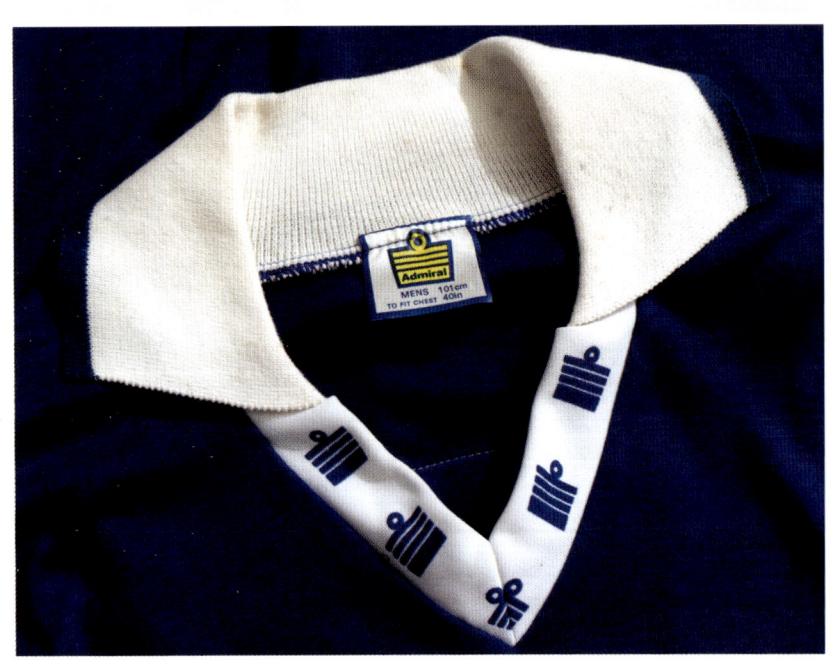

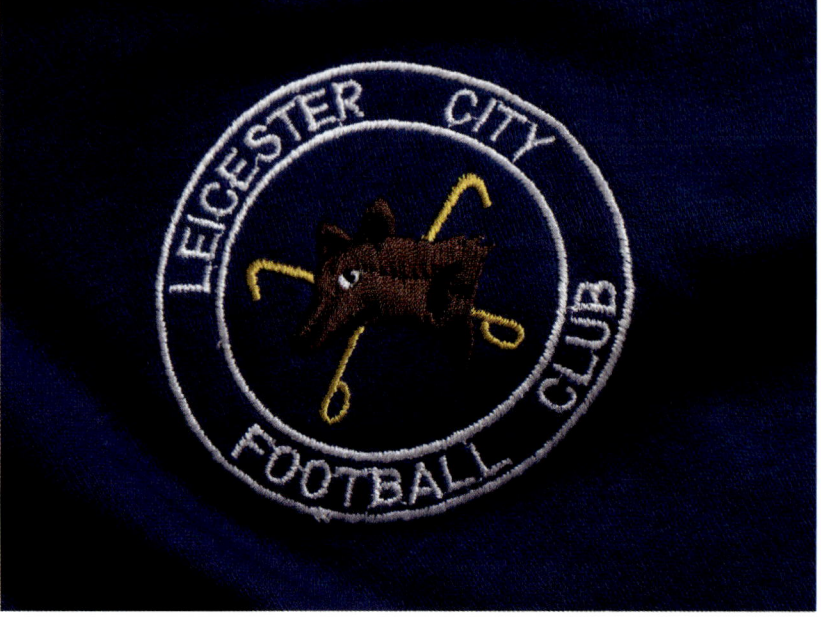

Two further versions, an inverted second kit, predominately white with blue accents (though it was hardly ever worn), and a red third option completed the new look. It was a kit unlike any other — and because it was Bloomfield's design, remained completely unique to Leicester City — it was never replicated at any other club, unlike many of Admiral's famous templates.

Sadly, the sensational new kit went a similar way to the Madrid iteration a few years earlier, and didn't inspire quite the bombast Bloomfield was looking for on the pitch. A sluggish start saw the team draw six times in succession — the season would end with 18 stalemates and 12 defeats as Leicester staggered to 11th. It didn't inspire any kind of consistency either — Leicester started each season of their initial association with Admiral with a different manager: Jimmy Bloomfield left the club in 1977 to famously lead the Admiral-clad underdogs of Orient to an FA Cup semi-final. His place was taken by Frank McLintock, who oversaw a fairly disastrous relegation to the Second Division in '77-'78, before Jock Wallace took the reins to see out the Admiral contract, frustrated by form and finances in his attempts to take Leicester back to the top flight. Nevertheless, there were green shoots of recovery in the iconic kit as Wallace's tenure began to take shape. Towards the end of the Admiral deal, a certain Gary Lineker would make his debut in it, on New Year's Day 1979 against Oldham Athletic, the 2-0 win a harbinger of better days to come — Leicester would end the decade back in the top division.

Admiral's adverts in *Shoot!* carried a tagline asking: 'Have you changed into Admiral kit yet?' Many were doing exactly that, but none of them looked quite like Leicester City.

Admiral shirt designer Lindsay Jelley's sketch of the 1970s Leicester kit design.

The importance of shirts
— Gary Lineker

Gary Lineker represented his home-town club with distinction from 1978-1985, scoring 95 goals in 184 appearances for Leicester City. Making his debut in Leicester's classic late '70s Admiral shirt, one-time golden boot winner and proud representative of the city Gary has also since returned to his Leicester roots as the menswear ambassador of global brand NEXT.

"Shirts are very important. Iconic even. When I think of Leicester and Everton, I think blue. White for Spurs and England. And I played at the biggest club in the world, Barcelona. The Barça shirt was incredibly special to see in the dressing room at the Nou Camp and to put on and play in.

"There wasn't a huge change in shirt materials or even in training gear over the course of my career, despite designs evolving. Football kits during my time as a player were for the best part functional and I was fortunate not to play in too many garish or questionable team strips.

"I would say as well that there is a lot more variety these days. Now of course, shirts have much more input on a technology front, with 'breathable' material, and a slimmer or more hugging fit. What is also different today is that shirts tend to be updated every single season. Years ago, a team may have had a home strip for two seasons or more and closer connections to manufacturers.

"My dream when I was a child was to play for my hometown club. Being able to achieve this was something so special and even now seeing the old Admiral shirt brings back wonderful memories. It was a special time in my young life." ●

A young Gary Lineker vies for the ball on his debut in 1979.

1970s

Dundee '76–'80

Words: Rob MacDonald

When Dundee signed with Admiral in 1976, the men from Dens Park could have been forgiven for thinking this was the very thing to help them not only bounce back from an unfortunate relegation the previous season, but also to break a very particular hoodoo.

They had tried with the kit before. As they rounded out the 1960s, Dundee suffered a semi-final defeat to Don Revie's Leeds United in the Inter-Cities Fairs Cup of 1967-68. It wasn't quite the European Cup semi-final heartbreak of 62-63, but it clearly left an impression as, like Revie's side, an all-white kit was adopted in 1971 following a season in which they lost a Scottish Cup semi-final to Celtic.

It didn't work, and semi-final defeats became an unwanted yet recurring theme. Dundee lost a Scottish Cup semi-final to Celtic in 1972-73, before a return to dark blue for '73-'74 saw them heroically lift the Scottish League Cup, but lose a second Scottish Cup semi-final to Celtic in as many years. In 1974-75, the peculiar hat-trick was complete when they lost a Scottish Cup semi-final, to Celtic. Worse was to follow, with relegation the following season, on goal difference, making them the first victims of the Scottish Premier Division's restructure.

In came Admiral, and in came arguably Admiral's most famous template, looking quite magnificent in red and white set against the famous dark blue. The liberal use of red on the shirt extended to stripes along the winged white collar and cuffs. As with many shirts of the time, there were some idiosyncrasies, and the famous Dundee monogram can be seen on some shirts photographed at the time, but not all. Likewise, the Admiral logo would usually be stitched on, but it appeared up to the applicant as to whether the badge would appear in white or yellow. Glorious inconsistencies were a sign of the times, and this is still a remarkably popular kit, save for the nipple-sanding chafing recollected by the then-schoolboys lucky enough to own the shirt with the stitched stripes.

One thing that remained consistent and stubbornly inglorious was The Dee's capacity for semi-final heartbreak and in Admiral's first season they were duly, remarkably, beaten by Celtic in a Scottish Cup semi-final for the fifth time in the decade. Consecutive third-placed finishes the First Division, the latter by only a point, were finally followed by a promotion back to the Premier Division in 1979. It would be the only year the famous Admiral kit graced the top flight as Dundee went straight back down, although after a couple of years of yo-yoing, they would become an established top-flight team. ●

1970s

Norwich City '76–'81

Words: Andrew Lawn

"Fashanu … Oh. Oh. Oh. What a goal. Oh, that's a magnificent goal."

Too right it was.

A few days before turning 19, Justin Fashanu, originally a Londoner but brought up by foster parents in rural Norfolk with his brother John, had just flicked the ball with the outside of his right foot, and left bewildered Alan Kennedy desperately trying to not fall on his backside. Having looped the ball up and away from a bobbly surface of part-grass, part-mud and part-sand, Justin swivels his hips in one fluid motion, drawing back his left leg and bang. There's power there, but it's more of a caress than a smash. Controlled. Smooth. Graceful. A white missile, with a streak of red panelling, the ball arcs towards the centre of the goal, but as Ray Clemence's despairing dive meets the initial trajectory, it seems to mock him, drifting away and nestling in by the left-hand post. With 10 minutes to go, it's Norwich 3-3 Liverpool. Late goals from Kenny Dalglish and Jimmy Case would give the visitors a 5-3 win, but few people remember that. Many, many more remember that goal, winner of the 1979-80 Goal of the Season award.

Justin Fashanu scores his wondergoal against Liverpool at Carrow Road on 9 February 1980.

1970s

1970s

Great goals deserve a great shirt, and City's that day is an understated beauty. Predominantly yellow, five stripes — alternating between a rich, deeply dark, green and yellow — adorn the oversized collar and sleeves. Behind the badge is a subtle green buffer, helping the yellow canary on the crest sing. A green band, bedecked with yellow Admiral logos creeps across the shoulders. On the back, the player numbers are solid green affairs, which provide a beautiful balance between front and back.

While Fashanu may have left us early, the iconic image of him, clad in an all-time classic Norwich City shirt, lives on in hearts, minds, and as a mural on a city pub. ●

Servette '76–'79

Words: Adam Bushby

'Tomorrow, Thursday, at 3pm, a football match will take place on the Plaine de Plainpalais, between 11 English from Lausanne and Geneva.'

These words were printed in an issue of *Le Journal de Genève* on 20 January 1869, and is likely the first mention of football in the local media. By the turn of the century, that kickabout between '11 English' had led to Servette becoming Geneva's largest club.

The English link was limited, even non-existent, over the ensuing 70-odd years until the seismic summer of 1976 — first, Spurs legend Martin Chivers transferred to Servette for £80,000, where he would notch 38 goals in his two successful seasons in Geneva. In 76-77, a Servette side spearheaded by Chivers lost 2-1 to Basel in the Championship play-off in front of 50,000 at the Bern's Wankdorfstadion. Big Chiv's final appearance for the club was the 1978 Swiss Cup Final victory over Grasshopper-Club Zürich, the first of the only back-to-back Swiss Cup wins Servette would ever achieve.

That same summer, Admiral produced what would be stone-cold classic kits for Servette.

A trademark maroon home shirt — elaborated with Admiral's usual panache, including a beautiful striped collar and cuffs — paired with royal blue shorts, and an all-white away strip, also with striped collar and cuffs and Admiral stripe on the sleeves — reminiscent of the mid-to-late-'70s Leeds shirt — were the uniforms worn by Servette's free-scoring side. Captain Gilbert Guyot was smitten: "This shirt was totally different from all the others we had before. It was beautiful."

If you're going to peak, you may as well do it in style and that's exactly what Servette did in 1978-79, sweeping all before them domestically in a truly glorious season. An unprecedented quadruple was only prevented from becoming a quintuple by the away goals rule in the Cup Winners' Cup against eventual winners Fortuna Düsseldorf in the quarters. The title win, though, was the club's first in 17 years, making the accomplishment all the more impressive.

Despite the loss of Chivers, who had headed back to England and Norwich City, former Servette player-cum-manager Péter Pázmándy assembled a swashbuckling side led by the adroit playmaker Umberto Barberis — Servette's three-time Swiss Footballer of the Year and star turn. He was ably supported by numbers one and two in the club's record appearance table, Marc Schnyder and Guyot, as well as Hans-Jörg Pfister, Piet Hamberg and Didi Andrey. It was a side for the ages.

The holy grail for football fans is when iconic season meets iconic shirt … 1978-79 was Servette's holy grail. ●

The flowing blonde hair of 'Joko' Pfister, Servette, c.1977.

1970s

Saudi Arabia '76–'78

Words: Adam Bushby

In many ways, the origins of Saudi Arabia's unlikeliest of unlikely wins against eventual World Cup winners Argentina at the Lusail Stadium outside Doha in 2022 could be traced to an equally unlikely blueprint created by an Englishman back in 1976.

After finishing a disappointing third bottom out of seven in the fourth edition of the Arabian Gulf Cup in April 1976, including a chastening 7-1 defeat to Iraq, Prince Faisal was royally fed up. He knew that desperate times called for desperate measures, or hugely expensive measures in any case. If Saudi Arabia were to ever eclipse historic rivals Kuwait, they would need a masterplan designed to shake the very foundations of football in the kingdom. But who to create it?

Step forward, Jimmy Hill.

Putting pen to paper on a three-year contract with an optional two-year extension, and lucrative advisory role to restructure and promote football in Saudi Arabia, Hill was well aware of the demanding expectations from his new bosses, especially given that he now held the keys to a £25m war chest: "In five years, you can't create a world-class team," he declared. "What is absolutely certain is that they will play far better than they're able at the moment."

A year later, when Hill was seeking a replacement for former Wolves boss Bill McGarry, his princely overseers mooted Bob Paisley, Brian Clough and Bobby Robson for the top job as national team coach — Hill brought in Ronnie Lane. Overseeing the training and coaching at youth levels was long-sighted, but not sexy, and it soon became clear that the royal obsession with immediate results was going to stymy Hill's plans. What's more, Lane had a penchant for barking out player's squad numbers rather than learn their "difficult" names.

1970s

Hill's team did manage to negotiate a kit deal with Admiral, using the tramlines template so popular back in the UK and one that Hill would embellish when chairman of Coventry City a few years later. A white shirt and shorts with green tramlines became the kingdom's home shirt, with the colour scheme reversed for the away strip; proof if proof be needed that sartorial excellence doesn't guarantee sporting success.

As well as cutting a dash in a stylistic sense, Hill's high point came when Saudi Arabia held the reigning European champions Liverpool to a 1-1 draw in a baking hot Jeddah in October 1978. All the more impressive given that the star-studded Liverpool side included Kenny Dalglish, Graeme Souness and Alan Hansen. Mind you, it was "walking football", Paisley would tell the *Liverpool Echo*, with the heat described as "terrific".

If the draw against top-class opposition was the acme of Hill's time in Saudi, a TV interview centred on the progress being made proved to be his nadir — he was filmed swatting away at a fly rather than ignoring it, thus deeply affronting his employers. "Apparently there was a huge fly problem in Saudi Arabia, of which I was completely unaware," Hill remarks in his autobiography. "My crime was that I should indulge in such a trivial action whilst in the middle of a television discussion on such an important topic."

Hill's star waned in Saudi, with the man from Balham admitting that it was a case of "too much money chasing too little talent", but it's certainly not a stretch to suggest that his three-year stint in the desert laid the foundations for the Under-16 World Cup win in '89, qualification for USA '94 and lifting the Arabian Gulf Cup for the first time the same year, Saudi Arabia's 2-1 win against Argentina at Qatar 2022 and the likes of Cristiano Ronaldo and Karim Benzema turning out in the domestic league.

Quite the legacy from a true footballing trailblazer. ●

1970s

West Ham United '76–'80

Words: Jacob Steinberg

There is something very West Ham about one of the club's rare golden periods managing to take in an agonising defeat in a European final and relegation to the old Second Division. Tragicomedy is an intrinsic part of their identity. Nothing can ever be straightforward for the club whose fans warm up for every home game by singing about bubbles almost reaching the sky, dreams fading and dying, and fortune always hiding, all of which is a pretty weird way of trying to gee up your team moments before they try to win a game of top-class football.

You see, learning how to deal with defeat is part of the deal with West Ham. Put it this way: have you truly lived until you've watched half the England team get relegated with 42 points? Do you really understand football until you've watched Steven Gerrard blast in a later-than-last-minute equaliser against your team in the FA Cup final?

And so to Prague. It's the 2023 Europa Conference League final and West Ham are taking on Fiorentina. Some say it's a tinpot trophy, but they're just bitter. They don't understand what it means when Jarrod Bowen scores his last-minute winner. They aren't there when the streets of east London fill out for the trophy parade the day after the final.

I took my four-year-old son to the parade. It was late and it took a lot of snacks to keep him going. In the distance, though, he could see West Ham's players celebrating on the balcony of Stratford Town Hall. He watched it, listened to the chants and got bitten by the bug. Ever the proud father, I welled up at him jabbering away about catching a glimpse of "Jaggered Bowens". After all, it had been 43 years since West Ham last won a major trophy. These moments don't come around often.

Forty-three years, though. Forty-three years since West Ham, resplendent in their white Admiral away kits, stunned Arsenal in the FA Cup final, Sir Trevor Brooking's early header enough for the second-division Hammers to get their hands on the trophy.

1970s

That sunny afternoon in May 1980 meant a lot. There's a lot of Admiral merchandise dedicated to that triumph in the West Ham shop next to the London Stadium. The cup final kit is something iconic, conjuring memories of the mazy Alan Devonshire dribble that led to Brooking's stooping header in the 13th minute, the indefatigable Billy Bonds captaining the side to victory and Arsenal's Willie Young chopping down a teenage Paul Allen when the 17-year-old was through on goal in the dying stages.

They were a one-off, Admiral producing them solely for the Arsenal game. You see the pointed claret and blue collar, the claret and blue tip on the sleeves and a crisp, unadorned white shirt, and the immediate thought is: "The funny thing about that goal is Trevor Brooking never scored many headers …". It looks modern and innovative. It stands the test of time. I didn't bother buying my son one of the new nylon kits before the start of the 2023-24 season; I got him a cotton Admiral home shirt, which he wears while charging round our kitchen, shouting "Goal for West Ham … it's No. 20 … Jaggered Bowen!"

Before Admiral, West Ham's kit was a simple affair: a circular collar, blue sleeves, claret body. They had brief success under Ron Greenwood in the mid '60s, the team of Bobby Moore, Martin Peters and Geoff Hurst winning the 1964 FA Cup and the 1965 European Cup Winners' Cup. In the league, though, there was never any consistency. This was the Academy of Football, not a winning machine. Decades on, arguments over style often centre around interpretations of 'The West Ham Way', a stick with which to beat any manager not committed to playing attractive passing football.

But maybe entertainment matters when you don't win a lot. European glory in 1965 would be followed by a barren spell, until West Ham, by now managed by John Lyall, reached the FA Cup final in 1975, which they won 2-0 thanks to a quickfire Alan Taylor brace.

A new deal was struck with Admiral in 1976, and the Leicester firm designed the kit for West Ham's Cup Winners' Cup final against Anderlecht that year. It was a major sartorial shift. The circular collar made way for a rounded one that displayed the Admiral logo on either side. A claret body and blue yoke was well received. The claret stripes running across the top part of the shirt added to the look. A centralised club badge — a castle and two crossed hammers — above the "Brussels 1976" embroidery completed it. The only shame was that West Ham lost 4-2 in a game famous for Frank Lampard Sr, the left-back, gifting the Dutch attacker Rob Rensenbrink a goal with a wayward back-pass.

1970s

The shirt, while remembered fondly, was consigned to history. Players received a single strip and were wearing a new design by the start of the new season. The crest was on the left and a pointed collar no longer showed the Admiral logo. A nice kit, however, was not going to score any goals or keep clean sheets. They might have looked the part but Lyall's West Ham began to struggle after losing to Anderlecht. They narrowly avoided relegation in 1977, but they weren't so lucky a year later. Having gone into the final day of the 1977-78 season needing at least a point against Liverpool to stay up, they succumbed to a 2-0 home defeat, ending their 20-year stay in the top-flight by a single point.

There was no kneejerk decision from the board, though. Lyall was given a chance to rebuild. He bought the goalkeeper, Phil Parkes, from Queens Park Rangers for a record £650,000. He signed the right-back, Ray Stewart, from Dundee United, and developed the striker, David Cross. Alvin Martin, the commanding centre-back, established himself as a first-team player after rising through the academy.

West Ham were patient. They were still in Division Two by the time they put together their cup run in 1980. Playing without fear, they took their fans on a thrilling ride. They survived a barrage away to West Brom in the third round, Parkes making some great saves, and won the replay. They won 3-2 away at Orient in the fourth round, saw off Swansea City with a 2-0 win at Upton Park and defied the odds to beat Aston Villa in the last eight. Ron Saunders, who would lead Villa to the First Division title in 1981 and the European Cup a year later, had signed the striker, Andy Gray, from Wolves for big money. But West Ham held firm and won 1-0 thanks to a last-minute penalty from the redoubtable Stewart.

Frank Lampard Sr in the classic Hammers home shirt.

1970s

115

The FA Cup is paraded around Wembley following West Ham's victory vs Arsenal, 1980.

They had a good team. They kept many of their best players after promotion, including Lampard and Brooking, an England international and their key creator. A few canny signings had them on the right track. West Ham were ready for their semi-final against Everton. They earned a replay when Stuart Pearson cancelled out a penalty from Brian Kidd, who was sent off early in the second half.

It was off to Elland Road for the reprise. Goalless after 90 minutes, the game went into extra-time. After 94 minutes West Ham broke, Brooking finding the languid Devonshire, a £5,000 signing from Southall four years earlier, on the left. Such a clever dribbler, Devonshire cut inside, linked with Pearson and ran through to score.

The bubbles soared, then drifted downwards. Everton levelled through Bob Latchford and penalties beckoned. Lampard's low winning header in the 119th minute is part of West Ham folklore. They were through to a final against Arsenal, the holders, and would defy the odds at Wembley.

It was their last time in an Admiral kit and they made it count. West Ham, the last team from outside the top-flight to win the FA Cup, would stun Arsenal thanks to Lyall's clever tactics, Brooking flicking in Pearson's shot, Geoff Pike's relentlessness in midfield and the brilliance of Martin and Bonds in defence.

It would be another 43 years before they experienced anything to rival that moment. But what a moment.

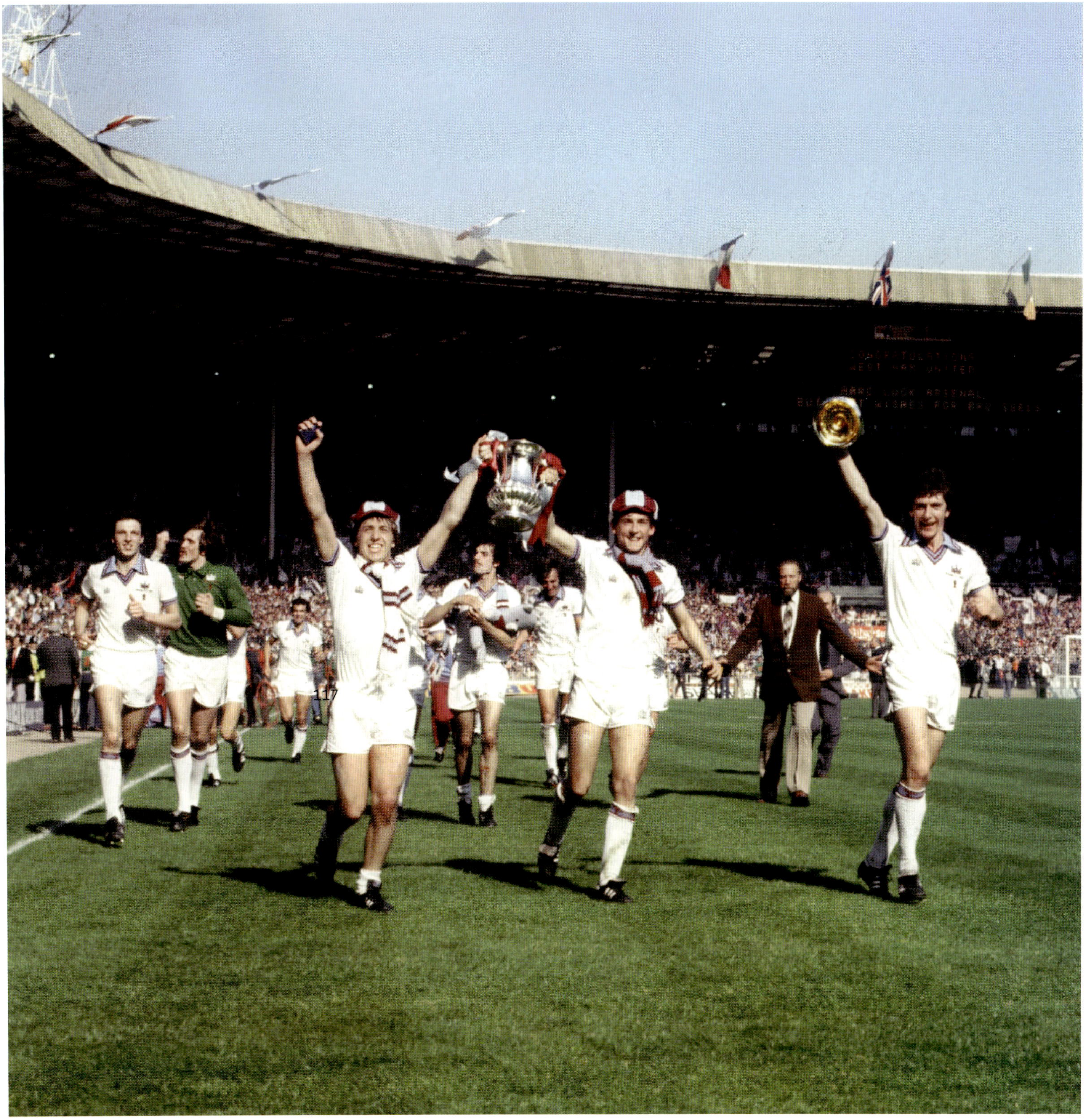
CONGRATULATIONS
WEST HAM UNITED

Without doubt, my favourite shirt
— Mick Clifford, Collector

The 1980 FA Cup Final at the famous old Wembley Stadium was the last competitive game West Ham used shirts manufactured by Admiral. Coincidentally, it was also the last time West Ham wore shirts made from cotton. Sadly, it was also the last time the club won a major domestic trophy.

Sir Trevor Brooking's 13th-minute stooping header was enough to bring the famous cup to East London, with West Ham beating the mighty Arsenal from the First Division.

This was, in no small part, down to West Ham manager John Lyall's changed tactics on the day, deploying striker Stuart Pearson more in a midfield role and leaving David Cross to battle it out with the two Arsenal centre-backs, Willie Young and David O'Leary, with neither defender seemingly knowing who was picking up who.

The iteration of the famous shirt used for the final featured a stunning embroidered club crest on the left breast. Embroidered in claret, with blue hammers, the type simply read 'Wembley 1980' underneath. It was all we needed. The Admiral logo was also embroidered directly onto the white away shirt, using their blue letters on a claret background.

The Admiral logo branding, running down each arm to the cuff, was a signature design they had produced for various other teams at the time and was, in short, magical. Even the production of the shirt on such an occasion was special — previous away shirts tended to feature an embroidered club badge and logo sewn directly onto the shirt itself, rather than this Cup Final treatment.

As a collector, and a West Ham fan, this was a vital shirt to me. In the days before social media and mobile telephones, I had tried to contact the West Ham players from that side, in the hope of purchasing a shirt, to no avail — most players wanted to keep them. But the search continued and during the next phase of the hunt, I found out some West Ham players had swapped with their Arsenal counterparts at the final whistle.

David Cross had exchanged shirts with Arsenal's number 6 that day, Scottish international defender Willie Young, whose shirt, and the spare long-sleeved version issued for the final, Cross still possesses. West Ham players were also issued with two shirts each, a long- and short-sleeved version, with all outfield players choosing to wear the short-sleeve version for the game.

I traced Young through his former club Nottingham Forest, who kindly informed me that the family was running a pub, Brancote Manor, located just outside of Nottingham. I clearly recall writing a letter to Willie, explaining about my collection, and my desire to get my hands on one of the most iconic shirts ever worn by West Ham United.

As time passed, I hadn't received a response, so in the end I called the pub and asked to speak to Willie, who informed me he wanted to keep the shirt within his family. But I wasn't deterred by the knock-backs and wrote to Willie again. After receiving my second letter, he called me on the telephone, agreeing to give me the shirt and explaining it was quits for his professional foul on Paul Allen, as the 17-year-old midfielder had been free on goal with only goalkeeper Pat Jennings to beat. Young had ruthlessly cut down Allen from behind, taking the obligatory yellow card issued by referee George Courtney.

The shirt worn during the 1980 Cup Final is one of the most recognisable and iconic West Ham shirts ever produced — and following the lengths I went to in order to get one, it is without doubt the favourite shirt in my entire collection.

1970s

Simply iconic — Alvin Martin

Centre-back Alvin Martin amassed almost 600 appearances for the Hammers over a 19-year period becoming a club legend in the process. He was a mainstay in the West Ham side that won the 1980 FA Cup. Manager Ron Greenwood gave Martin his England bow against Brazil at Wembley in 1981, while a Second Division player.

"Growing up as a fan, FA Cup Final Day was a must watch event even if your team weren't involved. It was the day that only if you were a Martian would you not be aware of it being Cup Final day! I remember the interviews afterwards, drinking milk provided by the sponsors, answering questions having won and not quite believing it was all happening to *me*.

"To see young current fans wearing a '70s or '80s West Ham United replica shirt shows respect for past teams and our club's history.

"Five years ago, a friend and I decided to commission a painting of the greatest West Ham United player I played with, with a view to printing a limited edition. The player was Billy Bonds — easy! Choosing the shirt was more difficult; there were a number that came into contention but after weeks of deliberation, we finally and categorically settled for the 1980 FA Cup final shirt. Iconic and worn by an absolute colossus, it is also a fantastic looking shirt.

"That red England Admiral shirt against Brazil [in 1981] ... my England debut at Wembley against a team containing Socrates, Eder and the great Zico, games that dreams are made of. I wouldn't swap that shirt, even for Zico's!

"I have kept a lot of shirts but have lost a few as well. In fact, I have my 1980 long-sleeved FA Cup shirt but, the shirt worn (short-sleeved) has gone missing. If anyone has any idea where it is I'd be grateful for its return and would gladly pay/swap for it.

"The shirts I do pride above the rest are World Cup '86 shirt worn vs Paraguay at the at the Azteca Stadium, and the great Dynamo Tbilisi shirt of [Ramaz] Shengelia when they came to the Boleyn and blitzed us 4-1 in the Cup Winner's Cup in 1981. Shengelia was some player." ●

Alvin Martin eagerly waits his turn to hold aloft the FA Cup.

1970s

Orient '77–'80

Words: Rob MacDonald

Rarely can an iconic kit have come together with an iconic season quite as memorably as for Orient in 1977-78. A home shirt that marked an almost complete departure from anything the club had sported before saw two thick red stripes run from the shoulder to the hem of a white shirt, the Admiral logo ensconced on the right breast and, in another first, Orient's logo sitting slap bang in the centre of the chest. Red collars and cuffs completed the design. The away shirt, pictured here, inverted those colours.

It was so good, they named the team after it. And they were so good, Orient's 'braces' team, that they reached the semi-finals of the FA Cup, seeing off Norwich City, Blackburn Rovers, Chelsea and Middlesbrough on the way.

"We were massive underdogs from the third round against Norwich City onwards", the much-missed Glenn Roeder told the *Football League Paper* in 2015, "we suddenly had everything to gain and nothing to lose". Gain they did, with Peter Kitchen scoring seven of their nine goals on the way to a colossal game against First Division Arsenal at Stamford Bridge.

The bubble was burst by a quickfire Malcolm MacDonald brace in the first half, but Orient's remarkable run remains their best ever in the FA Cup. The braces kit was reissued as a third kit in 2020-21 and remains a popular piece of retro design. ●

1970s

Tottenham Hotspur '77–'80

Words: Ian King

In the summer of 1977, when Admiral came aboard at White Hart Lane, few other clubs in the Football League needed some form of reinvention more than Tottenham Hotspur. Sixteen years had passed since they'd won the Double, and although there had been occasional successes over the decade and a half which followed it, it was clear by end of the decade that the team of 1961 had been a one-off, rather than the start of a dynasty.

Occasional cup successes papered over the cracks, which widened from a third-place finish in the First Division 1971 to 11th in 1974, each league season incrementally worse than the year before. The decline was so slight that you may not even have noticed it, what with the League Cup being won in 1971 and 1973 and the UEFA Cup in 1972.

But it was visible if you squinted. An aggregate defeat to Feyenoord in the 1974 UEFA Cup final was accompanied by violence in the stands, resulting in the club receiving a lifetime ban from European competition which was only commuted six years later; not that European qualification was often on the cards in those intervening years.

Bill Nicholson, who'd arrived as manager with a 10-4 win against Everton in 1958 and subsequently led Spurs to eight trophies in 16 years, including the Double, resigned the following September. The club's decision to sever all ties with Nicholson was one of what you could argue were a series of missteps, this one coming after chairman Sidney Wale was angered by Nicholson sounding out Johnny Giles and Danny Blanchflower about replacing him as player-coach and manager, respectively, without consulting him. Wale refused him a testimonial and the possibility of staying on as a consultant, until he returned with Keith Burkinshaw two years later.

Considering everything that Nicholson had done for Spurs, it left a sour taste in the mouth, and with five weeks of the season left to play under his actual replacement Terry Neill, it looked as though they were heading down, four points from safety under two points for a win, with just seven games left. But somehow, they made it. Five wins in their last seven games was enough to keep them up by a point above Luton Town and — hilariously for Spurs fans — Chelsea, at the end of a season which finished with a very congested bottom half of the table, just six points separating QPR in 12th place from Chelsea in 21st.

1970s

Sketch of the Spurs '77 home shirt, designed by Lindsay Jelley (right).

Ossie Ardiles starts another attack for Spurs (far right).

Things improved the following season, ninth in the league and semi-finalists in the League Cup, but 1976-77 saw a reversion to a couple of years earlier. Neill had left for Arsenal that summer and his replacement Keith Burkinshaw initially struggled to get to grips with a team that some in the media considered 'too good to go down', despite evidence to the contrary from the pitch almost every week.

An 8-2 defeat at Derby County in October was probably the nadir, but there were also home defeats against lower division opposition in both of the domestic cups — Third Division Wrexham in the League Cup and Second Division Cardiff City in the FA Cup — and this time there was no late salvation. Faced with six games in 14 days from 9 April, including matches on successive days against Arsenal and Bristol City, they won just once.

By the time they beat Aston Villa at the end of April 1977, it looked as though they'd still need to win both of their last two matches to stay up. The following Saturday they were beaten 5-0 at Manchester City; with practically everybody above them still having games in hand, a first relegation in 42 years was nigh. If anything, the mood at White Hart Lane for their final game was one of defiance, but beating Leicester City wasn't enough. The damage had already been done and despite the win, Spurs finished the season not just relegated, but bottom of the heap.

1970s

It turned out to be a shake awake for a club that seemed to have fallen asleep at the wheel, and the arrival of a new kit from Admiral during the summer of 1977 set that tone of regeneration. It certainly couldn't have been more of its era, with collars of the same aerodynamic properties as the wings of Concorde and manufacturer's logos running down the sleeves. The implied promise of such a design was that the 1977-78 season would be one of Saturday Afternoon Fever every weekend. If anything, the yellow and navy blue change kit, with two blue stripes jettisoning down from the shoulders, was even more rakish.

But as seasoned Spurs-observers already know, the big question is never whether they have the swagger. The question is usually whether they have the chops to back it up. The answer to this question, as seasoned Spurs-observers also already know, often ends up being no, but at the start of the season the early signs were encouraging. By the end of September, they were one of two remaining unbeaten teams and top of the table, though they lost the former record at Hull early in October.

The BBC's *Match of the Day* cameras arrived at White Hart Lane on the 22nd of that month for the first — and what turned out to be only — time that season, for their match against Bristol Rovers. October had brought two defeats in three games, with the previous Saturday's trip to Charlton ending in a particularly chastening 4-1 loss. But playing up for the cameras, Spurs delivered, recording the biggest win that the show had seen at the time, a 9-0 thrashing featuring John Pratt scoring four goals and Ian Moores three.

However, come the end of the season, Spurs ended up barely scrambling back into the First Division, winning just two of their last eight games. A crowd of over 50,000 turned out at White Hart Lane for a 1-0 win against leaders Bolton Wanderers in April, a match widely regarded as winner takes all, but this was a rare bright spot in a nervy, uneasy end to the season. Promotion was finally earned on the last weekend with a goalless draw at Southampton which took both teams up at the expense of Brighton & Hove Albion, with Bolton the champions. In the end, just four points separated the top four.

It certainly couldn't have been more of its era, with collars of the same aerodynamic properties as the wings of Concorde.

1970s

To say that Spurs' summer transfer activity upon their return to the First Division was revolutionary would be something of an understatement. For most of the previous five decades, foreign-born players had been prevented from playing in the UK unless they'd already been living in the country for two years, but in February 1978 the EEC ruled this unlawful and the FA tore up their ruling. This was not an uncontroversial decision. The players union, the PFA, argued that every foreign signing made was one less spot for a British player. Questions were asked in parliament.

But this was all to no avail. The attitude of clubs was already at clear odds with the player's union, and the 1978 World Cup was the obvious place to start casting a net to bring in some foreign-born talent. But it was still a shock when it was confirmed two weeks after the final that not one but two of the star names from the hosts and winners of the World Cup would be joining the newly-promoted Spurs.

Behind the scenes, Keith Burkinshaw had been tipped off about the availability of midfielder Osvaldo Ardiles by the Sheffield United manager Harry Haslam, who was trying to sign a 17-year-old wonderkid by the name of Diego Maradona. Haslam didn't get his target. Maradona, it later transpired, had been on the way to the airport when the transfer fee demanded by his club Argentinos Juniors suddenly leapt to a level that the Blades couldn't afford. But Burkinshaw returned not only with Ardiles, but with a further addition too. Having asked his new acquisition about the availability of other players, he was recommended another midfielder, Ricardo Villa, with whom Ardiles had roomed during the World Cup. The combined fee for the pair was £750,000.

1970s

As a snapshot, those pictures of Ardiles and Villa, resplendent in their none-more-late-1970s Admiral kits, speak of a very specific point in time.

They made their debuts at The City Ground against the previous season's surprise champions Nottingham Forest, and Villa scored the Spurs goal in a 1-1 draw. But things didn't quite go according to plan after that. The following Saturday, more than 47,000 turned out to welcome the new players for their home debuts against Aston Villa, but Villa (Aston, not Ricardo) won 4-1. A couple of weeks later, they were on the receiving end of a 7-0 defeat at Liverpool, a harsh reminder of how much more would have to be done if they were to get close to being title contenders.

That first season back ended up being a little underwhelming. Spurs finished 11th and it was clear that, although he'd had an immediate impact, Villa was struggling. The 1979-80 season was no improvement for either him or the club. This time around Spurs finished 14th. Long-standing goalkeeper Pat Jennings had left for Arsenal in 1977 and had never been successfully replaced. Struggling in front of goal, it wasn't until the summer of 1980 and the signing of a completely new attacking pair, Steve Archibald from Aberdeen and Garth Crooks from Stoke City, that fortunes started to change.

As a snapshot, those pictures of Ardiles and Villa, resplendent in their none-more-late-1970s Admiral kits, speak of a very specific point in time. Fashions moved faster than they do today. In 1977, after years of wearing little more than a white t-shirt with a cockerel on it, Spurs were brought right up to date. The Admiral kit came to represent a point at which matters on the pitch bottomed out at a club which had been slowly building up to a reckoning for some time.

In just three years, things had moved on. But what a three years it was. John Motson shouting "EIGHT!!!" on *Match of the Day*. A tense promotion scrap involving four teams, of whom only three could win, with two of them playing each other on the last weekend of the season. The sudden, earth-moving arrival of two World Cup winners. From South America! At the same time!

I arrived as a fan in 1980, with Garth Crooks, Steve Archibald et al. But I had that yellow Admiral change shirt, bought in a sale bin in a sports shop in about 1983. When I put it on, it felt like taking a trip in a time machine. At that time, three years felt like ancient history. These days, it feels like the blink of an eye. ●

Spurs' squad photo, 1979-80 (left).

Ricky Villa lets fly on the cover of a Spurs programme from 1979 (right).

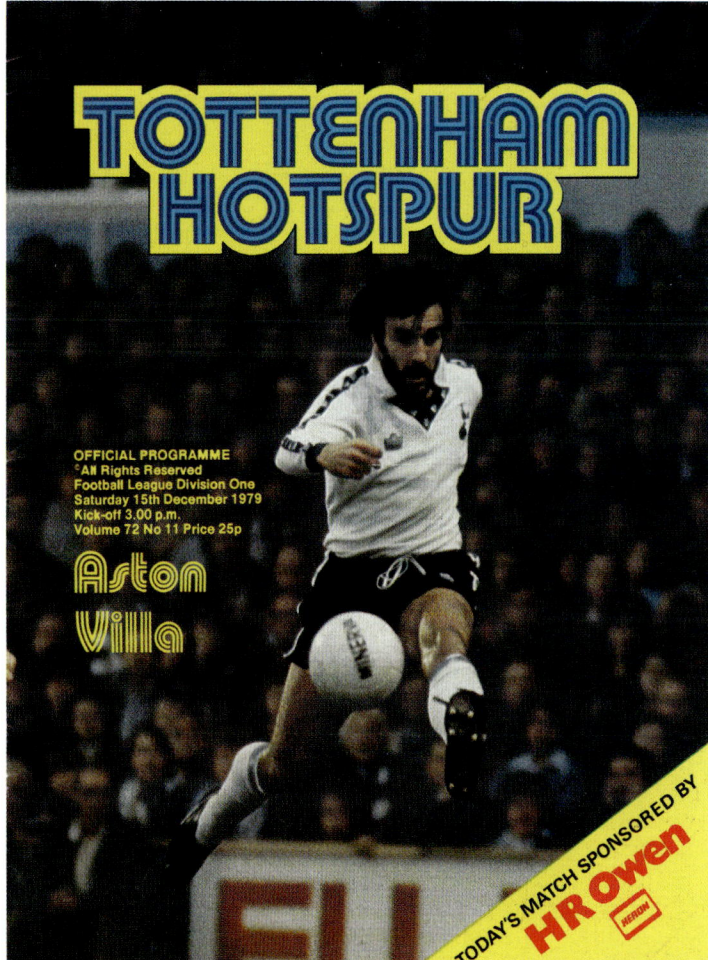

1970s

Crystal Palace '77–'80

Words: Rob MacDonald and Adam Bushby

As the replica kit market exploded, manufacturing for matchwear wasn't without its inconsistencies, most notable in a 1977-78 Crystal Palace team photo for which the players have seemingly been handed three variations of the same outfield shirt. It's a useful guide to Admiral's speedy evolution of Palace's iconic and beloved sash jersey — the gold Admiral badge on the right breast, followed by a red Admiral badge within the sash on the left breast, and then both manufacturer and club badges on the right and left side of the shirt, respectively, where they would stay for the next three years.

The design addition that stands out is the repeat tape (the Admiral logo in blue, on red) that ramps up the arm of both short- and long-sleeved editions from cuffs to neckline, which itself was changed from a wing collar to a simple 'v'. The tape and the design also stayed firmly in place until 1980.

The kit emerged in a lowly time for Palace, though they were massively on the up. They were 1978-79 champions of Division Two, having lost just four games under their young, charismatic manager, Terry Venables and gaining the win they needed in the final game of the season at home to Burnley to lift the title.

It was a sassy side, featuring a crop of exciting youngsters, such as Kenny Sansom, Terry Fenwick, Vince Hilaire, Dave Swindlehurst, Ian Walsh, Jerry Murphy and Paul Hinshelwood, wearing a sassy kit. These were exciting times at Selhurst Park as Palace's youngsters had also won the FA Youth Cup two years in a row (in '76-'77 and '77-'78).

At the end of September 1979, Palace played Bobby Robson's Ipswich Town. This was a side featuring several seasoned internationals, but Palace's upstarts played the reigning FA Cup winners off the park, winning 4-1. Implausibly, they went top of the First Division for the first time in their history.

They were even starting to believe they could knock Liverpool off their perch, the juggernaut that hadn't finished outside the top two for seven years. There was a sobering reminder that the anointed 'team of the eighties' had a long way to go to match their opponents at Anfield on 15 December, with the champions schooling the kids 3-0.

The flourish at the top of the league in 1979 was all too brief and the side never quite lived up to the early hype. Instead of dominating the '80s as they seemed destined to do, they would instead break up at the very start of the decade. Still, a star that burns brightly if only briefly is quite the thing to behold. For a while, that team and that shirt were the brightest of stars. ●

1970s

Malmö FF '78–'79

Words: Adam Bushby

It was a miracle that Malmö FF even got to Munich at all. 30 May 1979 is a date etched into the very fabric of the Swedish club, as is the name of an Englishman, though not scorer of the winner in the European Cup final that night at the Olympic Stadium, Trevor Francis, nor his charismatic manager Brian Clough.

Bob Houghton had taken over Malmö in 1974 fizzing with new ideas. Staffan Tapper was captain of the semi-professional side, all bar one born and raised in Skåne, the southern-most county in Sweden, and says Houghton was quick to throw out the rulebook: "Ninety-nine percent of all training was to be strictly on the pitch." Pressing was introduced that was "very hard and very high", zonal marking was debuted in Sweden, and Houghton's side would employ a high offside line to great effect — more of which later.

The results were instant — under Houghton's tutelage, Malmö won the Allsvenskan in '74, '75 and '77, and the Swedish Cup four times between 1974 and 1980, with Tapper his general on the pitch. Malmö's star had risen to such an extent that with Monaco, an Oleg Blokhin-led Dynamo Kiev, Wisła Kraków and Austria Vienna dispatched, they'd remarkably reached the zenith of European football.

A former team mate of Houghton's was sat in the stands in Munich as a guest of the Malmö head coach — a fellow English twenty-something by the name of Roy Hodgson, who had landed the manager's role at unfashionable Halmstads BK in 1976 on the personal recommendation of his friend. "They asked Bob Houghton if he knew somebody like himself, young and starting out, rather than contact the English FA to send over a more experienced traveller as it were, of which there were a few at that time," according to Hodgson. The two Englishmen had quietly but purposefully ignited a revolution in Sweden.

1970s

As they lined up against Nottingham Forest at the Olympiastadion, many of whom had done so together since their school days, the Malmö XI could have been forgiven for thinking themselves out of the contest before it had begun. Tapper recalls that they had 15 fit players, naming just four subs and, while eager to stress that it wasn't an excuse, that the irreplaceable duo of Bo Larsson and Roy Andersson missed the final through injury. There were also problems re-signing former captain Krister Kristensson, who had left Malmö to wind down his career at Trelleborgs in 1978, despite him playing against Austria Vienna in the semis. To compound matters, the captain himself left the field just over half an hour into the biggest game of his life, unable to recover from a broken toe sustained in training the day before.

The deadlock was broken when John Robertson beat two men on the wing in customary fashion and centred for the world's first million-pound player, Francis, to head home on the stroke of half-time. It was to be the only goal of the game — perhaps unsurprising given Houghton's by-now mechanical offside trap snared Forest a quite incredible 21 times.

But for Malmö, just getting there was a triumph in and of itself. On the expectation levels at the club after following in his friend Houghton's footsteps in 1985, Hodgson explains that they remained realistic. "Everyone regarded '79 very much as a one-off occasion which was getting harder every year." He added: "It was getting harder and harder for a smaller team to sneak through as Malmö did."

Domestically though, Hodgson would eclipse even his old friend. His arrival at Halmstads in 1976 heralded the start of a golden age; having never won the title, they did so twice in his five years at the helm. His five titles on the bounce at Malmö meant that the boys from Croydon wrote themselves into Scandinavian lore. Over the course of a decade and a half, the two men would have a profound impact on Swedish football in the round and Malmö specifically, so much so that "Bob's Hörna" (Bob's Corner) faces "Roy's Hörna" (Roy's Corner) at the Eleda Stadion to this day.

The squad of '79 remain as close as ever, with most of them making the trip to Munich once more in 2024, some four decades after the final, to receive an official UEFA plaque to replace the one handed to midfielder Anders 'Puskas' Ljungberg, which made it back to Sweden but as Tapper remembers, went AWOL, "and no-one knows what happened to it".

Tapper gave his iconic matchday shirt away to a good friend as a birthday present and doesn't know where it is now, a shame not only for sentimental reasons, but because it was the best shirt that he played in, according to the man himself. Malmö's sky-blue shirt was supplemented with white tape displaying the Admiral logo on the sleeves and a wonderfully '70s big, wide white collar — what's not to like? The only Nordic club to have reached the final of the European Cup or Champions League were also the best dressed. ●

Malmö FF face Nottingham Forest in in the 1979 European Cup final, eventually losing 1-0.
©Malmö FF/ Pierre Mens

Coventry City '78–'80

Words: Adam Bushby

Is the colour of a kit sacred? The answer is invariably yes, with a few notable exceptions. Although most football teams across the globe stick to the palate of their forefathers, some have dabbled in the dark arts of colour change, with varying degrees of success. Under the guidance of Don Revie, Leeds United switched to all white from royal blue in homage to all-conquering European champions Real Madrid. Revie led Leeds through a trophy-laden 13-year period. Brazil, haunted by defeat in the 1950 World Cup final, meanwhile, switched from white to the famous yellow a few years later in a bid to exorcise the demons of the *maracanazo* or Maracanã disaster and, well, the rest is history.

But what of the away shirt, that most fickle of garments? None can surely boast the level of infamy attributed to Coventry City's novel choice between 1978 and 1980. It's a tale that can trace its roots back to one infamous result that had a seismic impact on the club …

It was 25 November 1961 and Third Division Coventry had just been humiliated by the Southern League's bottom side, King's Lynn, in the FA Cup second round. Manager Billy Frith was duly shown the door by chairman Derrick Robins while King's Lynn landed a plum third round tie in the form of Everton. Things couldn't get much worse. Four days later, little did the Coventry faithful know that the new managerial appointment would shake the club and the game itself to their very foundations.

Jimmy Hill quit his role as chairman of the Professional Footballers' Association to take over at Highfield Road and four wins from his first five games hinted at things to come. It was Hill's primary intention to get Coventry to the lofty heights of the First Division as quickly as possible, but his plans for the club were all-encompassing.

"Chin set like a jousting pole against the world" is how Barney Ronay describes Hill in his book *The Manager*. The owner of the most famous mandible in football wasn't just out to change the fortunes of Coventry City; his stall was set for revolution. Ever the pioneer, Hill was not just content with his instrumental role in abolishing the Football League's maximum wage of £20 at the age of 29; there were worlds left to conquer.

1970s

A club seeking improved commercial terms, to rival their First Division peers, met a company in need of dispensing with a job lot of brown fabric.

High on Hill's agenda was Coventry's kit. Until 1962, they had played in different iterations of blue and white, but Hill, ever the innovator, orchestrated the razzmatazz of the 'Sky Blue Revolution', which involved changing the home strip to sky blue, pioneering pre-match entertainment and, after a few gins with club director John Camkin, penning the new club song to the tune of *'The Eton Boating Song'*. Fans were transported to away matches on sky blue buses and a sky blue train. The traditional matchday programme was reinvented as a trendy magazine. Attendances soared, cash registers kerching'd and the tired old ground was rebuilt.

By the 1968-67 season, Coventry had climbed from the Third Division to the First and were boasting the largest crowds in the Midlands. The Sky Blue Revolution had been an unqualified success. Then, on the eve of their baptism in the top flight, Hill stunned the Highfield Road faithful by announcing his departure for the bright lights of television.

It was on his heralded return as managing director in April 1975 that Hill's genius for spotting emerging trends came to the fore. It was inevitable that one of football's great innovators would seek out a company of equal vision to provide Coventry's kits. Enter Admiral, of course.

Admiral's venerated hourglass design graced many a kit during the firm's imperial phase in the mid- to late-'70s, with white taping that started just under the shoulder blade and ran to the bottom of the shorts, but it was apt that it was Coventry City, under their forward-thinking director that got the bandwagon rolling for the 1975/76 season in sky blue for the home kit, of course, and a red away version. This was a shirt that pushed the boundaries of football shirt design. It's easy to forget how plain shirts were in the time leading up to Admiral's majestic arrival. An embroidered club badge alone had adorned shirts described simply as 'plain', 'hooped' or 'striped' for 100 years or so, and often, not even that.

Then, in 1978-79, a story the origins of which could be traced to that humbling by Kings Lynn, unfolded. Hill was the one who signed off on one of the most infamous kit deals of all time as a club seeking improved commercial terms, to rival their First Division peers, met a company in need of dispensing with a job lot of brown fabric.

1970s

Though reticent to change Ipswich's home strip with the radical stylings proposed by Admiral's then-managing director John Griffin, manager Bobby Robson had been more susceptible to changing the away kit. Robson's initial enthusiasm for a brown kit had dampened by the time Griffin returned to Portman Road. In the middle of a bad run of form, Robson had seemingly come unstuck by the thought of being told that his team "look like shit and are playing like shit," Andy Wells writes in *Get Shirty: The Rise and Fall of Admiral Sportswear*.

Hill's skin was made of thicker stuff. After ringing Griffin in a fury having found out that West Ham were being paid £10,000 a year by Admiral to wear their kits, a full £3,000 more than Coventry were getting, he inadvertently gave the Admiral boss a solution to the Ipswich problem. Griffin absorbed Hill's spirited protestations and duly hung up the phone having agreed to match the £10,000, in return for Coventry sporting a new away kit.

> **I went to see the kit man to ask him what it was all about. And he said, 'that's what you're playing in today,' so I asked him, 'is there any chance I can get back on a plane to the States please?**
>
> — Steve Hunt, Coventry City

The *quid pro quo* resulted in Coventry trotting out in one of the most notorious strips of all time. The '70s were, by all accounts, a brown decade. Sepia, burnt umber, auburn, chestnut, russet, chocolate ... colours synonymous with the times; there were 50 shades of brown everywhere you looked. But on football kits? Absolutely not. Then again if anyone had the fortitude to take on the traditionalists, it was Admiral.

First worn at Derby County's Baseball Ground on 2 September 1978, the chocolate brown Admiral kit made an auspicious start, Steve Hunt scoring on his debut after swapping New York for the West Midlands. Ian Wallace netted the second that day as Coventry recorded a 2-0 win and moved into second place in the First Division.

Hunt was less than enamoured when he saw the kit that day. He told *Coventry Live*: "Living in the States I had a fair old sun tan, long blond hair — yes I did have hair back then — so I was looking a million dollars and I saw this brown kit and thought, 'it's got to be to warm up in, it can't be what we're playing in.'

"So I went to see the kit man to ask him what it was all about. And he said, 'that's what you're playing in today,' so I asked him, 'is there any chance I can get back on a plane to the States please?' But it's become legendary, that kit, and we won on the day, so hey ho!"

Steve Hunt, modelling a look befitting the '70s — moustache, long flowing hair and brown kit.

1970s

The 'Worst Kit of all Time'?

Or distinctive and boundary-pushing?

Although sported only around 20 times between September 1978 and late 1980, the kit took its place in the football kit pantheon/hall of shame, depending on your personal preferences. Admiral's dalliance with the club coincided with a period of unparalleled success for Coventry. Players of the calibre of Terry Yorath, Ian Wallace, Gary Gillespie, Hunt and the man who topped a *Coventry Evening Telegraph* poll to find the most popular Coventry player of the First Division era, Tommy Hutchison, all wore the sky blue and brown kits in the '70s and a seventh-place finish in the 1977-78 First Division season remains their second highest ever.

The Coventry chocolate brown away kit regularly tops lists of the 'Worst Kits of all Time'; however, surely the kit should be remembered for being distinctive and boundary pushing, a one-off and truly encapsulating of its era. Beauty may well be in the eye of the beholder but the proof of the shirt's pulling power is in the (chocolate) pudding — the brown kit's reputation has been burnished by the passage of time, nostalgia dictating that a retro version of it is one of Coventry's most consistent sellers in the club shop and original versions change hands for significant sums. For the notoriety alone, the shirt can be considered a success story. It's Admiral at their swaggering best.

1970s

Like bars of chocolate — Tommy Hutchison

Dubbed 'Mr Magic' by Coventry chairman Derrick Robins, Tommy Hutchison had eight successful seasons for the Sky Blues, voted supporters' player of the year a club record three times. 'Hutch' would play 355 times for Coventry after a £140k switch from Blackpool, scoring 30 goals and winning all of 17 caps for Scotland while at Highfield Road. Remarkably, he wouldn't officially hang up his boots until he was 46, after making more than 1,000 appearances in his career.

"It was definitely a big thing when Admiral came in. It also made me a bit of money as well. It was the start of pre-season and we used to go down to the local pub, Colin Stein and I — we lived in Allesley village — and we'd go in there and we'd found out what colour the kit was going to be, the new kit … So we said: 'We tell you what boys, we'll give you three guesses for a pound if you can name the colour of the next away kit' and not one of them got it. Even when we told them what the colour was going to be, they didn't believe us. I didn't care what colour we played in; I just didn't like the number 12 on my back!

"One of the first games we played in the brown kit was at Derby County and that was the worst ground in the league without a doubt. It was bare in the summer because there was a foundry in the corner, a factory or something, and everything that comes off it killed the grass. It was a bog all the time. Tommy Doc [Tommy Docherty] was the manager at the time and he started laughing because we had the brown kit on. He said he was hoping it was going to be sunny and we'd be like bars of chocolate and would melt. We beat them on the day anyway.

"When I went down for a book signing (*Hutch: Hard Work and Belief*), the lad who wrote it — a Coventry supporter, an ex-teacher — went to the club shop and he says 'is it alright if on the day of the game, we do a book signing in the shop?' and the woman says 'well, to tell you the truth, we've had quite a few doing it and they're not really that popular but you can put a table up if you want.' We came back to the ground for 11 o'clock for the book signing at the shop … they had police! The queue was halfway round the ground. They had to put fences up. Obviously, I just can't believe that. Any time I go there, it's as if I've never been away. It was brilliant." ●

The evergreen Tommy Hutchison, turning out in brown.

1970s

Admiral and the NASL

Words: Ian Plenderleith

Pelé, Franz Beckenbauer, Johan Cruyff, George Best, the New York Cosmos, and the leather tassels on the shirts of the Colorado Caribous. Mention the North American Soccer League — the first ever coast-to-coast professional football league in the United States and Canada, lasting from 1967 until 1984 — and those are the players and teams that will trip off the tongue of your average semi-informed fan. Stars, glamour, the Big Apple and ... a team that was forced to wear a shirt modelled on a cowboy jerkin.

The NASL was the third serious attempt to establish professional football in the crowded US sports market. This time they went large, by presenting a revolutionary but recognisable version of the game. The US had no stars of its own, so it imported them, mainly from Europe and South America. It played fast with the rules, awarding six points for a win, and bonus points for extra goals. There were playoffs and a championship final. The league decided drawn games through shootouts, where outfield players had seven seconds to dribble from the 35-yard line and beat the advancing keeper. A 35-yard line? That was an offside marker, designed to stretch the game a little more and void the negative tactics of the time.

And yet when people remember the NASL, they'll talk about those bloody shirts with the leather fronds, ignoring the fact that those jerseys only lasted one year, just like the moose-named team that wore them. Former Caribous goalkeeper Arnie Mausser remembers that the team "played in the gigantic Mile High Stadium with just a few thousand people, and a lot of the time it looked like there was no one there. The atmosphere was lacking. We used to have people poke fun at us because of the tassels, and we had these big five-gallon cowboy hats we had to wear on the plane for road trips."

Those jerseys and Stetsons were a one-off gimmick. A marketing fiasco that brought the team attention, right enough, but the wrong kind of attention. Failure followed mockery, as the Caribous won just eight games in that 1978 season, and finished bottom of the Central Division of the National Conference (whatever that was). They moved to Atlanta, but left the shirts behind. In their new home, the team wore Admiral.

Team names were displayed loud and proud on Admiral's NASL shirts.

1970s

The shirts worn by the Atlanta Chiefs in 1979 are a much better reflection of the NASL's true spirit. Like the game on the field of play, they differed from the rest of the world, but not conspicuously. The home kit is an unashamedly red, white and blue concoction that merely suggests the American flag, rather than waving and parading it. There's a red V-neck on a white shirt, with red and navy blue bars across the front, bearing the Chiefs' logo. If it was not for the tri-coloured stripes on the sleeves — a touch too much — then it would look like an extremely cool design. Even the red and blue lines at the bottom of the shorts work just fine.

In the early years of the NASL in the late '60s and early '70s, team shirts had mirrored their plain cousins around the world with straightforward, single colour tops and, eventually, numbers on the back. The reason for that was simple — there was no extra cash around to commission fancy designs, and the league was struggling just to stay alive from year to year. Even when investors started throwing money at the league in the second half of the '70s following the Cosmos' sensational signing of Pelé, they never sought to re-write the design portfolio, with the exception of the Caribous. Like the league itself, the shirts sought to innovate within the realms of an existing model, and many of those innovations took hold for good. Look at that Atlanta Chiefs shirt from 1979, for example. There's a number on the front, and there's a name on the back — something you didn't see outside of the NASL at that time.

In the 1960s, American Football teams had begun to make the sportsmen identify with their numbers by printing the players' surnames on the backs of their jerseys. They also printed the players' numbers on their sleeves, in addition to having them on the front and back. This was entirely for practical reasons — co-players, commentators, coaches, referees and spectators could now easily pick out who was who. The conservative minders of association football, as always, dragged their heels. British journalist Paul Gardner, who has covered the game in the US since the early 1960s, remembers how the NASL was the first to implement this simple scheme.

Putting numbers on the front of shirts was "a huge help to journalists and commentators, and to referees and to fans," says Gardner. "And names on the back. Numbers on the front made it so much easier — I was doing TV work, and the difference was enormous, everyone said it was a great idea." Gardner also says that he persuaded Fifa to do the same on international jerseys — "that was entirely due to me, because I kept on at them. [At the time] they said we've got more important things to think about, then I get a copy of *Fifa News* and I couldn't believe what I was reading: they started doing it, first for the U17 and then the U21 World Cup. [In the NASL], it made it easier for US journalists used to watching baseball players to cover the game — because otherwise they're saying: 'we don't know the game, we don't know the fucking players.'"

The NASL were the first to implement numbers on the front of shirts and names on the back.

1970s

So many British players were spending their summers on teams with novel names like the California Surf, the Chicago Sting and the Las Vegas Quicksilver.

An Admiral advert touting NASL shirts.

Also notable on the NASL jerseys is the prominence of the club logo, which often appeared where the sponsor's logo appears today — emblazoned across the chest. That was a must for a league which was seeking to gain a foothold in a hyper-competitive sports market, and where income through the gate from paying fans was still the prime source of funds. Embedding the team name in the consciousness of the locals was crucial when there were pro and college gridiron, baseball, basketball and ice hockey teams fighting for the same disposable dollars.

The fine orange Admiral shirts with the navy blue collar of the Detroit Express typify the NASL wardrobe, while the club itself is a classic reflection of the league's ultimately failed attempt to re-invent the game for the US market. The EXPRESS logo runs diagonally across the front of the shirt, sandwiched between the shirt number and the Admiral logo. The team was beholden to the ambitions of one Jimmy Hill (him again) and his son Duncan, who were convinced that the New World was the perfect place to improve upon the riches the former player and TV pundit had made working as a football consultant to Saudi Arabia. The Hills and their company, World Sports Academy, managed to sign Trevor Francis, who spent two summers — once the English season had finished — scoring multiple goals, while hawking the league, the game and the team through his exhaustive media work.

One of Europe's best strikers and an eye-catching uniform were not enough to save Detroit, who shipped money and folded after just three seasons. Hill and his company moved on, taking over the Washington Diplomats instead. Here they were much more efficient, and the team folded in the space of a few short months. Fittingly, the Dips' final shirt is a pale copy of its defunct Detroit counterpart.

In fact, many of the early NASL shirts were more like t-shirts with a club logo tagged on. With the arrival of identity players in the mid-1970s came identity shirts. The white New York Cosmos shirt with its green trim and iconic logo (reversed for the away kit) has been inextricably linked with Pelé and Beckenbauer ever since. The Tampa Bay Rowdies, fronted by the extravagant, long-haired, show-boating and shinpad-free flair of Rodney Marsh, stuck to a green, white and yellow colour scheme that was far enough removed from conventional shirts to be unique and eye-catching, but not overtly ridiculous like … oh you know, that cowboy thing in Colorado. Can the league's legacy ever escape it?

It's easy to see why Admiral signed a deal to manufacture and market these kits in Europe, with an advert touting: "Transatlantic Shirts. Have you got one?" With so many British players spending their summers on teams with novel names like the California Surf, the Chicago Sting and the Las Vegas Quicksilver, there was a perceived demand for US apparel being worn by home players. Like so much with the NASL, that was possibly another idea before its time. There was certainly no-one wearing an LA Aztecs jersey in my hometown.

Admiral's presence in North America around this time is frequent but fleeting. For one year, in 1979, the company produced the classic white Cosmos home shirt, but only tinkered with the trim — changing green to navy blue on the collars. They were much more radical with the away strip, abolishing the green shirt in favour of a deep navy blue number that was designed by Ralph Lauren "after consultation among club officials and Mr. Lauren", as the official press release put it. The club also clarified that "it had been felt for some time that green uniforms against the playing surface of the field presented visual problems for both the players and for television". Yet it's the Pelé-era green that has endured in the retro market.

The original press release announcing that a certain Ralph Lauren was getting involved with the Cosmos shirt.

1970s

Less successful, with hindsight, is Admiral's design for the Philadelphia Fury that same year. The Fury were co-owned by Rolling Stones tour manager Peter Rudge and Rick Wakeman of Yes, and attempted to ape the success of the Cosmos by signing bad boys like Frank Worthington and Peter Osgood, then letting them loose to paint the town red and create publicity. Unfortunately, the team didn't perform on the pitch with quite as much gusto and distracting outside influences could also be seen in the jerseys, which combined a yellow the colour of your great aunt's sofa with burgundy trim and massive, '70s-style white collars. The front placket is so deep that the '79 version of the jersey needed several buttons to hold the two sides together. It looks like a baseball creation, perhaps intentionally so. The 1980 take ditched the buttons, but it's only a very minor improvement. That was the team's third and final year. The money was gone, as were Worthington and Osgood, and the team's final home games were played out in front of crowds in the low four figures.

By contrast, Admiral worked much better in the Pacific North-West, where the British influence in the form of imported players seemed to chime with the temperate climate and an emerging base of loyal fans. NASL teams established in Vancouver (the Whitecaps), Portland (the Timbers) and Seattle (the Sounders) survived the league's post-collapse era in various forms and returned almost as saviours to boost and arguably rescue what was — in the early part of this century — the struggling and moribund Major League Soccer, the NASL's successor.

In 1978, Admiral re-fitted Vancouver with a white home shirt graced with its now signature curving stripes to the left and right, in navy blue and red. The away shirt reversed the colours, with red as the main player and the stripes in blue and white.

The following year, though, saw a whole new look — the stripes were dropped in favour of a navy and sky blue band across the chest, adorned with WHITECAPS in white. A royal blue version of the away kit features red Canadian maple leaves on the sleeves. This kit struck the right note and the overall design — remarkably — remains pretty much the same today. Only the word WHITECAPS has, of course, been replaced by a sponsor.

The company was less progressive with the Timbers' and Sounders' shirts, preferring not to fix what wasn't broken. In 1975, Portland wore a beautiful white mesh jersey, decorated only with the club's logo on the right of the chest and a small number on the left. The manufacturer's unknown, but could it have influenced the Cosmos jersey that appeared the same year? The following season, Admiral produced a version of this shirt, with the company's logo replacing the club emblem, and yellow and green stripes on the sleeves. Confusingly, the club also wore other versions of the shirt in the same year. Clearly, contracts were not exclusive, and Admiral's association with Portland appears to have run out after just this single season.

1970s

In that respect, Admiral's efforts to tap into the North American market were similar to the game's endeavours to coax 'the Yanks' to embrace soccer. They made partial inroads, with limited success, but left enough of an impression to influence later generations, or bequeath a legacy that was only appreciated when a fresh wave of investors decided that the time really had come for a significant number of North Americans to love the global game. The NASL was a glorious failure, an anarchic, fly-by-night operation that blazed, crashed and burned. Yet still it had an enormous impact on the domestic and world game, thanks to pushing new ideas and a willingness to re-think how the sport could evolve. Very much, in fact, like Admiral's approach to shirt design. ●

(Clockwise, from left)
Philadelphia Fury, Vancouver
Whitecaps, Atlanta Chiefs,
Minnesota Kicks.

1980

Introduction:
Adam Bushby

s

1980s

Spurs fans posing for the cameras before the FA Cup Final replay vs Manchester City, 14 May 1981.

Admiral would become a victim of its own success, eaten by the beast it had unleashed.

A decade that started with the US embargo on the sale of grain and high technology to the Soviet Union and ended with the spectacular fall of the Berlin wall spoke of 10 years of flux. It was bookended by a sense of trepidation on the one hand, and hope on the other. The spectre of mutually assured destruction hung in the air like a freezer's chill for much of the '80s, but the events of the night of November 9 1989 carried optimism far beyond the borders of Berlin, as the hammers and pickaxes smashed into the cinder blocks and barbed wire that had divided the German capital since 1945.

Closer to home, the gulf between the North and South in the UK was pronounced. The Square Mile boomed with the deregulation of the Stock Exchange in 1986 as vast wads of cash fizzed around the world's financial networks. At the same time, a sustained period of deindustrialisation, owing to cheaper manufacturing options overseas, meant the North was disproportionally hit as roots going back to the industrial revolution were pulled up and never adequately replaced.

Although Admiral was based in the Midlands, it didn't escape this new reality, with textiles going the same way as shipbuilding, steelworks and coal mining — it was far more cost-effective to produce goods in the Far East and import them into the UK, leading to a wholesale expansion of outsourcing. Jobs disappeared overnight as once-thriving businesses went to the wall.

Admiral would become a victim of its own success, eaten by the beast it had unleashed. Being the replica shirt trailblazer mattered nought to clubs wanting a more lucrative piece of the pie, and so larger companies simply blew Admiral out of the water; in 1984, the Football Association, for instance, renegotiated a new kit contract with Umbro worth a reported £1m a year over five years. Admiral couldn't compete and so the revolutionary shirt released in 1980 was consigned to the bargain bin.

As for consumers themselves, the '80s is forever associated with the rise of the young, urban professional, or 'yuppie'. These upwardly mobile upstarts were characterised as materialistic and self-absorbed, without a stake in the future or society. "The point is, ladies and gentlemen, that greed, for lack of a better word, is good," declared Wall Street's Gordon Gekko, the epitome of '80s cupidity.

1980s

Simple binary readings of the decade are, of course, destined to fail though and the huge impact of Live Aid, which was held simultaneously in London and Philadelphia, and the accompanying mass donations for relief of the famine in Ethiopia, disproved in part the theory that individualism had triumphed.

Football would have a huge influence on fashion during the '80s, with Admiral not being a beneficiary of this transformation. Liverpool fans, by virtue of supporting the most successful side in England, would come back from their trips to Italy or Spain laden with the latest leisurewear from abroad. Fans of rival clubs coveted these items and soon fell in line with their scouse counterparts — terraces were packed with working-class men looking the business. Designer brands were *de rigeur* and team colours and flares were out.

Off the terraces and onto the high street, the launch of MTV was pivotal in influencing fashion. Pertinently, 'Video Killed the Radio Star' by the Buggles was chosen as the first video to be broadcast on the new 24-hour platform for airing music videos in the USA on August 1 1981. Europe was slow to catch up and MTV Europe officially launched exactly six years to that day with an Elton John concert in Amsterdam at the Roxy Club. 'Money for Nothing' by Dire Straits was an obvious choice for its first song, featuring guest star Sting's refrain of "I want my MTV". The video's CGI graphics broke new ground and Mark Knopfler's booming riff confidently complemented the new direction of travel away from radio that MTV had spearheaded. The new style icons were Madonna, Prince, Debbie Harry, Duran Duran, Spandau Ballet, George Michael and David Bowie, although it was a push to expect firms to rock up to a dust up on the King's Road looking like Adam Ant.

Fans pack out Wembley for Live Aid, 13 July 1985 (far left).

A fan is accosted during a pitch invasion — a regular feature in the '80s (left).

1980s

Speaking of which, it would be remiss to discuss fandom in the UK in the '80s without reference to hooliganism. The effects of the miners' strike incited a generation of angry young men. Pitched battles between flying pickets and the police characterised the brutal, year-long war of attrition between the miners, led by Arthur Scargill of the National Union of Mineworkers, and the National Coal Board. The Conservative government would ultimately win, but the scale of the dispute later led journalist Seamus Milne to say that the strike "has no real parallel — in size, duration and impact — anywhere in the world".

Increasingly unsavoury events on the terraces, were occurring with alarming regularity. England fans ran riot in the unlikely surrounds of Luxembourg in 1983 after the English failed to qualify for Euro '84, a 4-0 win rendered useless after Denmark beating Greece earlier in the day. It was a regretful end to Admiral's association with the national team.

Increasingly unsavoury events on the terraces, were occurring with alarming regularity.

Further incidents inside and outside grounds up and down the country, and a dreadful reputation abroad, culminated in the bleak spring of '85. A shocking scene unfolded at St Andrews as Birmingham and Leeds United fans fought running battles on the pitch; missiles rained down from the skies; one policeman was dragged into the crowd and severely beaten; horses joined the hundreds of injured and then, worst of all, a young Leeds fan lost his life after a wall collapsed.

There was also a full-scale riot on the pitch at Kenilworth Road when Luton took on Millwall in the FA Cup quarter-final in March 1985. The level of violence was truly shocking. A knife was thrown at Luton keeper Les Sealey, golf balls flew back and forth between the two sets of supporters and at police, and a policeman had to be revived by a colleague, all the while being beaten up himself. Thirty-one arrests were made afterwards, while 47 people required hospital treatment. "A night football died a slow death" was how *The Guardian* described it, a day later.

Meanwhile England, favourites to host the 1988 European Championships, lost out to West Germany, a decision many attributed to the ongoing violence. The tragic events at Heysel before the Liverpool v Juventus European Cup final in May '85 were the final straw for the authorities. English teams were banned from competing in European competitions for five years, with Liverpool getting an extra year on top.

Some of the proposals brought in to curb the slide into oblivion are commonplace at grounds across the country nowadays — increased CCTV and all-ticket matches, and stronger police powers inside stadia, as well as a ban on taking alcohol into grounds. The tragedy at Hillsborough in 1989 and the ensuing Taylor Report would drive lasting change that was long overdue. The cloud that had enveloped the game was slowly, surely, starting to lift.

Violence from fans led to English teams being banned from competing in Europe for five years.

It was a decade of breathless transformation and deep contrasts. Take 1981, for example; the shattered glass and burnt-out cars that littered the streets of Brixton, Toxteth and Moss Side following widespread inter-city riots, juxtaposed with the genteel street parties celebrating the royal wedding of Prince Charles and Diana Spencer.

Teenagers got their kicks playing computer games on joypads, listening to cassette tapes and watching VHSes. The phones were big, the hair was bigger. And there was always a montage. Breaking from tradition, *Time* magazine named two non-humans as their Person of the Year, and they were both in the '80s — 'The Computer' became the first inanimate object to receive the accolade in 1982, followed by 'Earth' in 1988.

A brave new world had emerged, with the can-do attitude of the times being central to Admiral's repositioning as a key player that prospered in the football shirt market, even if not dominating it like the decade before. From the ashes of a game in tatters, within a country at a crossroad, came a new way of assimilating it. Football and Admiral would rise again. ●

Trouble flares at the Rous Cup England vs Scotland match, 1986.

1980s

Grimsby Town '80–'81

Words: Rob MacDonald

"May we wish you more 'Success on a Plate'", ran the headline in the Grimsby Town programme on 12 January 1980, as they unveiled Findus-sponsored shirts for the first time. And success followed — perhaps not on a plate, as they lost at home to Blackburn Rovers in the old Third Division that day, but certainly for the rest of the season. An away defeat to Colchester was the only reverse suffered among 13 wins and six draws to secure a second successive promotion.

If it was a period of success quite unlike any other — they also reached the League Cup quarter finals — then the Mariners certainly had a shirt to match. Rather than a boring old block in the centre of the shirt with 'Findus' in it, Grimsby and Admiral had gone all out and hand stitched the company's logo to each shirt in all its glory. Which is all well and good until you notice that their actual logo was a flag, replete with flagpole, and hand stitching doesn't give you the luxury of being 100% precise with the location of those sorts of things on different-sized shirts.

A year later, a new version of the shirt was introduced. A little apologetically, the launch article explained the change was because the traditional logo "proved difficult to see against the striped background". To avoid this, while remaining harmonious with Grimsby's iconic vertical black and white stripes, red lettering now ran vertically, just as the flag had done — a second unique first in as many years. Some pictures show the Admiral badge too, but this shirt was only a prototype and the actual home player shirt had no Admiral logo, to allow space for the lettering.

These are two iconic shirts in so many ways, their unique designs reflected in the fact that there are no known vertical FINDUS lettering shirts around today. But as with many shirts, they are preserved and imbued with meaning by what happens on the pitch, and with Grimsby's last championship coming in the flag kit 1979-80 season, that one-off design will not be easily forgotten. ●

Grimsby Town after beating Sheffield United 4-0. The result secured the Third Division championship and promotion, May 1980. Credit: Mirrorpix

1980s

FC Dordrecht '80–'81

Words: Adam Bushby

As midweek friendlies go, Chelsea's faithful would have been forgiven for giving the visit of a middling Dutch side from the Eerste Divisie on a crisp January evening, a miss. But they'd have been wrong. For the 4,211 hardy souls making the schlep down the King's Road to Stamford Bridge on 14 January 1981, it isn't remembered for the goals of John Bumstead, Alan Mayes (2) or Clive Walker in a 4-2 win.

Implausibly, the little-known club whose fans are nicknamed 'Schapenkoppen' (or the 'sheep heads') took to the field for the first of three practice matches at the start of 1981 with two World Cup finalists in their ranks, one of whom was a three-time Ballon d'Or winner. As publicity stunts go, getting Johan Cruyff and Rob Rensenbrink to swap the glitz and glamour of the North American Soccer League for a club that had spent most of its existence in the Dutch second-tier was audacious to say the least, but oil baron and financier Nico de Vries, who had changed FC Dordrecht's name to DS'79 two years earlier to appeal to the wider Drechtsteden region, had grand designs to shake up the football world.

Following the name change, De Vries quickly secured exhibition matches against Anderlecht and the LA Aztecs led by Rinus Michels and, crucially, starring Cruyff. De Vries then decided to put his not inconsiderable money where his mouth was. As Dutch journalist Frits Barend recalls: "It was very simple: Nico de Vries contacted [Cruyff's agent] Cor Coster and paid what Coster asked. We wrote about it in *Vrij Nederland* as far as I remember."

Reigning Eredevisie champions Ajax visited the Krommedijk in Dordrecht four days after the Chelsea friendly and one of the greatest players to ever pull on a jersey lined up against the club where he'd made his name, bedecked in the yellow and blue Admiral number of DS'79. Cruyff inspired a 2-1 win that day which, according to short-lived former teammate Harry van den Ham "was really only because of Johan". Dutch newspaper *Het Vrije Volk* was effusive in its praise of the 33-year-old too: "Time seems to stand still for Cruyff. Even when he walks relaxed across the field, he continues to radiate allure and his steps retain something compelling."

Cruyff's final appearance ended with a goal in a 6-1 thrashing of Charleroi in Belgium. And just like that, he was gone, opting for warmer climes in Spain with Levante. Never has Admiral's 'worn by champions' strapline been truer than in those three Dordrecht matches at the start of 1981. ●

A youthful-looking Johan Cruyff pulls on the Dordrecht shirt for a friendly vs Ajax, 1981. Credit: FC Dordrecht

1980s

England '80–'83

Words: Harry Pearson

In May 1980, England trotted out to face World Cup holders Argentina at Wembley wearing a new Admiral kit. The design — selected from a long list of 60 — was less fussy, more minimalist than previous incarnations. The flapping collar, a feature of jerseys for much of the 1970s, had been clipped off. A plunging continental V-neck was trimmed in red and blue. The polyester material was silkier, the blue and red yoke across the top of the chest brighter, than anything fans had seen before. The shirt seemed to glow beneath the floodlights, giving the players a saintly aura.

Perhaps that luminosity is the haze of dewy-eyed nostalgia, for at the time, the shirts appeared as popular as a piranha in a urinal. Watching the England players emerge from the tunnel, the BBC's headmasterly commentator Barry Davies wondered disapprovingly "quite why the England shirt should have the colours of the Union Jack remains a mystery". Nottingham Forest manager Brian Clough was, predictably, more outspoken: "I don't like it. It looks like one of my mother's pinnies". The *Daily Mirror* felt Admiral had taken commercialisation too far and ran a story on the price of the new kit under the headline "Strip Off!" Others claimed the England team looked like they were dressed in "clown outfits".

Today, the kit is regarded as a classic. It is ranked alongside those worn in 1966 and at Italia '90 as one of the greatest of all time. Original shirts sell for over £250; replicas still shift thousands of units per year. The half-sleeved jersey is viewed as the revolutionary harbinger of a new era in sportswear, the godfather of the modern replica shirt industry. Whether you share that opinion, or side with Davies, Clough and co, it is an undeniable truth that Admiral's shirt stood in marked contrast to the nation whose players would wear it. The jersey was sleek, smart, bold and modern. There was a hint of the Space Age about it, a gleam of Apollo 11 optimism. None of these were adjectives even the most blinkered patriot would have applied to England in the early 1980s. The country was crumbling, grey, dirty and filled with venom. If England had walked into a pub, you'd have left immediately before it caught your eye, snarled, "Do you want some?" and smashed a glass on the bar top.

1980s

The England '82 shirt is ranked alongside those worn in 1966 and at Italia '90 as one of the greatest of all time.

This feeling of flailing violently amongst the wreckage was echoed by the national football team. The glitter of '66 was long since faded. The friendly with Argentina was a warm-up for the 1980 European Championships in Italy, England's first finals tournament since Mexico 10 years earlier. Sadly, Admiral's new design — shorn of the company logo by pernickety Uefa officials — did not herald a new era. England drew their first game of the tournament with Belgium, as CS gas washed around the terraces of the Stadio Communale, Turin, following fighting involving elements of England's support. They were then sent home by the hosts in the next, courtesy of a Marco Tardelli volley. A consolation 2-1 win over Spain once again proved England's matchless ability to produce their best football in games that didn't matter.

Better times were surely around the corner. When England found themselves drawn in Group 4 of the 1982 World Cup qualifiers alongside Hungary, Romania, Switzerland and Norway, the nation cheered at their good fortune. "England have been handed a golden passport to the World Cup finals in Spain," crowed the *Daily Mail* after the draw, while the *Daily Telegraph* voiced the opinion that if England could not qualify from such a simple group, the national team should retire. The complacency combined jingoism and ignorance.

England would be piloted through these apparently placid waters by manager Ron Greenwood. The former West Ham United boss had succeeded Don Revie, after the latter had left for the Arabian Gulf in 1977. Greenwood was old-fashioned in manner, respectful, calm and reassuring — especially to the men who ran the English Football Association and quailed if they so much as heard the word "revolution".

1980s

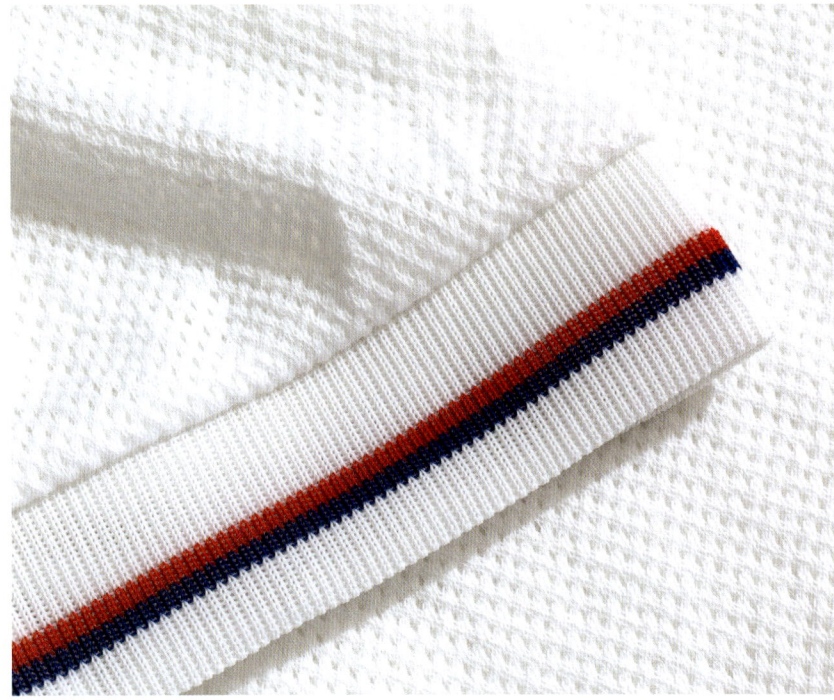

In his long spell at Upton Park, Greenwood had garnered a reputation as a technocrat and a moderniser. He had transformed the career of Bobby Moore by moving him to the left of a central defensive pairing, developed Geoff Hurst from a workhorse midfielder into a potent striker and discovered Martin Peters. But that was in another era. By the time he got the England job, Greenwood had moved upstairs at West Ham to become general manager. It was a wind-down role. It was said that, like his contemporary Bill Nicholson of Spurs who had resigned in 1976, he was disillusioned with modern football; the cynicism, greed and the hostility on the terraces.

Greenwood laboured under another great burden — he was not Clough. Old Big 'Ed was at the peak of his success, having won his second European Cup with Nottingham Forest in 1980. He was the people's choice, but — abrasive, opinionated and assertive — hardly likely to find favour with Sir Harold and the team at Lancaster Gate. "Cloughie would shake this lot up," people growled as they watched another tepid display by Greenwood's charges. The studied and balding England boss seemed colourless by comparison. As Geoff Hurst observed, Greenwood was a man who cared far more about "the finer points of the game than winning for winning's sake". That perhaps made him a better person, but results on the pitch are the benchmark for success in sport.

1980s

England's most incisive and cultivated player, Trevor Brooking, was the embodiment of the Greenwood philosophy. The two-footed West Ham midfielder had played much of his early club career under the England manager. He was a slow-moving, but highly skilled technician with a temperament as mild as custard. In the lairy, hairy world of 1970s football, the quiet, non-combative Brooking often looked out of place, a neat side-parting in an age of bubble-perms. It was noticeable that in the publicity launch of the new Admiral kit, Brooking was absent, his team mates Bryan Robson, Steve Coppell, Peter Barnes and David Johnson chosen to pose beside a model in the shirt and red sling-backs. That wasn't Trevor's scene at all.

Also absent from that photoshoot was England's bubble-perm-in-chief, the greatest English player of his generation, Kevin Keegan. Keegan claimed to be a man of moderate talents who had progressed by hard work. That he had twice been European Footballer of the Year while playing for Hamburg suggested that assessment was false modesty.

Other mainstays of Greenwood's starting XI were Britain's first £1 million pound footballer, the swift and tricky Trevor Francis, the traditional big target man, Ipswich Town's Paul Mariner, the young Manchester United midfielder Bryan Robson, his team mate the neat and tidy right-winger Steve Coppell, and Ipswich right-back, Mick Mills, who with his moustache, tan and no-nonsense barking manner seemed to be the role model for every male PE teacher in the country during the 1970s.

The rest of the team was less certain. Between the sticks, Greenwood seemed unable to choose between reliable Spurs keeper Ray Clemence and Forest's more athletic Peter Shilton. At left-back it was either Liverpool's Neal or Arsenal's Kenny Sansom. The centre-backs might be any two of Phil Thompson (Liverpool) the youthful Ipswich pairing of Russell Osman and Terry Butcher, West Ham's Alvin Martin or Manchester City's veteran stopper Dave Watson. The final place in the midfield alongside Brooking, Robson and Coppell was the most problematic. Those who favoured a cavalier approach advocated for Glenn Hoddle, or Terry McDermott, or Aston Villa's direct, pacy winger, Tony Morley. Those of a more conservative mindset pointed to Ray Wilkins of Manchester United or Graham Rix of Arsenal — both of whom played with graceful anonymity. Greenwood would toy with permutations of these players in qualifying without any of them doing enough to convince the watching public they deserved to become ever-presents. The turning point instead would come in the England backroom. In 1981, Greenwood appointed Don Howe as his assistant. The former West Bromwich and Arsenal full-back was so dour and humourless he made his quietly spoken boss look like Eddie Murphy. He was also the English game's arch-defensive pragmatist, a man to whom football was a game won not by enterprise, but by denial.

Bert Patrick (left) and Peter Hockenhull (right) pose with the Bobbies (Charlton and 'Bulldog').

1980s

England '82 shirts being packaged for sale.

Howe's arrival was months in the future when England began their World Cup campaign. By now, Admiral were in such financial turmoil a number of Fleet Street newspapers proclaimed that the opener against Norway at Wembley would be the final outing of the "my mother's pinnies" jerseys. Reports of Admiral's death proved exaggerated, however, while the complacency about Norway seemed fully justified. England swatted the visitors aside 4-0 in front of a half-full Wembley, Liverpool's McDermott scoring twice. The trip to Bucharest a month later proved problematic and England went down 2-1, the Romanian's attacking midfielder and Ballon d'Or nominee Marcel Răducanu scoring the opener. Back at Wembley in November, England scraped past Switzerland, thanks to a Marcus Tanner own goal, boos cascading down from the terraces at the final whistle. A 0-0 stalemate with Romania did nothing to quell a growing mood of anxiety and frustration. Yet England were still top of the group, level on points with Hungary (who had played one game fewer), when they flew out to play the Swiss in Basel.

I saw the game on the black-and-white TV of a backstreet boozer near Myrtle Street in Whitechapel. The experience was indicative of the mood of the time. Barely a dozen people had turned up to watch. England floundered pitifully. When the Swiss went 2-0 up after 30 minutes, English hooligans broke through the flimsy barriers separating them from the home support in the St Jakob-Park.

Admiral would be ahead of the game once more, launching the first adult-sized replica shirt in the spring of 1982.

Twenty Swiss fans were injured in the subsequent brawling. Police fired tear gas. As Brian Moore began the by now familiar condemnation of "scenes we do not ever want to witness in a football stadium", an elderly man behind me jumped from his seat and snarled some choice words of encouragement for the protagonists in the direction of the screen.

Things quietened down in the second period. McDermott pulled a goal back, but an equaliser could not be squeezed from England's lacklustre attack. After the match, FA Secretary Ted Crocker spoke of abolishing the England Travel Club (ETC), which had been launched three years earlier to stop hooliganism. That would have been a blow to Admiral who had, in another moment of innovation, designed polo shirts based on the 1980-launched kit for ETC members. The polo shirts were a clever addition to Admiral's range, because in those days, few adult fans wore replica shirts to matches — most kit manufacturers only made shirts big enough to fit children. Admiral would be ahead of the game again, launching the first adult-sized England replica shirt in the spring of 1982.

*Trevor Francis,
Ray Wilkins,
Trevor Brooking and
Glenn Hoddle posing
in the new strip.*

Following the defeat in Switzerland, England's hopes of reaching Spain hung by a thread. And the next game was against the group leaders, the undefeated Hungarians, in Budapest. England travelled to it after a series of disappointing performances in friendly matches and in the Home Internationals. The main issue was up front. Greenwood's team had not scored for close to seven hours. Incredibly, a Keegan-inspired side produced their best performance for years, easily defeating the Hungarians 3-1, the second goal a beauty from Brooking who wrong-footed a defender before driving a shot so firmly into the top corner it wedged in the stanchion.

It was widely agreed amongst commentators and pundits that Greenwood's men had "turned a corner". This was true. Unfortunately, sometimes when you turn a corner you run headfirst into a rampaging pig, or in this case Norway and Norwegian Broadcasting Corporation commentator Bjorge Lillelien.

Norway's against-the-odds 2-1 victory was masterminded by the veteran Tom Lund of Lillestrom, a player so talented Ajax had tried to sign him to replace Johan Cruyff, but what capped England's utter humiliation was Lillelien's reaction at the final whistle. The veteran broadcaster went off in a manner that made Muhamad Ali's response to knocking out George Foreman in Kinshasha seem like a funeral oration. "It is completely unbelievable!" he yodelled. "We have beaten England! England, birthplace of giants". He then went on to list some of the giants in a wild, emotional lilt. In the days before the existence of social media things could not "go viral", but somehow Lillelien's crazed excitement managed it.

After the Norway defeat, England needed a small miracle to qualify. Elimination would also spell disaster for Admiral — already rocking financially, they had projected sales worth around £4 million if Greenwood's team made it to Spain, more if they somehow got through to the last four.

If there were prayers in Lancaster Gate and Leicestershire, then they were answered by the Swiss, whose surprise victory in Bucharest sent the Romanian FA into a frenzy. They fired the entire coaching staff, including boss Stefan Kovacs who'd won two European Cups as head coach of Ajax. To make matters worse, the team's best midfielder, Răducanu, took advantage of Steaua Bucharest's trip to Borussia Dortmund to defect to the West. Romania needed to win their final fixture with Switzerland to dump England out, but leaderless and lacking their most creative player they drew 0-0. Greenwood's men now needed only to avoid defeat in their final match at home to Hungary to progress. Paul Mariner scored early and after a nervous hour, the game fizzled out. England were going to Spain.

Or were they? Because less than four months later, international events took an unexpected turn — on 2 April 1982, Argentina invaded and swiftly captured the British Overseas Territory of the Falkland Islands. And although war and sport are often falsely conflated, the sight of surrendered Royal Marines lying face down in Port Stanley under foreign guns and the shameful defeat to Norway appeared to many to be part and parcel of the same national humiliation.

1980s

The British Government debated whether to withdraw England (and fellow qualifiers Scotland and Northern Ireland) from the World Cup. The players expressed disquiet about making the trip while British troops were fighting. For a while, England's World Cup future — and that of Admiral — hung in the balance. Finally, it was concluded that withdrawal would hand Argentina a "moral victory over the UK". Greenwood's team would go to Spain, no matter what happened in the South Atlantic.

As it was, the Argentinean troops on the Falkland Islands surrendered on 13 June, the day the World Cup began. A ceasefire was declared on 14 June.

Football offered a welcome distraction from the war. England's main problem was that Greenwood would not be able to field his favoured starting XI for the early matches. Keegan was suffering from a persistent back problem and Brooking from a groin strain.

Their opener was against France at the San Mames in Bilbao. Greenwood's midfield was made up of three Manchester United players, Wilkins joining Robson and Coppell, with Arsenal's Rix on the left. It was a conservative selection (much influenced by Howe), but France, with a world-class midfield featuring Michel Platini, Jean Tigana and Alain Giresse, were not to be taken lightly.

Hoddle and Wilkins discuss a free-kick vs Czechoslovakia, 1982 (left).

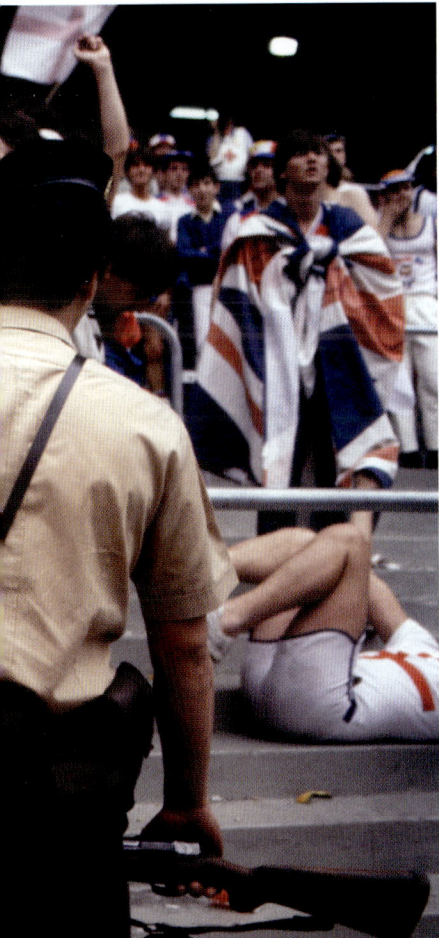

England fans descend on Spain in their tens of thousands to support the team (below).

As it was, England strolled past them. Robson scored with an acrobatic volley after just 27 seconds. The French equalised midway through the first half through Gérard Soler, but Robson drove England back into the lead in the second period and Mariner added a third. "Hello/Hello/England are back!/England are back!" chanted the travelling supporters. The press agreed. *The Times* thought the performance heralded England's "return from the international wilderness".

The match, played under the scorching afternoon sun, had drained the England players. Literally — Admiral had supplied them with standard issue polyester shirts. Overheated and perspiring, the Englishmen had lost a combined 84 pounds in weight during the 90 minutes. Two days later, Admiral sent out two sets of fresh, lightweight, breathable kit, made from Aertex material. A company seamstress worked overnight in the team hotel sewing on the three lions badges, the speed of the work reflected by the fact they were decidedly un-uniform in height.

In the next match against Czechoslovakia, a less sweaty England were so dominant Greenwood later claimed they should have been "5-0 up at half-time". As it was, they didn't take the lead until the second period and only then when Czech keeper Stanislav Seman bungled an attempt to collect Wilkins' innocuous corner from the left and presented a simple chance to Francis. England's second was equally fortuitous — Jozef Barmoš turning Mariner's through ball into his own net.

1980s

England line-up in their change strip at the Bernabéu in Madrid for their second group stage match v West Germany, 29 June 1982.

The final group match came against a feeble Kuwait side who had made headlines when the head of their FA, Prince Fahad ran onto the field and apparently persuaded the referee to reverse a decision in the 4-1 hammering by France. England were already through and were uninspired, Francis securing victory with an excellent solo goal. Prince Fahad stayed put.

Topping the group earned England a slot in the second group stage alongside West Germany and hosts Spain. Second place France went into a group with Austria and Northern Ireland. Beating Platini & co had been impressive, but it hadn't done England any favours.

Keegan and Brooking were still not match fit, so in England's game with West Germany, played on a brutally hot and humid night in Madrid, Greenwood reverted to the team that had beaten the French. England looked the better side for much of the match, but seemed held back by a fear of their opponents, or perhaps by the hand of Howe. Glenn Hoddle, who had impressed as a sub against Czechoslovakia was not brought on. The closest the game came to a goal was when West Germany skipper Karl-Heinz Rummenigge hit the bar with three minutes remaining.

Three days later, Franz Beckenbauer's team beat Spain 2-1. It meant England had to defeat the hosts by two clear goals to progress to the semi-finals. Keegan and Brooking were fit enough for the subs bench. Hoddle was there too, though he seemed to have little chance of playing.

It was another sauna-like night in the Spanish capital. Spain had been poor throughout the tournament, but now, already eliminated, they played expansive, attacking football. In the second period, with the players wilting in the heat, Greenwood threw on Keegan and Brooking with half an hour remaining. Watching, ITV pundit Jack Charlton felt relieved: "I'm much happier with Brooking coming on". The West Ham midfielder looked like he might turn things, dribbling brilliantly past a defender in the box, but Luis Arconada palmed his shot away. Then Robson surged down the England left and dinked in a cross to an unmarked Keegan, 10 yards out. The England skipper stooped to meet it. Firm contact would have sent it flying into the net, instead it glanced off the side of his head and a yard wide. Keegan pounded his thighs in frustration. "If we were going to win the World Cup, this was the one … " said Charlton. He was right. The game finished 0-0.

The stalemate brought down the curtain on England's World Cup and Ron Greenwood's career. The Admiral kit, launched against Argentina, would continue to be used until 1983, its last outing an away fixture against Luxembourg in another fruitless European Championship campaign. Unlike the campaign in Spain, all potential and no substance, the opposite can be said of the shirt, regularly voted the greatest of the national team's jerseys, whose legacy is assured. ●

1980s

Belgium '82

Words: Adam Bushby

It was one of the best bits of advertising Admiral ever did and it came free, courtesy of one Diego Armando Maradona. There's Maradona in the foreground, already one of the best players in the world at 21 and on his way to Camp Nou, carrying the hopes of a nation on his shoulders and poised like the most coiled of springs … and there's six, count them, SIX Belgium players arranged in a hurried cluster, terrified of what the little genius could do to them. It's a photo that perfectly encapsulates the sense of menace that Maradona possessed and the air of panic that paralysed the defences he came up against.

Or is it? The man who took the photo, Steve Powell, was on his inaugural assignment for *Sports Illustrated* and found himself time and again tracking the little Argentine, waiting for the magic to happen. The photo, according to Powell, is something of an illusion. What we're actually looking at is the moment Maradona has received the ball from a free-kick taken short, the Belgian wall fragmenting to block a potential shot. Why else would there be so many players from the same team so close to each other around one player? Once you know, you know.

Even being armed with this information does nothing to dull the impact of the photograph. It reveals a fundamental truth. That of an exquisitely skilled player with the world at his feet. It also showcases that beautiful Belgian kit in all its technicolour glory, one of the most iconic templates of all time. The Admiral logo sits not only on the right breast of the shirt but also down the yellow curved taping in black. Product design at its finest.

And it's easy to forget that Belgium actually beat the Argentines 1-0 through a goal by Erwin Vandenbergh.

A majestic Maradona faces six Belgian players. It worked, as Belgium ran out unlikely 1-0 winners.

1980s

This beautiful Belgian kit is one of the most iconic templates of all time.

The team wouldn't burn as bright as their shirts in Spain in the summer of '82, but then how could they unless they went and won the World Cup? Which wasn't as outlandish a claim as it first seems, given this talented Belgian side had got to the final at Euro '80, revelling in their 'dark horses' moniker and giving West Germany a run for their money, eventually going down 2-1.

After beating holders Argentina in the inaugural game of the '82 World Cup, Belgium limped to a 1-0 win over lowly El Salvador before drawing with Hungary to progress to the 12-team second round, where countries were drawn in groups of three.

In the first of these matches, a hat-trick from Juventus-bound Ziggy Boniek gave Poland a 3-0 win, before a 1-0 defeat to the USSR sealed Belgium's fate. Still, thankfully for kit connoisseurs, they flew home having played all five games in those glorious red shirts. ●

1980s

Hull City '82–'86

Words: Rob MacDonald

The early years of the '80s were disastrous for Hull City. The first Football League club ever to be placed into receivership was facing oblivion in February 1982, losing a reported £9,000 a week. With all 18 senior professionals and a further five youth players up for sale inside 24 hours, they remarkably continued to fulfil their fixtures until a saviour entered the fray.

That Don Robinson's professional wrestling name of choice had been 'Dr Death' may well have alarmed some of the Boothferry Park faithful, but it was more an indicator of his trademark bombast than any sinister omen. Robinson's *modus operandi* was to create headlines and promote the club everywhere he could, an ambition that extended from Hull to the panhandle of the USA and even, and I am being absolutely serious here, the moon.

"We'll be getting into the Third Division next year," he said upon assuming control, "and the Second Division after that, and the First Division, playing in the European Cup and if there's going to be a team playing on the moon … we want Hull City playing up on the moon."

Sometimes clubs can be invigorated just by sheer force of personality, and the first part of the lower-league-to-lunar-surface prophecy came true bang on schedule. Robinson appointed Colin Appleton manager, the two having worked together at non-league Scarborough, and clad in a sponsor-less Admiral kit, and with Emlyn Hughes briefly bolstering their ranks, Hull finished second in Division Four in the 1982-83 season.

Sponsorship was doubtless high on Robinson's agenda though, and the following season the logo of local kitchen manufacturer Hygena was added to the Admiral orange and red pinstriped shirt. Admiral had also introduced red socks upon becoming kit suppliers in 1982 — never one to miss an opportunity for hyperbole, Robinson said it symbolised the blood the players were willing to shed for the cause of Hull City.

With everything, especially their enigmatic chairman, looking up, there was still time for Fate to briefly whip the wheels off. On course for back-to-back promotions in 83-84 true to Robinson's prediction, Hull missed out on third place by a single goal on the last day — and by the time the players got back to the changing room, Appleton had resigned.

The legendary Hull City hardman Billy Whitehurst. Credit: Mirrorpix

1980s

The Associate Members Cup final — played at Boothferry Park three days later — offered a chance to salvage some silverware from the disappointment, but Hull were beaten 2-1 by Bournemouth, despite taking an early lead.

Nevertheless, glamour and success were waiting in the wings as part of a tie-in with a new sponsor, Miami-based airline Arrow Air. It already been teased earlier in the season with the visit of fellow Admiral alumni the Tampa Bay Rowdies, managed by Rodney Marsh, to Hull for the first leg of the 'Arrow Air Anglo-America Cup', which, perhaps unsurprisingly at this juncture, had seen Robinson don full cowboy regalia and ride round the side of the pitch on a horse pre-match to boost the carnival atmosphere. Hull had duly won 3-0. And a week after their cup final disappointment, they headed off to Florida for the return fixture.

Joining them with a camera was film director, screenwriter and Hull fan Mark Herman. The resulting film, 'A Kick in the Grass' is notable for a number of tropes bordering on the absolute classic, not least for the seemingly permanently bemused squad, among whose adventures are a visit to Disneyland, the hire of a stripper posing as an angry policewoman for a birthday party, which is worth the half-hour running time alone, and eventually being introduced to their new player-manager, an impossibly young-looking Brian Horton, who seems to introduce the concept of stretching before exercise to the whole squad.

Like every good film of the era, a training montage follows, before Horton prepares his charges for their only match of the tour with the immortal line: "As far as I know, the rules are just normal, no one's said anything to me". No one had said anything to Rowdies goalkeeper, the immaculately named Jurgen Stars, either as according to a match report he came out of his penalty area and picked up the ball — "a supreme no-no" — in the first 15 minutes. Nevertheless, 10 saves followed over the course of a match Hull would lose 1-0. They were, quite fairly, exhausted, a model aeroplane trophy scant consolation for a season in which they had fallen agonisingly short.

The tour did seem to stand them in excellent stead when the regular season rolled around. The loss of top scorer Brian Marwood to Sheffield Wednesday looked like it might be a problem on the opening day, as a 0-0 draw with Lincoln got them off to an underwhelming start. But step forward the legendary Billy Whitehurst.

A Hull City team photo in the famous Admiral/Arrow Air shirts. Future England manager, Steve Mclaren sits front row, third from right. Credit: Mirrorpix

A few things to know about Billy Whitehurst. He is generally considered to be the hardest of all the football hardmen, a former bricklayer who signed for Hull in 1980 for £2,000. He played some horrendous pranks on teammates and apprentices. In a game against Nottingham Forest, with 30 stitches in his face from a pub brawl, Whitehurst took a knock that opened the wound and apparently demanded the physio staple his face back together with real staples. He went back onto the pitch and played the second half with a hole in his cheek through which you could see into his mouth. And in 1984-85, he had the season of his life.

Between late October and early February, Hull didn't lose a single league game as a young team came of age. Whitehurst smashed in 24 goals in the campaign, 20 in the league, as a side containing Steve McLaren and legendary captain Garreth Roberts finished third, four points clear of Gillingham. With promotion assured by the time Hull played York in the last home game of the season, Robinson served champagne to supporters on the terraces. From the trauma of the early '80s, Hull were a club reborn.

It was fitting that Admiral enjoyed a similar flourish and Hull's 1984-86 shirt, complete with 'Arrow Air' sponsorship, was typical of the company's boundary-pushing approach even in testing times for a British manufacturer. An element of experimentation accompanied this second shirt of their tenure — the shirt sat somewhere between orange, yellow and gold but took a two-tone approach with fairly regulation 'shiny' stripes alongside darker, matte-finish ones, separated by the red pinstripes of the previous two years. An orange and red trim ran through the middle of the black V-neck collar, with plain black cuffs. A white away shirt with black pinstripes harked back to Admiral's glory days with the red logo on white taping across the shoulders.

They may not have made it to the moon, but Don Robinson and Hull still created a story for the ages, in a shirt that speaks volumes about the achievement. ●

The Tigers beat the Tampa Bay Rowdies to lift the infamous Arrow Air trophy (below).
Credit: Mirrorpix

Don Robinson hands out champagne to fans to celebrate promotion (bottom).
Credit: Mirrorpix

1980s

Leicester City '83–'88

Words: Rob MacDonald

To say there was a lot happening to Leicester City in the early 1980s would be something of an understatement. A promotion, a relegation, a genuine dalliance with Johan Cruyff, one of the greatest players ever to kick a ball, a 1982 FA Cup semi-final, lost to eventual winners Tottenham, and another promotion in 1983 meant that fans' cups were brimming, even if not completely running over.

Leicester earned the latter promotion from the Second Division in 1983 by virtue of a third-placed finish, a point ahead of Fulham. Although Gary Lineker had bagged 26 goals to finish top scorer in the division, the Foxes were five points behind Wolves in second and 10 off QPR in top spot. You might have been forgiven for thinking a season of steady-as-she-goes consolidation waited as they returned to the top flight, especially with a centenary season to follow in '84.

Not a bit of it. Out went the old and in came the new. A new club crest appeared, with the old fox and crop replaced by, depending on your interpretation of the relative mobility of a line drawing of a fox, the 'walking' or 'running' fox. A sponsor appeared on the front of the team's shirt for the first time, with the East Midlands arm of Ind Coope slathered across the torso (more on them later). And with Jock Wallace's departure the season before meaning his insistence on a particular kit manufacturer went too, Leicester returned design and manufacturing duties to Admiral. To a plain blue shirt, the local firm added a simple V-neck, but the real change was the subtle yet transformational vertical white pinstripes. The last Leicester kit to feature stripes had been worn in 1922, so it was quite a statement.

New-look logo? New commercial sponsor? Pinstripes? Leicester meant business.

Gary Lineker striding in stripes, vs Spurs in 1984.

1980s

On the pitch though, consolidation was certainly key, not least after Gordon Milne's side lost their first six games in a row (Lineker their only goalscorer in that time with two) and nine of their first ten. Thankfully, a decent run over the winter saw things stabilise slightly and although they only guaranteed their top division status with two games to spare, they finished 15th. Lineker would gain his first England cap that season and Paul Ramsey his first for Northern Ireland. The centenary season was almost a carbon copy — same shirt, same league position, Lineker this time scoring 24 rather than 22 but then departing for Everton at the end of the season. The end of an era.

As the club began life without its star, the Admiral shirt also saw changes. For the 1985 shirt, pictured here, Admiral upped the game yet again. Yes, there were still stripes, but where previously they had been white, applied by a process called sublimation printing (in which ink printed on to paper is fed through heated rollers under pressure, turning the ink into gas and fusing the colour to fabric), the new shirt was made using a process called jacquard knitting, scarcely if at all seen on football shirts at the time. Automation was key — machines producing garments could now be pre-programmed to knit 'dropping a needle' at certain points to create the jacquard effect and subsequently dying the material — resulting in the ability to create the two-tone effect between the matte and shiny finish on the Leicester shirts. It might have been one of the first football shirts to use this technique, but it certainly wasn't the last.

Having been the kit provider for all but four years between 1976 and 1988, the Leicester shirt was the carrier of a number of Admiral's new ideas and firsts as far as football kits were concerned. The jacquarding process was retained as part of the shirt design for a number of years, even beyond Admiral's engagement with the club, but not before they'd signed off with a few more updates. The iconic Admiral logo taping to the shoulders was another 1985 edit, followed by a herringbone-esque jacquard on the home shirt, instead of stripes, in 1987, also the first year of Walkers Crisps' shirt sponsorship. Last but certainly not least was the appearance of a yellow change kit for the first time in 1987, with thicker jacquard stripes this time. It was worn only twice, but set a precedent and frequently appeared as a second kit colour thereafter.

It was fitting perhaps that bringing manufacturing techniques to bear on design was pioneered by Admiral with its local club. As the club said at the launch of the 1983 kit, it was hoped that "fans will like the brand new kit and agree that it is original and modern. It is produced in Leicester, by Admiral, which must be a good thing".

The real change was the subtle yet transformational vertical white pinstripes. The last Leicester kit to feature stripes had been worn in 1922, so it was quite a statement.

1980s

"The most notorious shirt in the entire history of Leicester City Football Club."

Eagle-eyed Leicester watchers will know that there's one huge change not yet discussed (and I did promise more of Ind Coope) — the introduction in 1983 of, according to club historian John Hutchinson, "the most notorious shirt in the entire history of Leicester City Football Club".

"In some respects, it was a major piece of self-indulgence," says Alan Smith, marketing director of Ind Coope in 1983. "John McKeown, then and now a great mate, ran one of the Ind Coope pub companies in the East Midlands, and both of us were Leicester City supporters and season ticket holders.

"We knew people at the club at the time on the commercial side, the commercial director, and we met over dinner, Gordon Milne was there too, and we did that deal for two years. Towards the end of the dinner, we said there's just one thing we would be interested in — because Ind Coope's colours were quite distinctive, green and gold, was there any possibility that the away shirt could be done in our colours?"

Perhaps never has such an inauspicious enquiry had such an effect on a club or or a town.

"As a result of that," Alan continues, "the design, which I think was a tremendous design, was produced in the blue team colours, was also produced in the green and the gold. And Ind Coope were delighted about this, as you can imagine.

Everyone was a winner, until they definitively were not.

Leicester lost 13 league games in green, as well as two FA Cup matches. When they did finally win a game, beating Chelsea in the second leg of a 1984 League Cup tie, they still lost on penalties overall.

"It became very much the reason for losing! It was all over the *Leicester Mercury*, which in those days was a paid-for newspaper and pretty influential. If anything, it was probably fan pressure that brought about the end of the shirt rather than the players to be honest. The players later came out and said 'yeah it was awful and we hated it', but it was fan pressure that changed it, so it was quite democratic really!" ●

Tommy Williams keeps his eye on the ball vs Coventry City.

1980s

Derby County '84–'85

Words: Phil Lowe

Derby County kicked off the 1984-85 season, the 100th of their existence, in the third tier of the Football League, hoping to put the myriad financial difficulties of the previous two campaigns behind them.

Arthur Cox, who had just seen his Newcastle United side promoted to the First Division, surprised the footballing world by agreeing to join Derby after a disagreement with the Newcastle board. Waiting for him was a small squad of journeymen and youngsters who had just been relegated the previous season — to anyone vaguely familiar with the game, it was clear Cox would have his work cut out. A daunting season seemed to lie ahead, far removed from the gentlemen who strode out proudly in their colours to represent Derby County Football club for the first time 100 years previous.

Admiral came in as the shirt providers for Derby's centenary, and supplied a bespoke kit befitting the occasion: white shirts, blue shorts and white socks. A diagonal tri-colour stripe on the front of the shirt from the left shoulder comprised the founder club colours of amber, blue and chocolate. On the back, they wore deep blue numbers, though it must be pointed out that the original blue of 1884 was Cambridge blue (which is in fact more of a green), so perhaps not quite enough research was done at the time.

The away kit was the same design, but in a deep royal blue with white trim and white numbers and shorts.

The club badge of the Ram was redesigned to incorporate the wording 'Centenary 1884-85', and surrounded by a laurel leaf wreath, representing honour and achievement as often seen in Greek and Roman culture.

Local brewer Bass took over the shirt sponsorship, and their world-renowned red triangular logo sat nicely at the end of the shoulder stripe. Bass also produced a 'Celebration Ale' to mark the anniversary.

1980s

It represents a time of change and the beginning of a fightback; a renaissance.

Derby County's centenary tracksuit top and the home kit's stitched stripe and embroidered badge detailing.

1980s

Ultimately this was not a centenary that lived long in the memory for the action on the pitch — Derby finished seventh in Division Three — but better times were just around the corner.

The shirt, though, is appreciably more memorable. Iconic in its design, some might even say beautiful, it actually goes far deeper than that for fans. On the one hand, It encapsulates a moment in time where a club that had been Champions of England, not once but twice, just years previously, had fallen on financial hard times through mismanagement and had dropped down the Football League. On the other, it represents a time of change and the beginning of a fightback; a renaissance. And now, decades later, it is still one of the most highly sought-after replica shirts in not just a Derby, but any football shirt collection.

So yes, of course, this is a shirt. It reminds me of a time when I was 14 years of age, finally going to matches on my own with my mates, with no parental supervision. But it's not *just* a shirt. It's a living, breathing part of my youth, that has grown and stood the test of time just as I have. It will always be there, always be treasured, and I'm sure it will continue to be so long after I am gone. ●

Swansea City '86–'87

Words: Pete Jones

Swansea City kicked off the 1986-87 season back in Division Four, eight years since they were last there and with a story to tell that was scarcely believable.

After the shock appointment of John Toshack as player/manager in February 1978, three quick-fire promotions, a genuine bid for the First Division title (top with just eight weeks of the 1981-82 season remaining), followed by three relegations and a winding-up order just six months earlier at Christmas 1985, meant the dwindling Vetch Field faithful were somewhat shell-shocked.

Nevertheless, a spirit of optimism greeted the appointment of Terry Yorath as manager. Young, ambitious and, like his fellow Cardiff-native Toshack, a veteran of that truly iconic Admiral Wales strip of the late 1970s.

Talking of strips, Swansea fans like theirs fairly simple — all white with a hint of black — so when the club received its first Admiral kit it was universally welcomed, recalling the beloved strips that had been incumbent when the Toshack revolution began, and the first to feature a coveted embroidered crest — previous shirts offering vinyl or felt badges had cracked or crumbled. It was truly a thing of beauty.

So we were all dressed up, but did we have anywhere to go?

Well, Yorath certainly didn't have the same tools Toshack had been blessed with in 1978 — exciting youngsters like Alan Curtis, Robbie James and Jeremy Charles and Anfield on speed-dial for the likes of Tommy Smith and Ian Callaghan. Far from it. The remaining relics of the Toshack era — Nigel Stevenson and Dudley Lewis — struggled to shine without international-class players around them, stars of the calibre of Leighton James, Bob Latchford and the popular Yugoslav duo Džemal Hadžiabdić and Ante Rajković long gone, replaced by lower-league journeymen and untried youngsters.

Yorath's team was a mix of youth and experience, although there's experience and then there's Tommy Hutchison, still going strong while seemingly of pensionable age. However, despite the generation gap, the veteran Scot struck up an almost telepathic understanding down the left flank with the thrilling 19 year-old Terry Phelan, a free transfer from Leeds who would be ever-present for one glorious season before a big-money move to Wimbledon's Crazy Gang.

An 18-year old Jason Ball poses in a pristine Swansea kit.
Credit: Swansea City FC

1980s

207

Yorath's squad blended a mix of youth and experience.
Credit: Swansea City FC

A strong first half of the campaign saw Yorath's men sitting third in the table at the turn of 1987, exceeding expectations and giving Swans fans belief that maybe a Toshack-style ascent could be on the cards again. There was even a Cup run of sorts to enjoy. Non-league Wealdstone — who took us to a replay — and Slough Town were dispatched before a "glamour" third round tie with West Brom — two divisions higher — was secured at a rain-soaked Vetch. There were few highlights in the years after the Toshack era, but this certainly stood out, a pulsating, late 3-2 win over the Baggies in front of a bumper (10,000!) crowd. The fourth round draw was kind to us, a home tie with Hull offering a realistic chance to progress yet further; alas the visitors nicked a 1-0 win in a game we could and should have won.

An injury crisis in March precipitated a slump in form and saw the manager pressed into action — despite not having played a competitive game for several years. "Not many get past me in training," Yorath reassured the press ahead of a doomed trip to Molineux, Wolves winning comfortably by four goals to nil. It might have been far worse had the rampant Steve Bull not been out injured.

A 2-0 win over Cardiff at Easter — always welcome — left Yorath's men as outside play-off contenders, but an uncharacteristic five straight defeats rendered the season-ender at home to Lincoln meaningless. The 2-0 win mattered not to Yorath or Swansea, but had dire consequences for the Imps, as they became the first club relegated to the Conference. Cruel on Lincoln, but it would have been perversely satisfying for Swans fans to put the hurt on someone else for a change, the previous four seasons yielding three relegations and a last-day survival.

So, all things considered a mid-table finish was something to luxuriate in for the beleaguered Swansea faithful, and the foundation was laid for Yorath and his men to go one better the following season and clinch promotion via the play-offs to Division Three. ●

1980s

1990

Introduction:
Adam Bushby

1990s

English football had dragged itself, knuckles and nose bleeding, kicking and screaming, into the 1990s.

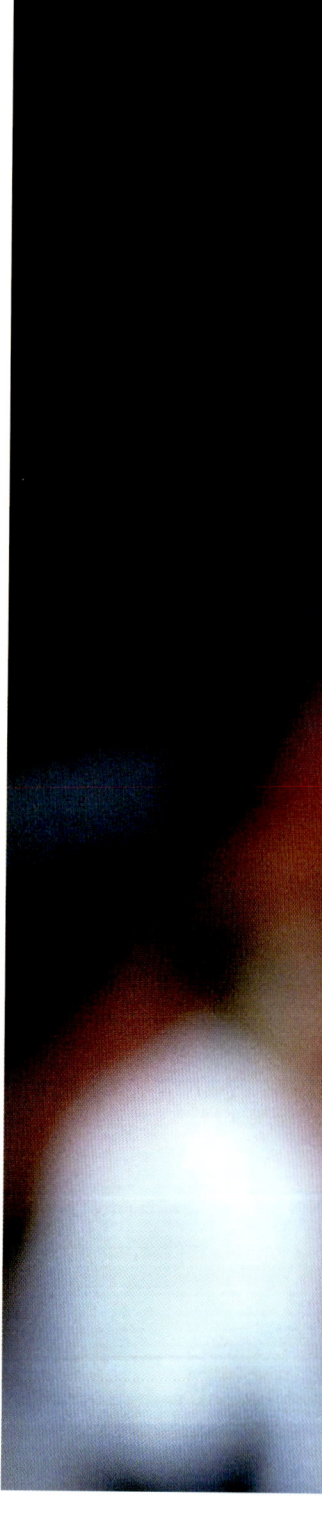

The waterworks famously flowed for Gazza during Italia '90.

The year started with the emotional rollercoaster, from an English point of view, of Italia '90. It would turn out to be four weeks that would change the face of English football for good.

A tournament perhaps shorn of the quality that its name commands in the footballing canon now exists as a series of easily digestible moments. Gazza's tears, Ciao (the mascot), Pavarotti singing 'Nessun Dorma', Totò Schillaci, 'World in Motion', and the unadulterated joy of Cameroon and a jiggling Roger Milla ... flashes of memories from an era-defining summer.

Nostalgia has had its way with Italia '90, positioned as it was when English football collided with music, zines and fashion in a creative surge, a perfect storm that very soon would add the homemade cool of *Football Italia* and the crossover appeal of Nick Hornby's *Fever Pitch* to the mix. Supplement the birth of the Premier League with the advent of Britpop, the effervescence of Euro '96 and the rise of 'Cool Britannia' and you had not only a new type of football but a new cultural currency, one that was outward-looking, inclusive and panoptic.

But how did we get here?

In 1984, the average attendance in the English top flight had dropped below 20,000 for the first time since the First World War. Football historian and author David Goldblatt describes the decline as "one long, plaintive, sorrowful, nostalgic goodbye to industrial working-class England". The prognosis was undeniably bleak as a new decade approached. "A slum sport played in slum stadiums and increasingly watched by slum people who deter decent folk from turning up," was how *The Sunday Times* denounced football in 1985 in the wake of the Valley Parade disaster. But then the final Taylor Report was published in 1990 and out of the ashes of the tragedy of Hillsborough, a line was drawn under a century in which fans had been stuffed into crumbling terraces, held in unsafe pens and caged by high perimeter fences.

Since the Premier League lion roared into life in 1992, cajoled into the public consciousness by the five-year TV deal struck with BSkyB for a then mind-blowing sum of £304m, football hasn't really looked back. Look at the iconic Sky launch with its 'Whole New Ball Game' schtick ... and spot the four Admiral shirts in the line-up. Admiral may not have been top boys anymore, but their reputation still preceded them, reuniting with the reigning champions Leeds United, once again. North of the border, Admiral and Glasgow Rangers also had a hugely successful relationship between 1990 and '92, the side led by Graeme Souness winning the league in both seasons, along with a League Cup, followed by a Scottish Cup.

1990s

Fever Pitch, a memoir on fandom first published in 1992, meanwhile, fed off the boom in interest in the game post-Italia '90. It would go on to sell over a million copies in the UK. Along with Pete Davies' seminal *All Played Out*, written at a feverish pace after the author had immersed himself with Bobby Robson's England squad in Italy for a month, the books helped sell football to a new audience. They spoke to a generation of fans unfairly maligned as uncouth, beer-swilling, working-class louts, of their irrational quirks and obsessions, and their ability to both intellectualise and laugh at the ridiculousness of the object of their passion. They also spoke to a ready-made audience of non-football-affiliated individuals who wished to understand more about the intricacies and idiosyncrasies of the national sport.

"It was a mad gamble to write it," Davies remembers. "I had no clue what would happen — but a decent book about football? There weren't any, so why not?"

Channel 4's *Football Italia*, hosted by James Richardson, extended this theme. Coinciding with the year that the Premier League was born, this witty, knowing show not only showcased the sexiest league in the world, Serie A, to supporters brought up on the kick-and-chase style played on boggy pitches in Blighty, but provided a portal into beautiful Italy, replete with espressos, the pink pages of *La Gazetta dello Sport* and Attilio Lombardo doing the lambada, over an iconic soundtrack.

By the middle of the decade, the interstitial space between football and music had never been so blurred. Replica shirts became ubiquitous. From Noel and Liam Gallagher wearing their Manchester City shirts as cover stars on *NME* as Oasis became the biggest band in the world, to the Spice Girls wearing their team's kits for the pages of *Shoot!* and *90 Minutes*. Music and football were feeding into each other's sensibilities and aesthetics like never before.

Fireworks, sumo wrestlers and dancing girls — the inaugural Premier League season saw it all.

The soundtrack to the summer of 1996 was provided by David Baddiel, Frank Skinner and the Lightning Seeds. 'Three Lions' was unashamedly nostalgic, featuring iconic commentary from the past 30 years. When the song played before England's semi-final against Germany, the Wembley crowd belted it out like it was the new national anthem. But as Gazza strained every sinew to reach a cross from Alan Shearer that he was never going to get on the end of, the "30 years of hurt" refrain got that bit longer. As a forlorn love song, the enduring appeal of 'Three Lions' is that there are few songs that have captured the nuanced brass tacks of the collective British psyche.

At the time of its recording, Baddiel and Skinner sang of just '30 years of hurt'. We can nearly double that now.

1990s

Another song that would chime with an increasingly confident country, D Ream's 'Things Can Only Get Better', was adopted by New Labour as its election theme tune in the run up to the monumental 1997 polls. Everyone knew it was only a matter of time before they were anointed as the party of power. It came to pass in a landslide victory.

With a rhetorical flourish, Labour leader Tony Blair had already set out his vision to "make this the young country of my generation's dreams". Blair playing keepy-uppies with Kevin Keegan, then in charge of one of the most exhilarating teams in Europe, Newcastle United, certainly helped feed into this narrative.

Kevin Keegan and Tony Blair share a game of head tennis, 1997.

The people's game and the self-styled 'party of the people' had never had such a symbiotic relationship.

The people's game and the self-styled 'party of the people' had never had such a symbiotic relationship either. Labour's was a cabinet and inner circle full of football fans. Alistair Campbell has never been shy of divulging his love for Burnley, while Andy Burnham is a staunch Everton fan. In Scotland, there was Gordon Brown and Raith Rovers, while Scottish Labour MP Brian Wilson wrote the official history of Celtic. Then-deputy PM John Prescott regularly turned out for the parliamentary team in the 1970s; his ghost writer, the venerable Hunter Davies said that "despite not being very skilful", Prescott's "strength was in kicking people".

In the 1990s, we saw the rise and rise of the internet as we all went online. To a degree at least. Still in its infancy, it had novelty appeal and crucially, centred on input, as an information tool, rather than having an onus on carefully curated output, as would later become the case. The decade would be the last one where people still looked up, rather than down at their phones. New technologies proposed solutions rather than caused problems. Google launched in 1998 and all bets were off.

There is one thing perhaps key to understanding the appeal of the '90s to a contemporary audience, and it's best represented by the considerable national buy-in to the ideal of Cool Britannia. Everyone had an opinion on albums like 'Parklife' and 'What's The Story (Morning Glory?)', and the work of the YBAs (young British artists). Proletarian totems as curry, smoking and Sunday morning kickabouts became *de rigueur*. Life was fun again and everyone was invited. If football had become a cultural outpost in '80s Britain, a decade later, it had become part of the national furniture. ●

1990s

Rangers '90–'92

Words: Alasdair McKillop

The 1990s were a good time to be a Rangers fan — club legends were created generously and lasting memories were made. The decade's early years were marked by the transition from revolutionary success in the late 1980s to established dominance, culminating in a record-equalling ninth consecutive league title in 1997.

The story must rightly begin in 1986, when Graeme Souness was appointed player-manager after several years in which Rangers had scuffled with no great purpose. Accustomed as he was to success, Souness was determined to pull the club up by its bootstraps. He understood that a return to past glories would only be achieved by forcefully applying new attitudes in changed circumstances, not by tolerating mediocrity in the guise of tradition.

To his own considerable talents was added inherited good fortune. Ibrox had been vividly transformed in the years after the terrible disaster in January 1971. By the time Souness arrived, slouching terraces had been replaced by firmly upright stands. Only in the enclosures flanking the tunnel did fans watch games on their feet because they had no other option.

The stadium was arguably the finest anywhere in Britain and a place where prospective players could be made to feel like they'd already gained access to the future of football.

Souness and Rangers also benefited from the casting into the wilderness of English teams because of the tragic events that preceded the 1985 European Cup Final. Scottish clubs were now in a position to offer English players the chance to play European football — but only if they had the imagination and resources to adopt such a bold strategy. Under Souness, Rangers had both. And so, in striking fashion, movement was reversed on the well-travelled migratory pathways from north to south as Rangers signed high-profile English players. First Chris Woods and Terry Butcher in the World Cup summer of 1986; later, Trevor Francis, Ray Wilkins, Gary Stevens, Trevor Steven, Mark Walters and Mark Hateley. The seismic signing of Maurice Johnston in 1989 proved three years in power had not extinguished a happily disruptive spirit.

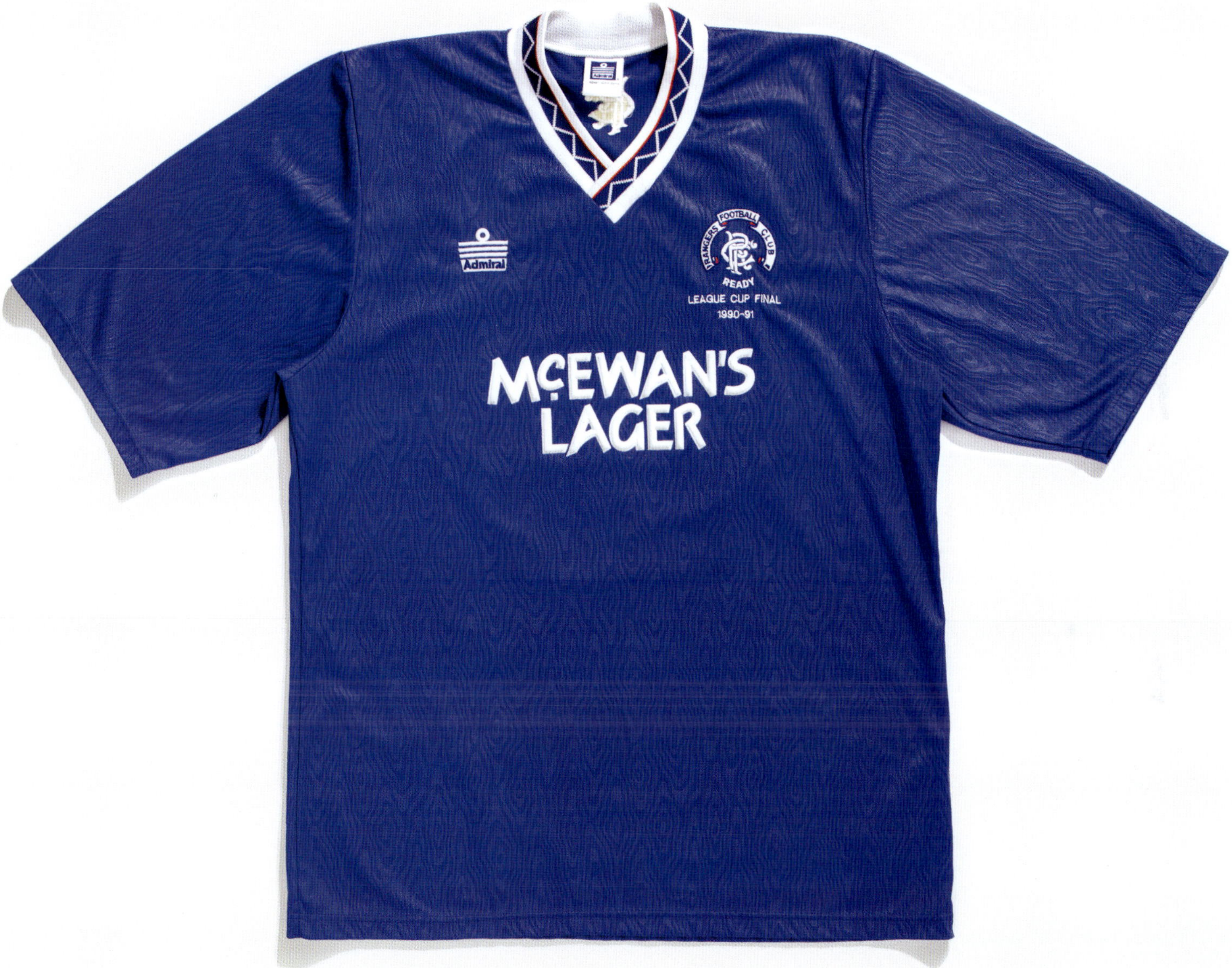
Admiral
RANGERS FOOTBALL CLUB
READY
LEAGUE CUP FINAL
1990-91
McEWAN'S
LAGER

Souness led Rangers to the league title in his first season – the last had been in 1978 — and again in the 1988-89 and 1989-90 seasons. With four games of the 1990-91 season remaining, he left Rangers to replace his former teammate Kenny Dalglish as manager of Liverpool. His final trophy was the League Cup, which had been won against Celtic in October 1990 thanks to a Richard Gough winner in extra time. Walter Smith, who had served as assistant to Souness, was given the job of seeing the team through the last league games and maintaining the slender points advantage over Aberdeen that would deliver the title.

Narrow wins against St Mirren and Dundee United — the club where Smith had assisted Jim McLean before joining Rangers – were followed by a deflating defeat at Motherwell, which meant Aberdeen travelled to Ibrox as league leaders for a title-deciding match on the last day of the season. It was a game that set the course of years. Hateley — signed the previous summer from Monaco, but not yet embellished with the swishing Samsonite hair that would, in future, make his headers resemble a tailed-comet adjusting the position of a weakling moon — scored two goals, one either side of the break, to win Rangers a third consecutive title and stabilise an emerging dynasty. Smith would later describe the victory as the finest moment of his two spells as Rangers manager; the fourth of what would eventually be nine unbroken titles was secured more comfortably the next season.

Ally McCoist contributed mightily and won his first Golden Boot, with Hateley almost as potent and Alexei Mikhailichenko appearing regularly on the scoresheet during the second half of the campaign.

McCoist and Hateley combined for a 2-1 victory over Airdrie in the Scottish Cup Final, Celtic having been dispatched by means of a single McCoist goal in the semi. With Smith firmly in place and buttressed by silverware, Rangers moved out to meet more radical changes in British and European football, caused by the creation of the Premier League and the Champions League, having successfully passed through a period of transition without losing the momentum created in previous years.

The Admiral kit of those two early '90s seasons was a model of simplicity that doesn't feel beholden to its time on the surface, but look a little closer and there is a subtle jacquard of a cross section of oak, chosen to symbolise the dominium the club had over the rest of the league. Understated and composed, it allied itself professionally and discretely to the singular focus on victory that characterised Rangers during the Souness and Smith tenures. The blue was a fearsome shade, like skies only seen in another country. The neckline was encircled by a white trim with a glancing line to suggest it was neatly tucked into itself at the front, in the style of a scarf worn under a coat. The white was overlaid with a further blue band scored with a sharp, angular zig-zag line, again in white. The effect brings to mind, albeit with the colours reversed, the detailing on the famous main stand at Ibrox designed by Archibald Leitch.

1990s

(Clockwise from top left) Front and back detailing on Rangers' 1990-91 League Cup final shirts, back and front of League Cup final walk-out tracksuit tops.

Further down and opposite the Admiral logo is the Rangers crest with unfurled scroll at the top and the word 'Ready' at the bottom. Finally, there was printed, not without small touches of character, the name McEwan's Lager as the appointed sponsor of that and several other shirts from the nine-in-a-row period. Note the punctuated airborne rise of the 'c' in McEwan and how the 'A's angle in a way that suggests they'd had one too many. Over the shoulders of the white change kit were dagger thrusts of red and blue.

The legacy and meaning of any football kit — draped as they are, somewhere between military and gang uniforms — depends to a great extent on the deeds committed in the act of wearing them. In terms of this Admiral shirt, Rangers fans fondly recall a classic, worn by great players who achieved great things for the club.

Its simplicity is iconic — Mark Hateley

Mark Hateley played 218 times for Rangers from 1990-95, scoring 112 goals and, with Ally McCoist, forming one of the deadliest strike partnerships in Europe. Clad in Admiral from 1990-92, Rangers picked up the third and fourth of their nine consecutive titles, the 1991 Scottish League Cup and a Scottish Cup in 1992, their first for 11 years.

I'd been away for six years — three years in Italy and three years in Monaco — and I bumped into Graeme Souness, who was Rangers manager, by accident in Casino Square at the 1990 World Cup as he was travelling up to see Scotland play in Genoa. So it was a really strange occasion, just a casual bump into a manager who'd been trying get you a couple of times before, so at the third time of asking, I said yes.

Graeme's thoughts on football and the way the game should be played is exactly the same way as I think the game should be played, basically you leave everything on the pitch and have no regrets; that was his ethos and wherever he went he was successful. And I think that's why he got the players to go to Rangers, you know there were a lot of England players — Terry Butcher, Chris Woods, Gary Stephens, Trevor Stephen, myself — all given the opportunity to win titles, go to cup finals, and obviously the inaugural Champions League in which we put out an English club, Leeds United. So, proving all the doubters wrong made it a great time, a really successful time, with a really successful kit.

It's a simple shirt and its simplicity is iconic. But they are always measured by success. In the period that I was there, and the kit was worn, I think we won everything that was available to win, the only thing we didn't win was the Eurovision Song Contest! So it's a great kit and one that was worn with pride. But it also carries expectations — the fans expect you to win every game, they expect you to win them with class, and they expect you to win scoring lots of goals, which we were fortunate enough to do.

Once we'd broken the hoodoo of not winning the Scottish Cup, you know, it became free-flowing, the dam had burst — we won another one very shortly after that and did a treble as well. And with 52,000 at Ibrox every other week — they were carrying the whole team and carrying the shirt. That shirt now, on a matchday, is still worn, that's how famous it became. It's a classic retro shirt — simple, glorious in carrying the badge, that's what Rangers fans do. I've still got mine and you carry it proudly because it's got great memories. For me in particular, Rangers was where my whole career came to fruition. ●

Mark Hateley celebrates with the Championship Trophy for Rangers, 1991.

Motherwell '90–'91

Words: Adam Bushby

Epic games — *truly* epic games — are by their very nature, rare beasts. Throw in more than a little jeopardy, triumph, tragedy, the unexpected, the heroic, the seemingly impossible … the Scottish Cup final on 18 May 1991, is a rare beast indeed.

On first glance, there is nothing extraordinary about the claret and amber shirt that Motherwell sported in the 1990-91 season. The Admiral logo sits proudly opposite the badge and there is a sophisticated vertical stripe on each shoulder in claret, with a smaller white one running alongside it. Local car sales tycoon Ian Skelly added his name as the sponsor to the jacquarded shirt. Urbane but unremarkable. There was nothing unremarkable about the game it will forever be associated with though.

Leading the two sides out in front of a crowd of over 57,000 at Hampden for the 106th Scottish Cup final were brothers Tommy and Jim McLean. Quite something for a game free of the Old Firm. But the solemn look on the two managers' faces betrayed a deep sense of loss — their father died a week before the so-called 'Family Final' and they entered the arena sporting black ties and an agreement that whoever emerged victorious would keep celebrations respectful and to a minimum.

Loss was something the town of Motherwell knew all too well. The final played out against the backdrop of the planned closure of the Ravenscraig steelworks, the largest hot strip steel mill in Western Europe. The shockwaves of the announcement were felt all over Lanarkshire as thousands of skilled workers and their families faced the prospect of having their livelihoods destroyed. Carrying the hopes and dreams of supporters is one thing, what about a whole town?

The McLean brothers knew the power of football as a release. In his autobiography, Tommy acknowledged that "what we never lost sight of, no matter how tough a time it was for the McLean family as a whole, was that the Cup final made an awful lot of people very happy".

Jim McLean's Dundee United were strong favourites, with memories of European Cup semi-finals and Uefa Cup finals fresh in the collective mind, and veterans of the latter (Maurice Malpas and Dave Bowman) still in the starting XI. They had also beaten Motherwell three times out of four in the league and had finished the season two places above them in fourth. Then again, Motherwell had Davie Cooper, a man with magic in his boots. "A Brazilian trapped in a Scotsman's body," as Ray Wilkins put it.

Motherwell players celebrate victory in the Scottish Cup final vs Dundee United, 1991.

1990s

The final began at a breathless pace. United had the ball in the net within a minute, Hamish French latching on to a Jim McInally pass and slotting under Ally Maxwell, but the goal was disallowed. Freddy van der Hoorn then thudded a 25-yard free kick against Maxwell's right-hand post; it flew across the goal but somehow stayed out.

So far, so one-way traffic, but the Steelmen came into the game and with half an hour gone, the script was flipped and Motherwell grabbed the first goal, Iain Ferguson booming a header past Alan Main into the top corner from Jim Griffin's inch-perfect cross. Motherwell swarmed over their more illustrious counterparts until half-time, but couldn't add to their lead.

Cue the next layer of drama. Early in the second half, Maxwell ran out to intercept a Dundee United cross, but was met by the formidable frame of The Terrors' John Clark. The damage, it would turn out, was extreme: Maxwell would later find out he'd suffered broken ribs and a ruptured spleen. There was no substitute keeper on the bench so clutching his shattered rib cage, wincing with pain and struggling to breathe, heroically, Maxwell stayed on for most of the second half plus 30 minutes of extra time.

The pendulum would swing both ways during normal time. Moments after Maxwell's injury, Dave Bowman's daisy cutter nestled in the corner with Maxwell clearly in huge discomfort. 1-1. But Motherwell were unbowed. A teenage Phil O'Donnell netted and then Ian Angus put the Steelmen 3-1 up.

It was Dundee United's turn to fight back. Two minutes later, John O'Neil reduced the deficit to set up a grandstand finish. The men in white peppered Maxwell's goal with crosses but despite his agony, the keeper held firm ... until two minutes to go. A gigantic boot up the pitch by Main bounced up into Motherwell's box with snow on it and Darren Jackson beat Maxwell in a foot race to head it into an empty net as the keeper was cleaned out once again.

Fourteen seconds left. Fourteen seconds and suddenly it was 3-3. A breathless contest showed no signs of taking a breather as the two teams headed into an additional 30 minutes. There was the quaint sight of the Motherwell backroom staff coming on to the pitch with some fine China and a kettle so the players could have a brew.

Motherwell players celebrate victory as referee David Syme signals the end of the game.

A teenage Phil O'Donnell holds a scarf aloft — the Motherwell legend tragically died after collapsing on the Fir Park pitch in 2007.

When an iconic shirt became an immortal one.

Four minutes into the first period of extra time, substitute Stevie Kirk maintained his record of scoring in every round, nay, coming off the bench to score in every round, heading beyond United striker Darren Jackson on the line from a Davie Cooper corner to make it 4-3. A sea of claret and amber limbs and flags and scarves cascaded down the terracing at Hampden. The match that had everything still had time for Maxwell — who by now had completely given up on taking goal kicks — to pull off a miraculous save from seasoned Scottish international Maurice Malpas at close range. He would eventually end the day in hospital.

Although there was a sense of loss amid the celebrations, from the personal to the collective, with poignant photos showing the bus parade passing the Ravenscraig steelworks that would be demolished a year later, Tommy McLean's side had brought a moment of light back to the town. The victory is etched into the fabric of the club, with three of the heroes of the Scottish Cup final victory of 1991 having stands at Fir Park named after them — manager McLean, as well as O'Donnell and Cooper, both of whom would tragically never make it to their 40th birthdays.

There would be plenty of other great games that featured this Admiral shirt, but for Motherwell fans, it is about one exhilarating afternoon at Hampden when they got their hands on their first major honour in 39 years. It is when an iconic shirt became an immortal one. ●

1990s

Admiral and the Premier League

1990s

The Premier League

Words: Daniel Gray

As in any class photograph, our subjects' smiles vary from the convincing to the sheepish via the downright terrifying. There is the top row nuisance with a grin that suggests he has taped a 'Kick Me' sign on the back of the lad in front's shirt. Next to him, the school bully apparently attempts to shatter the camera lens with a lethal stare.

Some grudgingly show a full cargo of teeth, as if remembering motherly instructions. One or two seem to have their eyes closed — caught in a flash, mocked forevermore. Each of those seated clasps his hands as if begging or in prayer or clumsily milking a cow. There are fresh haircuts — glossy curtains with precision centre-partings, crisp fringes surely measured with crooked bowls, fluffy blow-dries soon to be eyed by nesting chaffinches. All wear bright, spotless and brand-new uniforms.

Each of them left school some years ago. Now, they are the captains and sirens of Liverpool, Sheffield United and Ipswich Town, of Crystal Palace, Oldham Athletic and Everton and more. Head boys Butterworth and Bradshaw, Sinton and Salako, and 18 others have gathered to tell us that Sky Sports and the Premier League are alive and kicking.

It is 1992, a whole new ball game, top-flight football's Year Zero. The autumn term will soon begin.

What of those uniforms, those polyester threads of belonging, that each of the classmates wear? Canary yellow blazes cheerfully and then the viewer becomes waylaid in the Magic Eye morass of Coventry Sky Blue. There are frills which entrench these garments in the early 1990s just as a top hat might signify the Victorian era: shirt sponsorships from photocopier and fertiliser companies, or computer and washing machine brands no longer alive; long-sleeved goalkeeper tops with padded shoulders and elbows, the chain mail of the six-yard box making stoppers look like so many armadillos; and laced collars, banned in some schools for the threat of strangulation if you believed the macabre rumours of the day.

(Clockwise, from left) The Premier League home shirts of Leeds United, Middlesbrough, Wimbledon and Southampton.

1990s

The rightly-sainted Admiral logo appears in abundance, as if a child has gone berserk with a new ink stamp set.

I still have mine: a Middlesbrough Admiral home kit from 1992. The shirt's ICI logo — a disc the size of a small pizza that is made from some kind of rubber felt — rests snugly on the crest of a stomach that 30 passing years have awarded me.

This shirt was unlike anything Middlesbrough supporters had seen before and have worn since. It remains a meticulously detailed offering. Broad white epaulettes lend the air of a boxer's sweat towel draped over the shoulders. The rightly-sainted Admiral logo appears in abundance, as if a child has gone berserk with a new ink stamp set. It is seen numerously on sleeve ribbons and woven copiously into the red fabric, the word BORO appearing each time at its base, a textile mantra. A further neat red and black pattern lines the collar, though mine remains uneven due to an unfortunate ironing incident in 1994. The shorts, too, boast appealing minutiae — a red band on one side, then a triangular strip on the other, plus patterned strings still curiously long enough to lasso cattle with. I never did figure out how to tie them without the peril of them tripping me, or an opponent, up.

This kit was built to last. On some cold days I still wear the socks. Pulling on their faded white cuffs with thin blue hoops summons yesterday's heroes: jinky John Hendrie and his lanky co-star Paul Wilkinson, tireless Jamie Pollock with his tongue hanging out or Derek Whyte, newly arrived from exotic Scotland. I think too of tiny Tommy Wright huffing and puffing on the wing like a minor *Thomas the Tank Engine* character. The shirt's unusually generous 'short' sleeves seemed from some angles to reach his wrists in the style of those on a monk's robe.

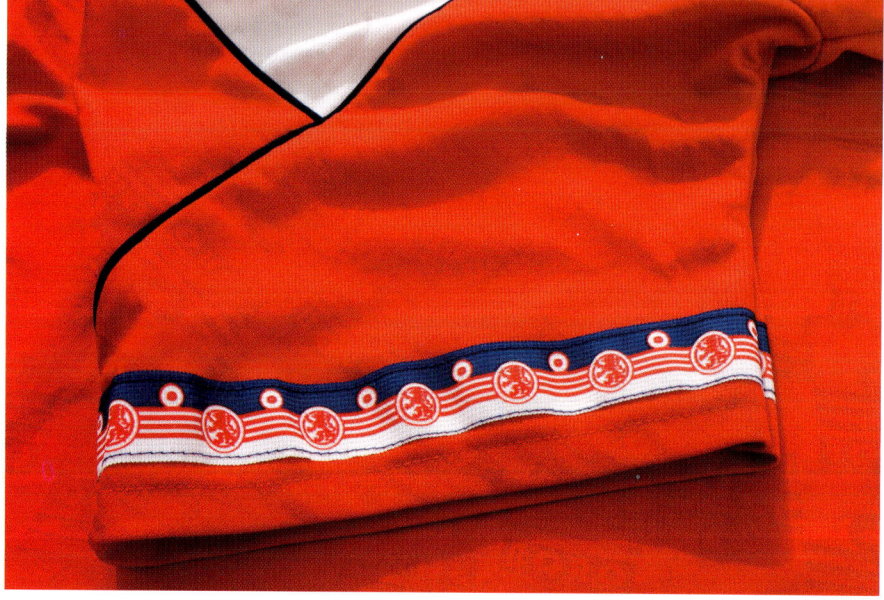

Our youthful brand snobbery quickly disappeared. We loved this kit. Plus, our Dads were around to tell us of Admiral's heritage; of Leeds United, of England and of Coventry in furniture brown. Today, young supporters spend handsomely to procure ICI health hazard shirts of their own, or buy retro replicas. As I sit wearing mine now, polyester static rising and crinkling, I wonder if it could become part of my pension plan.

Perhaps Admiral's scheme was to capitalise on the rebirth of football. What started at Italia '90 was now to be continued by Sky two years later. The other three teams in the maiden Premier League that the oldest British sportswear brand had captured were Southampton, Wimbledon and — most significantly — the reigning champions, Leeds United, final winners of the old First Division.

In this rekindled romance, Admiral would not only supply the West Yorkshire club's kit, but also be their main shirt sponsors. 'The League Champions Wear Admiral' boast matchday programme adverts from the time. It was a relationship that just felt right — two old flames, back together.

Second-generation Admiral Leeds made their debut at an incandescently bright Wembley in a Charity Shield duel with Liverpool. Their plain all-white kit seemed to radiate in the August sunshine. From distanced television cameras, each player was a Catherine Wheel let off early. There were intricacies to the kit, not least a dramatic medal-like collar and dappled sleeve and short ribbons, but the overall impression was of a smooth and classy return to simpler days.

Leeds United celebrate beating Liverpool to win the Charity Shield, 1992.

Complexity was reserved for Leeds's second and third shirts. As with Middlesbrough's change kit offerings, a majority of the fabric was clustered with a glacial, skiwear-like block pattern. It is hard to emphasise quite how much we who were 11 or 12 adored these shirts. They felt like some kind of graphic representation of all that we loved. Lucky old Dorigo and Fairclough, and Strachan, Batty and Speed. And isn't a mark of a good kit that, when we think of it, we can instantly populate it with numerous players?

That convention holds for Admiral Southampton too. Their deckchair shirts beckon thoughts, in particular, of questionable hair — Glenn Cockerill with his off-blond mullet caught five years past its sell-by date, a roadie without his band. Francis Benali's CDT teacher moustache. Terry Hurlock, coal black locks lapping red and white stripes like seaweed through an incoming tide. 'Now Southampton's beefy tough guy,' says Hurlock's Panini sticker description in that season's album. You would not have messed with him, and neither would his barber.

What of the fourth club, Wimbledon? Now in a second Admiral season, their sponsor-free blue home and red away strips were uncomplicated and effective, as if inspired by their team's playing style. Both had shoulder flashes which gave the impression of unruly teenage schoolboys and their slack rucksack straps; again, team kit matching team character.

Like Boro's and Leeds's, all were likeable outfits, resolutely of their early '90s eras. Many of us have hardly moved on and in our heads, Southampton will always be sponsored by Draper Tools, and we will forever have a nervous tick which makes us blurt the phrase 'utility man' whenever we hear or see the words 'Paul Warhurst'. In kits and the times they conjure are comfort, and there is nothing wrong with that.

We early label snobs must have quickly fallen for Admiral because it was not just their shirts we chose as Christmas and birthday gifts from the club shops of Ayresome, Elland Road, The Dell and Selhurst Park. Their noble logo appeared on pencil cases and t-shirts, on school rulers and flags, on casual jumpers and drill tops. The latter, in this early portion of the decade anyway, were stiff and uncompromising training jerseys sported by players in pre-match warm-ups and kids in the park. Donning one felt, somehow, like wearing a punishment or serving a minor stint of National Service, and yet this was a sought-after item. I am convinced that snow used to take fright and bounce off them.

From the old terraces of our beloved and shabby grounds, and on relaunched *Match of the Day* (did anyone you know actually have Sky?), we watched this new version of football. In reality, little of consequence to us supporters was different from before. Small, material changes had to be deciphered — variances in the match ball, new-fangled sleeve patches, the fact that Dave Beasant had undergone a haircut. Little wonder so many of us obsessed over kits.

The 'crazy gang' of Wimbledon (above).

A classic advert for Southampton kits, early '90s (below).

1990s

On the second Saturday of the season, I saw Middlesbrough wallop Leeds United 4-1 at Ayresome Park. When we got back to our Vauxhall Astra, a shell-suited man was in the passenger seat, stealing the car radio. Little could be more early-1990s than that. It was already Leeds's second Admiral Derby — on the first day, the champions had beaten Wimbledon 2-1.

I remember the 4-1 — and the car thief brandishing his screwdriver, possibly a Draper Tool — with clarity. The season review VHS and online videos sharpen this vivacity. Watching the game again recently while researching this article led me to ponder other Admiral clashes of that 1992-93 season. I recalled a win against Southampton and not being allowed to attend due to it falling on a school night, and a victory against Wimbledon of which we missed the end due to more vehicular drama — my Dad had that awful sinking feeling that he had left his wallet on the car's dashboard. There was a lot of car-related fretting that season. We went to Elland Road, too, where the New Eric Cantona — a robust Norwegian named Frank Strandli — scored in a 3-0 home triumph.

Who would, I wondered now, have been champions of a 1992-93 Admiral mini-league? The First Lords of the Admiralty, if you like. The answer: Leeds United, some consolation perhaps for their actual fall from Champions to 17th place, and their European Cup exit to Glasgow Rangers. Boro, incidentally, would have finished second, as opposed to their 21st place Premier berth, and a return to the Football League.

The following season, second-tier Boro stuck with Admiral and their ICI panel and were now one of only four Division One teams with squad numbers and player surnames above them. The future was creaking into view behind an underwhelming, mid-table season. Soon would come Bryan Robson and then the Riverside Stadium, Juninho and all. The bottom half of Boro's Admiral strip lives on in the consciousness of many, though — it is those shorts and socks that Robbo is wearing in his famous smart/casual unveiling photo. It says much for Admiral that their products look good even with a blazer and tie.

After the last game at Ayresome Park, a club shop bargain bin was stuffed with blue Admiral Boro away shirts. Each cost a fiver. My Dad bought two. They still fit us now. Nearly.

From left: David Batty, Chris Whyte, Lee Chapman and Gary Speed (top left).

Joyous Southampton fans cheer a goal at The Dell (below left).

Vinnie Jones gets ready to launch one for Wimbledon (below).

1990s

Remembering those first shirts — Alan Shearer

Alan Shearer made his debut for Southampton in 1988 and became Britain's most expensive footballer when he moved to Blackburn Rovers at the start of the Premier League era. He would go on to become the competition's all-time record goal-scorer with 260 goals.

The reason I went down there was to put that first team kit on — Southampton had a really successful youth development scheme where they were bringing lots of kids through and they still do now, it's still a huge part of who and what they are, so I wanted to play at the Dell and wear the first team shirt and get into that first-team dressing room.

Pulling on the shirt, I wouldn't say I had nerves but a bit of excitement and apprehension I guess — although you put the kit on in the youth team and the reserves, it's a lot heavier and feels a lot different when you're putting it on for the first team.

The start of the 1992 season definitely had a different feel, but I'd be a liar if I said I knew how big the Premier League was going to become. It felt different for many reasons; one because we'd started a new league and two, I was moving away to Blackburn after my best season in a Southampton shirt and I was about to become Britain's most expensive player, or I was, so I knew that the spotlight was going to be on me.

Shirts became really popular, without doubt I started to see more replica tops wherever we went, whether that was actually in the town or in the football grounds. And there's no doubt that from 1988 to 2006 when I retired, they had become a little bit more refined for us too. They certainly weren't as heavy — it was better not to be carrying a huge wet top around on you when you're sweating or when it's raining, they were definitely better aerated and more up to date when I retired.

I loved the old red and white Southampton tops with Draper Tools that were a sponsor on there. Those shirts were iconic — I remember Kevin Keegan and Mick Channon and all those guys wearing the red and white top so that to me was Southampton.

The shirts that really stand out to me are the ones that I wore when I first went to the football club. The first shirt I signed for when I went to Southampton was obviously the red and white one, and then the Brown Ale one with Newcastle, and obviously the McEwan's Lager at Blackburn when I signed there, so I always remember the first shirts that I wore. ●

Shearer wheels away with Neil Ruddock after yet another goal.

1990s

Heart of Midlothian '92–'93

Words: Grant Young and Adam Bushby

It had all started so well. Heading to the Stadion Evžena Rošického in Prague for the first round, first leg of the Uefa Cup on 16 September 1992, Hearts fans were buoyant. Five wins, two draws and one defeat in the league saw them second only on goal difference to Rangers and there was a genuine belief around Tynecastle that the club could go one better than their runners-up finish of the season before. The classy Admiral strips worn in 1991-92 had seen a change of sponsor from Miller Homes to Strongbow and seemed to be a good luck charm.

A 1-0 defeat was far from ideal however — these were the days of away goals — so the Jambos knew they needed to score at least one in the return leg and, preferably, shut Slavia out, or else hope for an extra time winner or face the lottery of penalties. If Slavia found the net, Hearts would need two more than them. Permutations and headaches.

Gary McKay, the legendary record appearance holder for Hearts, opened the scoring in the 10th minute with a 16-yard side foot after a lung-busting run and Tynecastle was rocking. For two minutes at least — Jaroslav Silhavy's finish took the wind out of Hearts' sails.

"Like being kicked in the groin at your birthday party," was how Archie McPherson described it in commentary. But two fine headers from Ian Baird and Craig Levein sent the ground into raptures with a 3-1 score line at half time enough to send them through. Hearts sank in the crowd though when Czech Republic international Pavel Kuka scored with a deft chip over keeper Henry Smith. They were heading out ...

Cometh the hour, cometh the man. Yorkshireman Glynn Snodin to be precise. When a free-kick was awarded 25 yards out with 10 minutes to go, the wee man with a penchant for ferocious set pieces had Hearts supporters praying for the net to bulge, more in hope than expectation. The net didn't bulge, as it happens. Instead, Snodin's thunderbolt arrowed into the stanchion, a goal from the second it left his boot. Cue pandemonium. Snodin would later tell the *Edinburgh Evening News* that he thought to himself "'just aim for Eamonn [Bannon]'s shiny head'" — Bannon was stood in the wall and got out of the way of Snodin's rocket in the nick of time before his "shiny head" was separated from his shoulders.

1990s

The rollercoaster of the Slavia Prague tie was to be the high-water mark of an ultimately second-rate season. After the highs of the previous year, the team's fifth-place finish was a bitter disappointment. McKay candidly acknowledged that the squad struggled to align themselves with Joe Jordan's tactics at Tynecastle: "Collectively the players hadn't perhaps bought into Joe's vision. The same players who had worked so hard for the previous management team of Alex MacDonald and Sandy Jardine may not have applied themselves with the same vigour for the new man". This misalignment led to collective frustration, affecting both the club and the manager. Jordan's tenure ended abruptly following a morale-crushing defeat to Falkirk in the Scottish Cup.

McKay reminisces about the 1992-93 season with a mix of emotions. His memories are woven around the iconic Admiral shirt, a dark maroon jersey adorned with jacquarded Hearts badges. To Gary, this kit wasn't just fabric; it was "a symbol of identity and unwavering passion to the club I had supported all my life".

But what is football if not moments and memories? Ask a Hearts fan to remember the '92-'93 season and it isn't the nine winless games to close the season with a whimper. It's the Crazy Corner living up to their name on a wild September night under the floodlights. It's Glynn Snodin's screamer. It's that iconic strip. ●

1990s

San Marino '92–'93

Words: Adam Bushby

Can a shirt be associated with one goal and one goal alone? What if that goal was scored more than 30 years ago? What if it's still the most famous in your history?

England had travelled to San Marino with shallow hopes of qualification for USA 1994; defeats away in Oslo and Rotterdam meant they needed to win by seven clear goals, as well as cross their fingers that Poland would beat the Netherlands. England at least had form in Bologna's Stadio Renato Dall'Ara, David Platt volleying past Michel Preud'homme to put Bobby Robson's men into the quarters at Italia '90. Back then, England were in charge of their own destiny, but this was only little San Marino, who'd only ever scored two goals in their entire history … right?

"The stage is set for England's last and decisive match in this World Cup qualifying group," John Motson began, in his match commentary for the BBC. "England in red, San Marino in blue, England needing to win by a seven-goal margin and hope that Poland can do them a favour in Poznań against Holland."

Referee Mohamed Nazri Abdullah blows his whistle. San Marino kick off.

"I'm sure you're aware now what's at stake. And Nicola Bacciocchi the number nine picks the ball up straight away and San Marino launch the first attack. Oh and a mistake by Stuart Pearce and San Marino have scored! I don't believe this!"

Motson wasn't the only one.

Eight point three seconds is all it took for Davide Gualtieri's life to change forever. That's computer science student Davide Gualtieri. Eight point three seconds had gone and in a game that England needed to win by seven clear goals, impossibly, a Stuart Pearce back-pass to David Seaman fell short of its target, leaving Gualtieri to stab home. England trailed one goal to nil against a team of part-timers from a country whose population would fit comfortably inside the Stadium of Light.

The shirt that made history. Well, for eight seconds anyway.

1990s

> **Gaggles of Scotland fans have made the pilgrimage to the computer store Gualtieri owns over the years to pay their respects.**

Right-back for the English that night, Lee Dixon, later revealed that he reacted to Gualtieri's bombshell opener by bursting out laughing. That the game ended 7-1 in England's favour was incidental as the Dutch beat Poland 3-1 in Poznań anyway. Incidental for the English in any case (not so much for Graham Taylor, who quit "with great sadness" six days later). For Gualtieri, that goal — at that point the fastest goal in World Cup history — and that blue Admiral shirt are celebrated to this day. And not just in his native San Marino. Gaggles of Scotland fans have made the pilgrimage to the computer store Gualtieri owns over the years to pay their respects.

It's serendipity that such a historic goal should be scored in such a classic kit. Tiled across the sky blue shirt is the Admiral logo, jacquarded into the fabric, with a flocked badge and a series of dark blue and white daggers dominating the lower portion, and covering the left shoulder. It's the definitive shirt, befitting the definitive goal.

So can a shirt be associated with one goal and one goal alone? For a team that has a solitary win under its belt in 205 at the time of writing and has scored just 30 goals, that goal against England in 1993 was monumental … just ask Davide Gualtieri:

"At first, I wasn't aware how much of a big deal the goal against England was at all. It took a few days for me to understand how big my goal had been. Newspapers kept writing about it and how fast that goal had been. The resonance of it all became bigger and bigger as the days went on.

"I know a replica kit celebrating 30 years of that goal is being made and I think it's great. Wearing your national team shirt is always something special, because it's like you are carrying and representing your country around the world. It's really fantastic. This also means a lot to fans, who ask for autographs on the shirts they're wearing and for the players' shirts. The shirt is a symbol.

"You always feel a bit nostalgic. I still train a little club here in San Marino to remain in football. When I meet up with my former teammates, we feel a bit nostalgic because we had a great time together, lived some unique experiences that not many have had and had a lot of fun; we were very lucky from that point of view. In terms of my personal career, maybe I could have done a bit more, but I really have no regrets and I can look back with satisfaction and gratitude. I often think of that goal and the shirt I was wearing with immense pleasure — the memories will stay with me forever." ●

1990s

Birmingham City '95–'96

Words: Rob MacDonald

Whether or not Karren Brady expected to be modelling a new club shirt for photographers a week into her role as Managing Director of Birmingham City is anyone's guess. But, in the middle of the pitch, although flanked by new signings, Brady is the focus of attention at the launch of an interim kit in March 1993.

David Sullivan had acquired the club, then in receivership, a month earlier and installed Brady as Managing Director at only 23. She faced a barrage of misogyny from the outset. Up and down the country, women weren't allowed in boardrooms, opposition fans were vicious and even the club's own players seemed to struggle to get their heads around how to respond.

The other new faces come the start of the 1993-94 season were Admiral, who wasted no time making their mark. Birmingham's new home shirts alone were a sight to behold — jacquarding by now was such a ubiquitous part of kit design that variations of the Admiral logo in the background of the shirt barely registered, overtaken as they were by white chevrons and stripes on the sleeves. On the collar, more subtle double blue piping appeared at the edges, as did buttons, with 'Blues' embroidered on the left side.

Just as notable was the club's appointment of Barry Fry as manager that season — Fry would lead the Blues to promotion out of the Second Division at the first time of asking, with the Football League trophy completing a lower-league double.

A simpler 1994-95 version was all blue, with a jacquard repeating crest and a white collar and trim on the sleeves. The neckline carried the date 1875 in a nod to the club's formation — relatively understated compared to its predecessor. Not so its successor.

This 1995-96 shirt truly had something for everyone. Jacquarding, of course — but applied to a revived, though barely-used, 'BCFC' monogram from the 1970s. The monogram was writ large across the right-hand side of the shirt but then also repeated in diagonal rows everywhere else, with 'the blues' interspersed between. Presumably there was just no room for the Admiral logo, which — in the only known instance of this for any manufacturer — found itself simply printed across the neck like a clerical collar, without the famous nautical lines.

Mid-90s Birmingham City was certainly a club that raised eyebrows and there's little argument that the club was transformed under Brady. To succeed as she did, firstly making Birmingham profitable and then overseeing their rise to the Premier League, she had to throw everything at it. Admiral's kits followed suit. ●

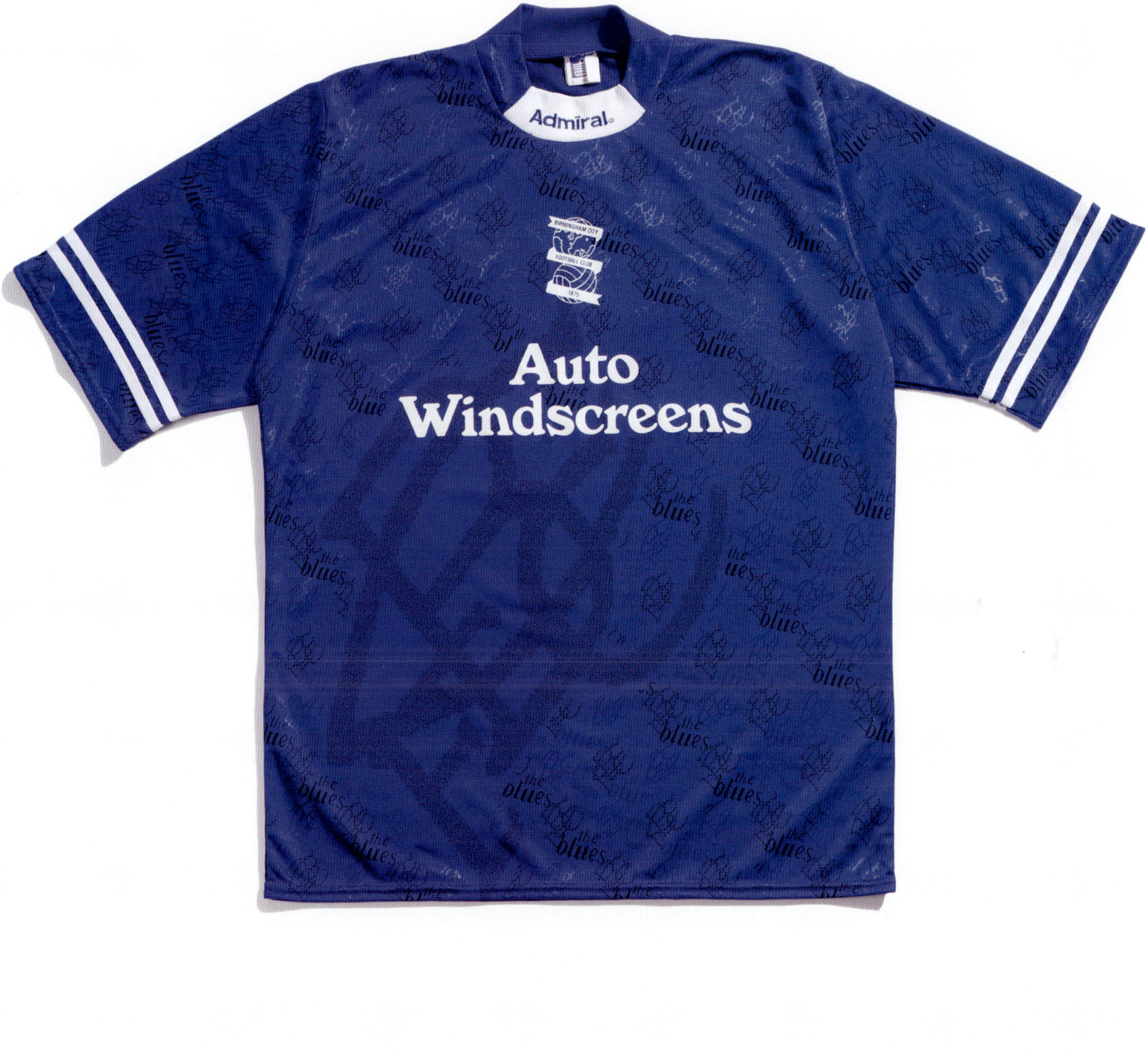
Admiral
BIRMINGHAM CITY
FOOTBALL CLUB
1875
Auto
Windscreens

1990s

York City '95–'97

Words: Adam Bushby

Giant-killing
noun.

the unexpected defeat of a sportsman, sportswoman or sports team by an apparently inferior opponent.

It is one of English football's greatest traditions and holds a quasi-liturgical resonance in the annals of the game. If Manchester United were a giant in 1995, then York City were, let's say, unequivocally not a giant. Languishing second bottom in the third tier, my hometown team had rolled into Manchester looking to avoid humiliation. As it happened, one team was to be humiliated on the evening of 20 September 1995 … A scarcely believable night on the other side of the Pennines saw York score three goals without reply against a United side featuring David Beckham, Ryan Giggs, Brian McClair, Lee Sharpe and Denis Irwin. If there was a collective bout of imposter syndrome in the away end as the game kicked off, it had been well and truly dispatched as it ended. There couldn't have been more magic in the air that night if Old Trafford had been filled with 30,000 David Copperfield impersonators.

That blue Admiral shirt with the white squares on the shoulder and right sleeve remains indelibly etched in my mind's eye. I had just witnessed my first giant killing in the flesh on my 12th birthday.

1990s

Paul Barnes (arms aloft) and team celebrate a famous win over Manchester United in 1995 (top).

York City players in jubilant mood in the dressing room after another famous scalp — this time Everton a year later (above).

York's former right back and club legend Andy McMillan cites the game as being as remarkable for the players as it was for the supporters: "I remember the old Trafford game very well as it was an unbelievable night for the players, the club and especially the fans — the noise was deafening at times," he recalls. "I remember coming out for the warm-up and seeing all the fans and the shirts in the away end." York rode out the barrage from United's big guns, losing 3-1 at Bootham Crescent in the return leg, but through 4-3 on aggregate.

A year later and we were at it again.

York City 3 Everton 2. The second division side deservedly through after a 1-1 draw at Goodison. 'Easy, Easy," we chanted, again. We invaded the pitch, again. We'd killed giants, again.

"Everton at home was such a great game," remembers McMillan. "I won MOM and was given a bike — probably the weirdest prize I ever received. I actually injured my neck and couldn't turn my head either way but there was no way I was going to miss that game, so I never said anything to the physio or to Alan [Little; the manager]."

"I wish I'd kept my shirts in hindsight", McMillan says. "I still see the old shirts when I sometimes go to a game now and it does bring back good memories. Admiral are so iconic."

Mention Admiral or the Coca Cola Cup to any York fan over the age of 35 and they'd be lying if they said they weren't conjuring memories of those giant killings in the '90s and the crisp red home shirt with navy collar. Simple yet classy. And, aahh, the old badge. Just the tonic when you've just lost to Wealdstone at home in the Conference. ●

The first York kit I ever saw in the late 1970s will, for me, be the (red and!) blueprint for what all the club's kits should look like. Simple, stylish, smart, with the always essential V-neck and collar. I remember being particularly excited when Admiral returned to City in the mid 1990s and they didn't let us down!

One of the club's best strips ever was worn by our last properly good team, including in famous League Cup successes against Manchester United and Everton.

– Guy Mowbray, commentator

1990s

200

Introduction:
Rob MacDonald

2000–

A fan wearing the England '82 shirt at the 2002 World Cup.

They spent at least $100 billion on it in America. Internationally, the cost was thought to have been three to five times that amount, just to prepare for, and then correct, faults. All for something that, in the first days of a new millennium, became derided as a joke, a hoax, or some kind of misplaced IT programmer hysteria.

But, stereotypically at least, IT programmers don't tend to be the type given over to hysteria and the millennium bug, or simply 'Y2K', was a very real concern. By December 1999 it had been a live issue for some time — responses and active testing was underway as early as 1995 — and by 1998 the G8 and UN were coordinating an international effort. On New Year's Eve itself, UK flights were cancelled in case of failures seeing them drop from the skies.

As quickly as public awareness had grown around the bug though, it dissipated. Speed was the overriding factor the world hurtled into the 21st century — technology rapidly advanced, taking almost everything with it. Y2K even gave its name to a fashion trend at the time, with monochromatic designs complemented by metallic accents aiming to reflect increasingly sleek consumer tech like the iPod.

Most broadly, the dawn of 'fast fashion' meant that consumers really could keep up with design and high fashion, with garments in similar styles now mass produced, at low-cost, and available off-the-peg on the high street not long after being seen on the runway. Affordable clothing became an increasingly relevant battleground for designer brands themselves, who also had to adjust to the new pace of consumption.

They also had to adjust to a completely new landscape as social media and online marketplaces and communities gained first a foothold, then almost complete dominance in how customers and collectors went shopping. Never before had so much been instantly accessible, shareable and reviewable, and communities sprang up dedicated to the collation and proliferation of fashion and clothing of nearly every genre and type.

The first two decades of the 21st century were marked by a global mash up of a variety of styles, but there was still a tendency to look back in time for inspiration and revivals of '70s, '80s and '90s trends all surfaced and resurfaced. Sportswear had also been edging its way into the day-to-day, firstly in the form of tracksuits, baseball caps and trainers becoming ubiquitous among young men. Later on in the 2010s, this was propelled further by an explosion in 'athleisure', but another significant market combined the two trends and was hugely significant for Admiral. As customers who had been the original targets of replica shirts in childhood reached a certain (nostalgic) vintage, a market materialised for those designs to be revisited, reimagined and resold. Shirt collection remains a vibrant, thriving pursuit.

As customers who had been the original targets of replica shirts in childhood reached a certain (nostalgic) vintage, a market materialised for those designs to be revisited, reimagined and resold.

2000–

New Prime Minister Gordon Brown starts a Year 11 football match, 2006.

Consumer spending wasn't free and easy throughout though, and came into sharp focus in 2008 when a catastrophic global financial crash heralded the beginning of the end of 11 years of Labour governments. Having led Labour to three successive election victories, Tony Blair left in 2007 and Gordon Brown assumed office. His proactive response to the crisis that engulfed global markets was widely admired, but recession was unavoidable, which, combined with earlier public misgivings about indecisiveness over a snap election and the 10p tax rate, saw his popularity wane.

Labour were replaced by a Conservative-Lib Dem coalition in 2010 and the referendums began. The 'Alternative Vote' was rejected by voters in 2011, before Scottish voters said 'no' to independence in 2014. The next general election in 2015 was won outright by the Conservatives and the defining moment of the decade came with a referendum on Britain's EU membership in 2016, in which 52% voted to leave. The rest, as they say, is history.

Wales fans revel in their first major tournament for 58 years, at Euro 2016.

2000–

An altogether more fulfilling type of history was made on the football pitch in the 2010s, at least. Wales ended a 58-year wait for a major tournament by qualifying for Euro 2016 in France, then went on to top a group containing England and incredibly reached the semi-final before succumbing to Cristiano Ronaldo, Nani and Portugal. Serial attendees England threated to deliver on a young team's promise with a World Cup semi-final in 2018 and a home Euros final in 2020, only to lose out in extra time and on penalties respectively. Scotland also broke a long-standing drought by qualifying for Euro 2020 through the playoffs via consecutive penalty shootout victories, and then in a sure sign of the apocalypse (and I say this as a Scotland fan), breezing through qualifying for Euro 2024, losing only once away to Spain.

Wales ended a 58-year wait for a major tournament by qualifying for Euro 2016 in France.

Manchester United's era of dominance came to an end with the departure of Sir Alex Ferguson as manager.

Domestically, the Premier League had absolutely no issue with an extra zero at the start of the new millennium as the sale of rights to Sky Sports and NTL tipped extraordinarily over £1 billion for the first time in 2001 (and since reaching nearly £7 billion in 2023). New viewing options became available to the public as streaming services gained a foothold in the market too. Technology influenced coverage too, with a new style of punditry delving into unprecedented detail supported by multiple camera angles and CGI. And just as in the fashion world, online communities including Twitter, Instagram and Facebook, which gave anyone who wanted to the ability to interact with the clubs, players and leagues, meant that in next to no time the brand had truly gone global.

On the pitch, increasing investment changed the face of the game still further. Manchester United's era of dominance came to an end with the departure of Sir Alex Ferguson as manager in 2013 — they were (unsurprisingly) unable to repeat their treble of 1999, but still collected eight Premier League titles, an FA Cup, three league cups, another Champions League and a Club World Cup in those 13 years. Although United were no strangers to spending, the mega-riches of Chelsea and Manchester City hoovered up eight of the next domestic titles, with only Liverpool and, seismically, Leicester City, interrupting the processions.

Women's football also became a powerful force in the 2010s — the inaugural Super League kicked off on 13 April 2011 at Chelsea's home ground, Imperial Fields, where the hosts lost 1-0 to Arsenal, who would go on to take the title. Chelsea would have to wait until 2015 for their first championship, although they have since gone on to win five more, making them the most successful club under the 'Super League' banner. Since 2017-18, WSL matches have frequently been broadcast live by a series of channels. Internationally, England stole the show, performing well at a series of tournaments before winning a home Euros in 2022 and reaching the World Cup final in 2023.

As a result of a tumultuous two decades, clubs and brands have increasingly embraced a new way to be they were (unsurprisingly) unable to repeat their treble of 1999, but still collected inclusive, creative and innovative, sustainable and local, built on values. Admiral's renaissance from 2011 to now relies on a mix of heritage and innovation and has been revitalised thanks to a string of inspired collaborations, several of which are celebrated in this section. The Admiral kit builder, another recent development, completely opens up the process, allows you to design a kit for a team at any level, selecting from 12 shirt types for which there are around 80 customisable design templates. Fifty years may have passed, but Admiral's focus on individuality and pioneering design remains firmly intact. ●

Alex Ferguson lifts his final Premier League trophy, 2013.

2000–

Bristol City '01–'02

Words: Mark and Paul Watson

The beauty lies in its simplicity. A totally red shirt with sponsors 'DAS' in a white circle. The away was just the reverse of the home. While other shirts, like the famous Spider-Man shirt of the 1993-94 Dry Blackthorn Cider and Thorn Security sponsorship era, which was made by the club's own label Nibor (Robin backwards), may have been flashier, the 2001-02 Admiral kit won hearts for its purity. It also somehow looked like the shirt of a bigger club; you could picture City wearing it in the First Division, rather than Division Two where we were stuck.

This was before the days of shirts being slowly and artfully trailed on social media, so the first proper look at the kit was when it was already being worn by the likes of Brian 'Tin Man' Tinnion, the ever-present Louis Carey and, of course, Tony Thorpe, for an opening day 3-0 win away at Northampton Town.

There's nothing sweeter than an opening day win. So often by the end of the first 90 minutes of the season we'd have written off our entire campaign, but in 2001-02, Danny Wilson's men romped to victory thanks to a hat-trick from Thorpe.

Thorpe, who joined City for a then-fortune of £1 million but was worryingly packed off on loan to Reading, ended up being a great investment, scoring a remarkable 51 goals in 128 games. At times he was a force of nature, at others he would disappear, but he's still remembered with fondness by fans who over the years watched the likes of Steve Jones, Steve Torpey and Kevin Nugent labouring in attack. Not to mention Bas Savage — we should probably never mention Bas Savage.

As fans filed out of the Atyeo and Dolman Stands to the compulsory 'One For The Bristol City' by The Wurzels on a warm August afternoon, after a 3-1 win over Swindon in the second match of the season, we believed this could be the year we escaped the Second Division. But despite some brilliant spells, a slightly thin squad tailed off and could only finish seventh, just outside the play-offs. Maybe we were also distracted by the glamour of a run in the LDV Vans Trophy that took City to the Area Final, and defeat against Cambridge United.

2000–

265

But it's almost impossible to picture that 2001-02 shirt without picturing Scott Murray in it. Specifically, Murray's delirious joy after netting a brace against Cardiff City at Ninian Park in a 3-1 triumph in the Severnside Derby. After squeezing his second goal in at the near post, Murray wheeled away with his hand to his ear, delighting in silencing the home fans with an expression reminiscent of the great Marco Tardelli after his goal for Italy in the 1982 World Cup final. It summed up Murray perfectly — bags of flair, but also a passion for the club where he became a legend, racking up 91 goals, over 400 appearances, and taking on a position as kit-man after his playing career.

It was to be a period of near misses for the club on the pitch. We traded the heartbreak of missing out on the play-offs for heartbreak *in* the play-offs. However, in spite of that, I defy any City fan to look at the 2001-02 shirt and not remember the good times. ●

2000–

Wolverhampton Wanderers '02–'04

Words: James Bird

Life is short and quick, and days become weeks become years before you have the chance to stop the rot and really think about it all. But when you do, it's the first times that often become the thick, vertical markers on the constant horizontal timeline. The first time you rode a bike (fell into the thorn bushes in my nan's back garden), the first time you go away with school (walked around a lake at night and cried for hours), the first time someone kisses you (closing credits of Shark Tale in the cinema, no tears, no tears), the first time you drive a car.

I think that the first time I loved a Wolves team was in the 2002-03 season. I'd loved players before: the embering years of Steve Bull, Ludovic Pollet with his head bandaged up, Mohamed Camara legging it up and down the left-hand side. I'd loved moments too: 17-year-old Robbie Keane's two debut goals in 1997, our cloggers against Arsenal's velvety Nicolas Anelka, Marc Overmars and Christopher Wreh in the FA Cup semi-final at Villa Park the following year.

But none of that came close to what the team managed to do in May 2003. We got promoted to the Premier League, and we were wearing this shirt.

By the time I was closing in on my teenage years, I'd been going to Molineux regularly and I think I understood all of it more. The smell of smoke and beer and pies and bad breath, the ground groaning with men, the punch of boot on ball and the piercing white of the floodlights. I was less intimidated by the massiveness of it all, and more embalmed by it. And, we'd started winning.

The team was a classic Championship pic 'n' mix. There were the young, local, green shoots of hope: Joleon Lescott, 20 now, and in his third year of being far too good for anyone that came near him; Matt Murray, cool, calm, only 21, and about to play his last full season for a long time before his knees gave way. There were the steady heads: Mark Kennedy, Shaun Newton, Alex Rae, Paul Butler. There were the men of significant glory: Paul Ince and Denis Irwin drafted in to play 40 games a season like the late 30s didn't exist.

2000–

269

Wolves players celebrate taking the club to the Premier League for the first time, beating Sheffield United 3-0 in the playoff final at the Millennium Stadium.

We were Wolves, we were going up, and we were wearing a shirt that said 'Doritos' on it.

And then there was my hero: George Ebialimolisa Ndah, a player who could part the swirling ocean of a football pitch like Moses. He was direct, elegant, with legs that were far too long for a footballer, legs that invited angry tackles from frustrated defenders and fast-twitch muscle strains. This was his first proper season back after having his leg broken during the Black Country derby, and he was unplayable: pitch-length odysseys, winners in the FA Cup, a man we sang "George Ndah, my Lord" about.

And all of this was happening, all of it: the promotion, the pic 'n' mix, the odysseys, while wearing a shirt that said 'Doritos' on it.

The shirt itself is glorious, you can see that. Strong folded collar with old gold trimmings, black side panels, a sewn-on Admiral label in the bottom right, and a '90s-ish oversized fit. We were Wolves, we were going up, and we were wearing a shirt that said 'Doritos' on it.

Life is short and quick, but when I stop my finger on the vertical marker just before the timeline goes teenage-carnage, I close my eyes and see this shirt. I see George Ndah picking the ball up in his own box against Preston and doing it all on his own. I see Joleon Lescott getting there first over and over again. I see Paul Ince at the Millennium Stadium, lifting the trophy, waving at Sir Jack Hayward, and taking us to new first times. ●

2000–

Leeds United Women '05–'06

Words: Maisie Adam

I love Leeds United. And I really do mean 'love', in its truest form. I love them come rain or shine, through the good times and the bad, whether I agree with their decisions or not. They've broken my heart more times than I can count, yet I keep going back, and why? Because the good times make it all worth it, because I really, truly, love them.

Leeds United is an intrinsic part of my entire family. We've always followed Leeds, at the games, on the telly, through the colours we'd wear both on matchdays and day-to-day life, and in our local community. This one-club city — and any of the tiny towns or villages within a 20-mile radius of it — has always prided itself on its deep-rooted connection with the football team inhabiting our beloved Elland Road. All Leeds, Aren't We?

That team though, had always been a team of men. That's what Leeds United was to me; in fact, that's what football was to me. I had no idea about a women's side. Football was the beautiful game, but it was a man's game. Or so I thought.

When I was 12 years old, I went to Elland Road for another painful fixture, as Kevin Blackwell's side had somehow managed to go from third place in the Championship in the first half of the season, to gaining just four points from the possible 18 left for the taking. Leeds were yet again in a rut, and the mood at the ground was sour. But as I sat in the back of my uncle's car on the way home, flicking through my matchday programme, I came across something I'd never seen before. A women's football team. A professional women's football team. And best of all, a LEEDS UNITED PROFESSIONAL WOMEN'S FOOTBALL TEAM!

Here were pictures of female players in a Leeds kit — and what a kit. Brilliant white with vertical blue and yellow pin stripes, the Admiral logo on one side of the shirt, and that iconic club badge shining proudly on the other. The only difference to the shirt I had (the men's kit) was the sponsor; on this one the White & McKay whiskey brand was replaced by something called "Empire direct.com"... but I had no idea what that was or its significance (they sponsored the women's team for two years after Ken Bates cut off the funding in 2005), because the only websites I ever used were Myspace and *www.ZacEfronFanClub.com*.

2000–

A Leeds United women's team, stood there in an iconic kit, preparing to play in the final of the greatest domestic tournament of all, at one of the most notoriously tough grounds? This was bloomin' exciting.

I was enthralled by this team as I read about their journey. They had got to the final of the Women's FA Cup for the first time in their history and had an almighty task ahead of them for the final. They'd be playing six-time champions Arsenal, and on top of that, the match was to be played at the one ground I was never allowed to go to for an away day. Millwall's The Den.

Suddenly, in the back of that car, my feelings of bitter disappointment from the game were being replaced by something else. Hope? Inspiration? Nerves for a team I had never known existed until about 10 seconds ago? I couldn't quite identify how I felt, because I had never seen this before. A Leeds United women's team, stood there in an iconic kit, preparing to play in the final of the greatest domestic tournament of all, at one of the most notoriously tough grounds? This was bloomin' exciting.

I told my family all about it. They too were intrigued and excited, but also just as unaware of Leeds' women's side as I had been. How had this happened? We were Leeds through and through, and we weren't aware of this incredible squad — why?! After all, we're All Leeds … Aren't We?

Obviously, I now know all the reasons I wasn't aware of them until that point: all the years of underfunding, underrepresentation, ignorance and indifference to the game's existence from major broadcasters and sporting bodies. That these women were playing a game that yes, had always been a huge part of my family's — and my city's — identity, but that it was also a game that women were banned from playing professionally for 50 years. Of course, it wasn't in the same position as the men's.

2000–

I say this now, because as I have grown, so has my attachment to the women's game. But at the time, I was 12 years old. So I put it down to something like "they must play on a school day", or "their games must be on one of the fancy channels that we don't get, like the cricket" or "maybe everyone else knew about it and I didn't, like that time everyone else had seen *Anchorman*, and I couldn't understand why everyone at school kept saying 'I love lamp'".

My family and I sat down to watch that FA Cup final. And, as heartbreaking as it is to type my memories of the 5-0 defeat, it was a game that contained everything you love football for. It was heartbreaking, exhilarating, frustrating, and inspiring. In that game I saw, for the first time, players that changed the face of women's football in this country and on the international stage; Sue Smith, Rachel Yankey, Lianne Sanderson, Alex Scott and Kelly Smith (whose 77th-minute penalty still lives rent-free in my mind).

2000–

I wanted that Leeds shirt so badly. I wanted to wear what that team had worn.

I wanted that Leeds shirt so badly. I wanted to wear what that team had worn, playing in such an iconic game, at the highest level. But alas, I had that kit already, but the men's version, and the idea of asking my Dad — a man who nearly went into cardiac arrest every time he saw the price of a new Leeds kit — for the same shirt but with a different sponsor, was frankly ridiculous.

But I love that kit because I loved that squad and what it represented. That kit was the first time I saw someone like me in football. It's synonymous with a turning point for me as a football fan; it was the moment I realised football wasn't a man's game that I happened to enjoy. It was for everyone. After all, we're All Leeds, Aren't We.

A bittersweet shirt — Sue Smith

Sue Smith began her career at Tranmere before playing for Leeds United for eight years from 2002-2010, appearing in the famous Admiral kit in the women's FA Cup final in 2006. She later played for Lincoln Ladies and Doncaster Rovers Belles, and won 93 caps for England, scoring 16 goals.

Playing for Leeds you always felt the support of the fan base — whether you played for the youth team, the women's team, or the men's they would always follow you. Obviously the Cup Final result wasn't what we wanted, but I do remember the incredible support from the fans, you could see and hear them and yeah, there were a lot of white shirts, the kind that we wore, which obviously gives you a huge boost walking out in front of thousands watching …

I think it's important to know the history of a club and know what's happened before you, whether that's in the women's game or the men's. Allan Clarke presented us with sock tags like the men's team wore when they won the Cup in 1972, and I've still got mine along with my shirt, it was all really nicely done.

Shirts had massively evolved. When I first started playing at Tranmere, we just had the men's kit and even when I first played for England, we had the men's kit — I've got a picture of me on my debut in the big shirt, big shorts. At the time you just do what you can, you might roll your sleeves up, you might tuck your shirt in — it's only when you get a women's kit, something that actually fits you properly, that you realise how much it helps. And the Cup Final shirt I remember being fitted, being a women's size, it wasn't too baggy or anything like that. Thankfully Admiral had moved things forward by that point!

I do think the way a shirt looks as well is quite important — you always have your favourites — with Leeds it's probably the white home shirt of course, the Cup Final shirt, just because you see a lot of fans wearing that, it's the one that's completely synonymous. I've been quite lucky that all my shirts have been nice!

The 2006 shirt does have a particular meaning, although the result makes it bittersweet. Obviously to get there was amazing, and the build-up around it, and the actual occasion was great when you reflect on it, so the shirt itself is of course something I've kept — getting to a cup final is a big deal and it's massive in the women's game in particular. I have got it, I have kept it along with my England debut shirt, I scored a hat trick against Spain and I've kept that too — there are definitely certain shirts that do mean more to you. ●

Sue Smith (left) faces up a free-kick in the FA Cup final, 2006.

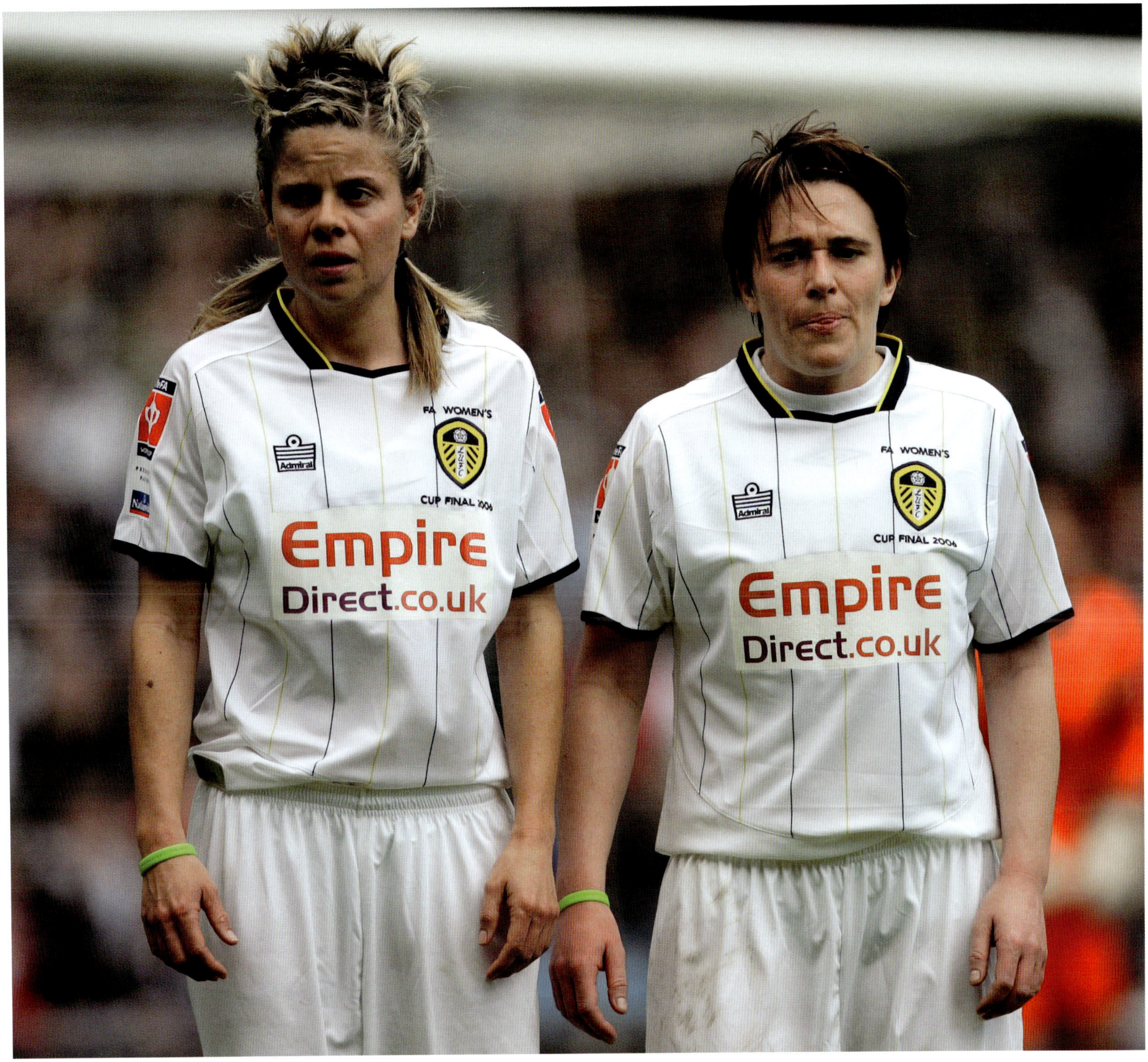
Admiral
FA WOMEN'S
CUP FINAL 2006
Empire
Direct.co.uk
Admiral
FA WOMEN'S
CUP FINAL 2006
Empire
Direct.co.uk

2000–

Tampa Bay Rowdies '13

Words: Adam Bushby

The Tampa Bay Rowdies are dead, long live the Tampa Bay Rowdies. As phoenix clubs go, the new iteration, founded in 2013, is remarkably similar to the original, sharing a name, logo and other intellectual property.

Admiral delved into its back catalogue with the design for the 2013 North American Soccer League (NASL) season, which was heavily reminiscent of the classic 1981 template for the home and away shirts, barring a couple of updates. A smaller modern collar replaced the previous flappy version, and as defending NASL champions the Rowdies added a second star under their collars to complement the one won in their inaugural season (1975). The home shirt remained green with yellow hoops on the sleeves as it was in their late '70s heyday, during which former QPR and Man City legend Rodney Marsh dazzling his adoring public for four seasons.

"Football in England had become a grey game, played on grey days by grey people," Marsh famously said, as he swapped the persistent drizzle of Manchester for the scorching sun of Florida. He was contacted by Elton John's agent in 1975 as the rock legend looked to lure Marsh to the club he part owned, LA Aztecs.

Enjoying the VIP treatment at an Elton John concert at Dodger Stadium, Marsh was tapped up by Campbell's Soup heir George Strawbridge, Jr, who persuaded him to move to the Rowdies instead. Rumours that John penned "Don't go breaking my heart" a year later in response to Marsh's betrayal have been neither confirmed or denied.

Marsh wasn't the only trailblazer. One of the first black players to grace the English top-flight, West Ham cult hero Clyde Best, wrote himself into club folklore with his last-gasp goal over Portland Timbers — a side he would later join — to guarantee the Rowdies' first NASL championship. London to Tampa remained a well-worn path for talent, former Wimbledon and Brentford forward Carl Cort scoring in Soccer Bowl 2012 under the tutelage of former Luton stalwart and thrice-capped Englishman Ricky Hill. Hill's son Shane also turned out for the Rowdies under his father.

The Rowdies class of 2013-14 couldn't quite match the championship-winning heights of a year prior, finishing three points behind Atlanta Silverbacks in fourth in the spring season, and third in the fall iteration as a Marcos Senna-inspired New York Cosmos swept all before them. Still, at least the shirt looked good, even if the team couldn't add a third star to it. ●

Rowdies fans getting ... rowdy before a game, 2013.

2000–

Gibraltar '13–'14

Words: Adam Bushby

Despite a rich footballing history in Gibraltar stretching way back to kickabouts with the British garrison in the late 1800s, and a first friendly in 1901 against the military, the tiny British Overseas Territory had to wait until 2013 to play its first ever recognised international.

Lining up against Slovakia at the Estádio Algarve on 19 November 2013, Gibraltar weathered the storm to record a 0-0 draw after being welcomed as the 54th member of the UEFA European Football Family, as well as the smallest but one by population (only San Marino had fewer citizens at the time). It was apt that Gibraltar relied on their rock at the back, former Manchester United defender Danny Higginbotham, who was named man of the match. Higginbotham qualified for Gibraltar through his maternal grandmother and it didn't harm his chances of selection that the manager at the time, Allen Bula, was his uncle.

Gibraltar sported a red Admiral kit for this historic match, augmented with a four-stripe diagonal watermark and a stylised white stripe running underneath the crest. The white-blue away and navy third kits both used the same design. The framing of the Gibraltar Football Association (GFA) logo was dubbed a "defiance strip", inspired by the "defiance, tenacity and sheer strength of the people of Gibraltar", according to Admiral.

Customs officer Roy Chipolina scored Gibraltar's first ever international goal in a 4-1 defeat by the Faroe Islands in March 2014, and the minnows' first ever victory came against Malta three months later, making the Admiral shirt a truly iconic one associated with a raft of firsts.

Gibraltar would need to wait until 2018 for a first competitive international win, beating Armenia 1-0 in the Nations League group D4 with a goal from Roy's cousin, prison officer Joseph Chipolina. The only shame was that they didn't do so wearing this celebrated shirt. ●

2000–

AFC Wimbledon '14–'16

Words: Andi Thomas

There's no correct way to play Football Manager. It's a single player game, for the most part, and so you can define the parameters of your own pleasure. Want to steamroller everybody as Paris Saint-Germain? Have at it. Want to manage PSG and Manchester City, then sell all the former's stars to the latter at hilarious knockdown prices, for even more efficient steamrollering? That's between you, your conscience, your gods, and your laptop.

But still, there is a correct way. Ethically, morally … you know there is. Start at the bottom, work to the top. Take the lowliest little club to the highest heights: all FM stories are their own adventure, but those are the true epics. Started unemployed, did you? With no reputation to speak of? Be still my beating heart.

As such, the sponsorship deal between AFC Wimbledon and Football Manager (or Sports Interactive, or Championship Manager) isn't just the longest running in the Football League. It is also the most appropriate. Admittedly, AFC Wimbledon haven't yet won 10 Champions Leagues in a row using a janky 2-6-2 formation. Or even the FA Cup. But clambering up from the Combined Counties League Premier Division to League One is about as close as modern football will permit.

They weren't even in their sponsor's game when they started out again.

It is, perhaps, impossible to imagine modern football without Football Manager. The game is there, you suspect, in the origin stories of the analytics nerds and the amateur experts, the hipsters and the ITKs. Some clubs use the databases, and all receive applications from FM players when the manager's job comes up ("I've no IRL experience, but…"). The launch of each seasonal update is an event marked by a frenzy of content and hype, joy and fury; it's rather like deadline day, only with a bit less shouting.

But perhaps, too, it is impossible to imagine modern football without AFC Wimbledon. Without all that led to AFC Wimbledon: the forced dislocation of Wimbledon FC; the institutional contempt for the club's fans and anybody else that complained; the creation of the new club in Wimbledon; the peculiar arrival of the new club in Milton Keynes; the opening of the new Plough Lane just down the road from the site of the old. None of it should have happened, but it all did, and perhaps one consequence of that can be seen in how we imagine football clubs today. The answers that we came up with then inform the world we watch football in now. You can do a lot to a football club, if you can afford it. Almost anything. But you can't do that.

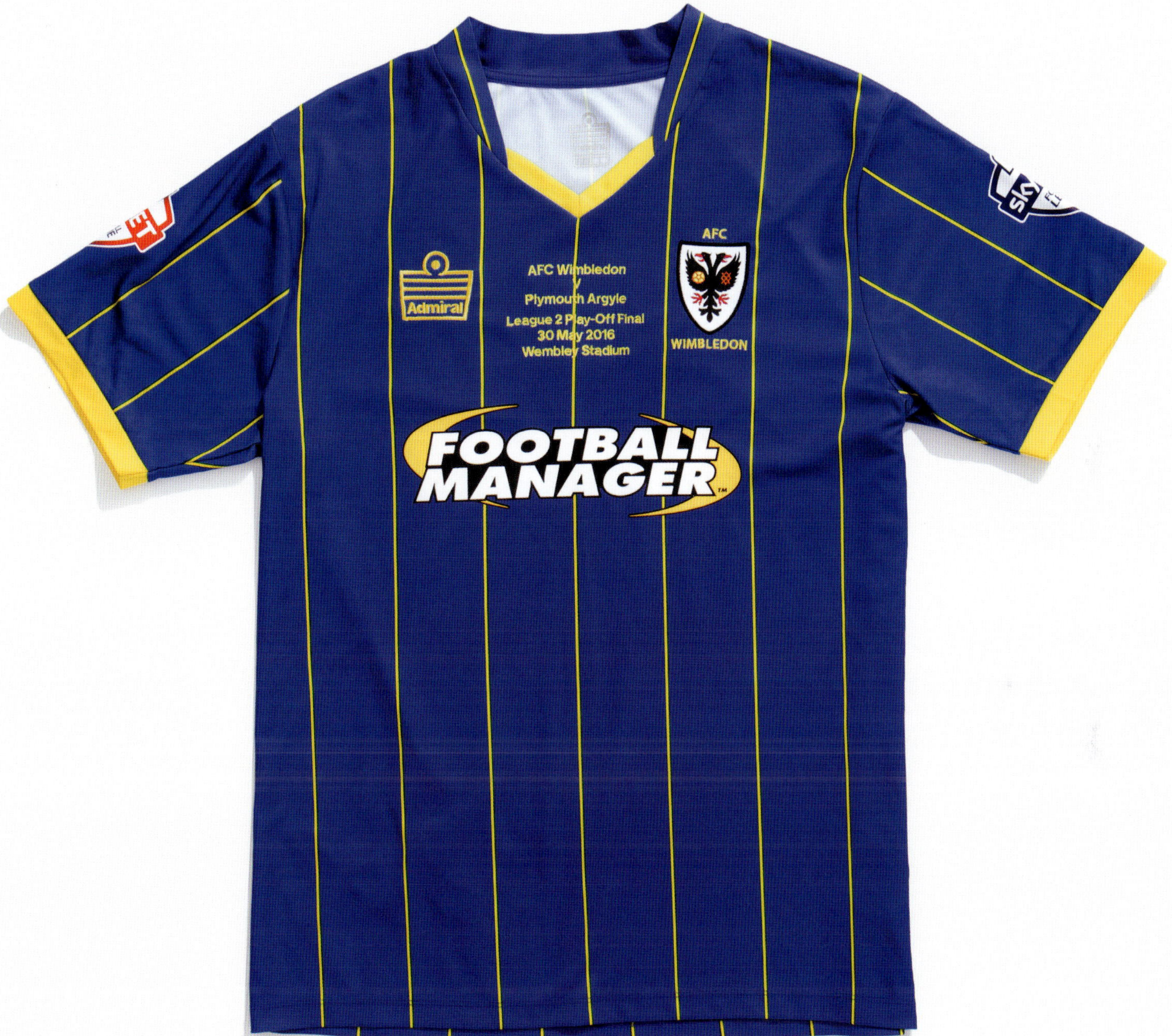
Admiral
AFC Wimbledon
v
Plymouth Argyle
League 2 Play-Off Final
30 May 2016
Wembley Stadium
AFC
WIMBLEDON
FOOTBALL
MANAGER

Suppose Wimbledon had gone quietly. Suppose the fans had done as they were meant to do, accepted that their interests were not the wider interests of football, and drifted off to their closest non-league side, or to Crystal Palace, or to a bitter, nostalgic yearning. Suppose the AFC project had, for one reason or another, never quite clicked into place. Seems lunatic in hindsight, of course, with Wimbledon-in-Wimbledon once again a normal football club with all the mundane things that go along with it: a shiny new stadium, a Womble mascot and concerns about promotion or relegation just like the rest of us.

Would we have seen more and bigger franchising? (A Budweiser advert released a decade after the unpleasantness joked about moving Arsenal to the Peak District.) Would we have seen the same splenetic reaction to the Super League, which promised not a physical departure but a sporting one? As the arguments about Wimbledon and Milton Keynes played out through the late '90s and early noughties, the broader nation — the part of it that likes football, anyway — was forced to consider what a football club is, and why, and who gets to decide that, and the importance of place in it all.

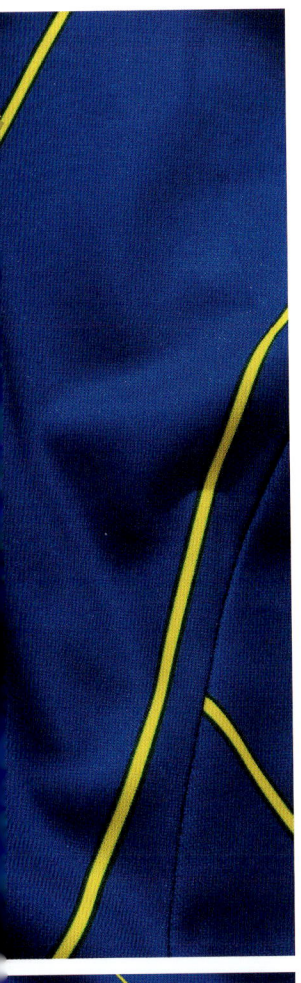

It's a fine blue, isn't it? Bright and rich and classy. Tastefully threaded with yellow pinstripes.

For that's what was established, along with a new club. A founding principle: a football club is of a place, and moving it is not just controversial, but existentially problematic. It will not be the same club. Clubs have moved, of course, before and since; some historically, before football was really settled, others more recently and more quietly, without the scandal. But there was a victory in Wimbledon's defeat, a sleight of hand. They went and moved the club, but when they got to where they were going, it was empty.

It's a fine blue, isn't it? Bright and rich and classy. Tastefully threaded with yellow pinstripes for Admiral's first effort, which AFC wore while winning promotion to League One, and then thin pale hoops for two years of staying up. Anybody growing up in the '90s might have presumed that Wimbledon FC wore dark blue, a grim and forbidding navy, but they wore the bolder shade from just after World War 1 through to 1993; they wore it all through their march up from non-league, and they wore it to Wembley when they humbled Liverpool.

AFC's first shirt, for the 2002-03 season, was designed by Marc Jones, founder member and football kit enthusiast: "I copied the 1975 kit design ... it was blue with yellow underneath the sleeves. I intentionally made the kit look like the one that non-league Wimbledon famously wore against Leeds to say to people, 'don't worry, we've been a non-league club before and last time we were in this position, we were a great, famous side'. That was the Wimbledon that the world started to understand and know about." The blue is making a statement. Us again. ●

2000–

Queen's Park '20–'22

Words: Rob MacDonald

Even for Queen's Park, this was historic. Most shirts designed to celebrate heritage or anniversaries tend to only flirt with the past, revising a colour here, a few lines there, an old logo perhaps. But when there's as much history to work with as there is around Queen's, Scotland's oldest club and the 10th oldest in the world, it's a shame to leave too much of it out.

"We knew the history and importance of the club to Scottish football and we had an open brief to create something bold to represent that," says Scott Dawson, who with creative partner Robb McAulay designed the away shirt. The result — more than 4,000 dots representing every Queen's Park result since joining the Scottish League system in 1900-01 — covers 112 seasons of league football, during which time the club had remained staunchly amateur, even as professionalism swept across the game.

There was a reason it was billed the #MostHistoricKit upon release. In 2019, 91% of members had voted to take the club professional after 152 years, meaning they could sign players to longer-term contracts and crucially, offer deals to players emerging from their renowned academy, whose notable recent graduates Andy Robertson, Lawrence Shankland and Aidan Connolly all moved from the third-tier amateurs to the SPL for nothing. The two seasons for which the shirt would be worn would also be the last of their sponsorship by AG Barr and IRN-BRU, themselves incorporated in 1901, which had been in place for 25 years, one of the longest associations in Scottish football.

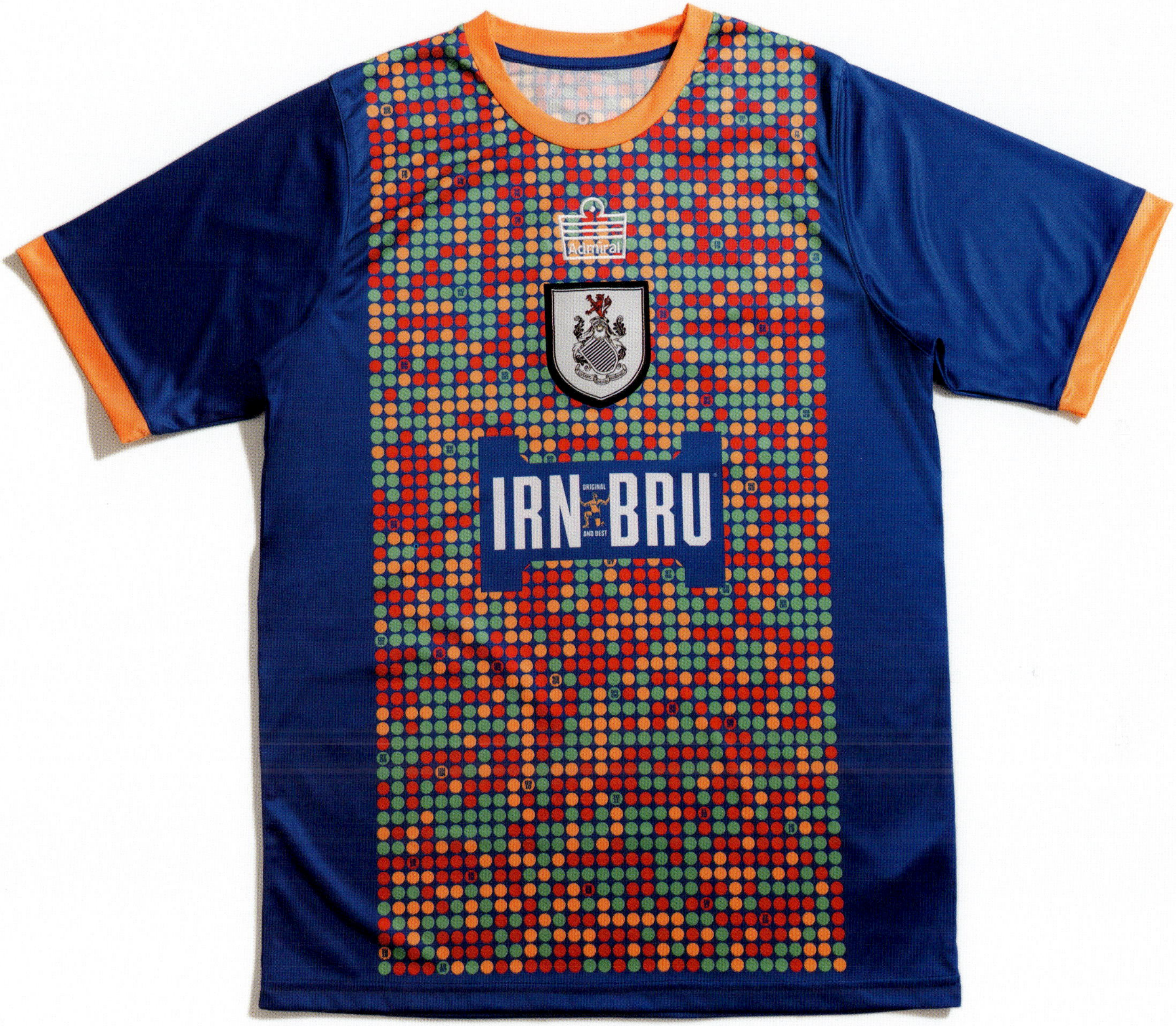
Admiral
IRN BRU
ORIGINAL
AND BEST

More than 4,000 dots represent every Queen's Park result since joining the Scottish League system in 1900-01.

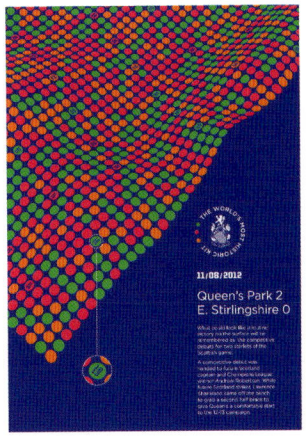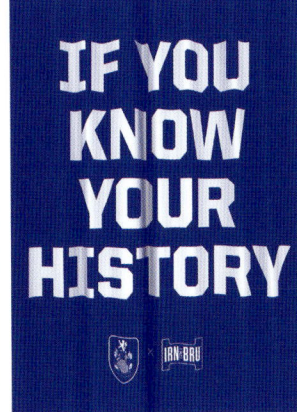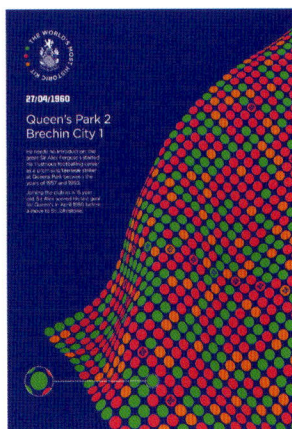

The shirt was backed up with a campaign, marrying key results from Queen's Park's history with the corresponding 'dot'.

2000–

The first fully professional Queen's Park team donned Admiral for the truncated, 22-game 2020-21 League Two season and stormed to the league title by 16 points. Despite some growing pains in League One the next campaign, they came good in the end-of-season playoffs and were promoted again thanks to Simon Murray's extra-time penalty against Airdrie. Back-to-back promotions from the fourth tier to the second — even for Queen's Park, pretty historic.

Two such successful seasons would certainly have added a bit more green to the shirt, with an extremely bold approach to results leading to some fears that, as amateurs among generations of professionals, the red-orange-green coding for defeats, draws and wins might lead to an overwhelmingly red hue (the overall results table actually reads 1,409 wins, 952 draws and 1,853 defeats). But when you're faced with sourcing and coding 56 seasons on each side of a jersey, manually, you just have to wait and see.

"It was pretty painstaking to research and design", says Scott. "We did try to work out some kind of algorithm so we could enter the data and it would be applied to the shirt automatically, but it didn't really work … so each individual dot was set and coloured by us. It did give us a bit more control over checks and making sure that we were representing each result correctly and in the right order. There was a lot of cross-checking!"

But they knew, said Scott, that the idea was worth it. The shirt is all about the detail — as well as every fixture being recorded on it, they are done so chronologically, with the dates of each season noted on the circle of that season's first game. History begins on the back in 1900 and ends in 2020 on the front. The base colours, IRN-BRU's distinctive blue shirt with orange accents, would have been notable enough, so too the centralised embroidered Admiral logo above the club crest and IRN-BRU logo, but it's the sublimated dots that place the shirt among the most notable collaborations of them all. And for Queen's Park, it's yet another piece of history. ●

Admiral x The Square Ball

Words: Daniel Chapman

Many great traditions begin with someone stepping forward into the future, and where Leeds United and Admiral helped establish the seasonal marketplace of desirable designer footballer shirts in the 1970s, our Leeds United fanzine and podcast, The Square Ball (TSB), has its own football shirt heritage thanks to some bold business at the start of the 1990s. That's what brought TSB and Admiral together, looping back into the past of our fanzine, our city, and our football club.

The blurbs we've written for the shirts we've made with Admiral all begin with, 'The Square Ball is not, technically, a football club. But if we were, we'd design really nice football shirts.' The Square Ball is, technically, a football fanzine, founded in 1990 and publishing ever since; the current custodians, of which I'm one, took it on when that ever-present record looked like breaking in 2009. It was hard for us as long-term readers and writers to imagine Elland Road, specifically the tunnel connecting the two ends of Lowfields Road beneath the M621, without someone holding copies of TSB in the air and patiently explaining to wary punters that, no, it's not the programme.

So, we undertook to take it into the 2010s. Somehow, we're still taking it into the 2020s, still in print, still cheap, now with a digital version, a long-running podcast, and our own football shirts.

Although it's a relatively recent phenomenon for entities that are not technically football clubs to make what are technically football shirts, we were taking TSB back to its origins, as an in-house diversion of a what's on guide. The 'Events' staff were increasingly preoccupied by United's march up the Second Division, inspired by Howard Wilkinson, Gordon Strachan and most of all Vinnie Jones, and anticipation for the World Cup, Italia '90. Their base was in Aire Street Workshops, and brightly coloured adverts in the magazine, offering football shirts for sale, shared the same address, and the same people.

Olivia Smart of Leeds United Women wears the shirt inspired by the Lowfield tiles.
Credit: The Square Ball/Lee Brown

2000–

I can't make any claims that Arkwright Sportswear was the first retro remake footie shirt company, or the first importing what an advert called 'Wacky shirts from around the world!'. But I can tell you that my first copy of TSB, bought by my doubtful mum after I insisted that anything with a photo of Eric Cantona on the front had to be worth £1, opened my 11-year-old eyes to ways of looking at football I'd never found in MATCH! or Shoot!. For one thing, I didn't know that all the words I heard in the playground but wasn't allowed to say were being printed in magazines to insult Manchester United fans.

For another, I didn't know what or where a 'Fortuna Sittard' could be found, or why a 'Cruzeiro' shirt would have stars on it and a big Coca-Cola logo, but as I spent hours gazing at these brightly coloured polyester creations being modelled in the smudgily printed adverts — these 'wacky shirts' from who knows where — I felt myself yearning for a Nova Horizonte home kit, years before I heard Half Man Half Biscuit singing of desire for a Dukla Prague away kit.

Where actual clubs have to make sure their kit designs have wide appeal, football fanzines are free to indulge.

That advert became something like a checklist, as when Sampdoria came to Elland Road for the pre-season Makita Tournament. Leeds were the English champions, giving a first run out to their technologically advanced new Admiral kits, and after David Batty had finished scrapping with Roberto Mancini, I could go back to the advert and confirm, yep, that's what a Sampdoria is. The Arkwright retro gear was harder to decode: these were just drawings, of a smiley badge inside a Stone Roses style flower or a cigarette card printed on an XL-only white tee. Among the 'International '70s shirts', a Penarol shirt 'as worn by Pedro Rocha' is still one I need Google for. As for 'Wicked 50s shorts, as worn by Matthews and Lofthouse', that's one throwback idea yet to come back into fashion.

The rest of it, though, easily passes any Instagram test, where the same Fluminense shirts are still in demand with people who, like me, stood no chance of persuading our parents to send off a £36.49 cheque or postal order to a suspect looking address in Leeds, for a hideous football shirt of some club we couldn't pronounce from a city we couldn't find on a map. Now we're grown up enough to do joined up writing in our own chequebooks, but haven't grown out of lust for 'Kaiserslauten (H)'.

That feeling is present in our collaborations with Admiral. Where actual clubs have to make sure their designs have wide appeal, football fanzines are free to indulge. While the club could never put red on a new Leeds shirt, we — well, I still can't quite believe we got away with a scarlet-and-black halved tribute to Newell's Old Boys, but that's how much Leeds fans love Marcelo Bielsa. Then there's the blue, yellow and white tile design that someone in the council Highways department once decided would spruce up a forbidding pedestrian underpass, that became the backdrop to thousands of TSB fanzine transactions for over 30 years. When transferred to fabric by Admiral the design brings together club, place, fans, and fanzine, and TSB's contribution to the football tradition of seeing the future in retro. ●

2000–

Simon Rix of Kaiser Chiefs mid-practice, donning the away shirt.
Credit: The Square Ball/Lee Brown

Admiral and music

Words: James Brown

When I came up with the idea for *loaded* magazine in the summer of 1992, I had two words at the top of everything, 'music' and 'football'. There were a load of other things I wanted to include, but they were the big loves of my life and I wanted them to be the foundations. To me, the magazine would be about me and my mates who went dancing in clubs, jumping up and down at gigs and doing the same on the terraces. In particular, I thought about the audiences of two iconic British bands, New Order and before them, The Jam.

Both audiences had thousands of largely young lads who were as likely to be singing along to 'Eton Rifles' or 'Bizarre Love Triangle' as they would be chanting for their favourite stars from the stands of Maine Road, Stamford Bridge, Elland Road, Anfield, Old Trafford, Highbury, or wherever their weekend took them.

Both cultures revolved around obsessive devotion to their act or team, both involved easily attained and affordable tribal fashions, and both allowed large gangs of fans to unite and share their passion for great music and great home and away days. Gigs lasted 90 minutes and, obviously, football matches did too.

To me, this wasn't rocket science; in the mid-'70s when I was watching my first World Cup, in West Germany, the hair lengths of footballers and pop stars were indistinguishable. George Best had attained the status of the rock and roll footballer in the '60s and in the years that immediately followed there was a procession of fancy Dans — Alan Hudson of Stoke and Chelsea, Stan Bowles of QPR, Tony Currie of Sheffield United and Leeds, Charlie George of Arsenal and Derby County, and Frank Worthington of Bolton and Leicester City, who looked as good on the pitch as they did off it — none of whom resembled the traditional blazer and Brylcreemed sportsman of old.

These players had charisma, were exceptionally talented and some of them had a reputation for tossing it off, falling out with managers and failing to capitalise on their undoubted abilities. They were footballers with the arrogance and cockiness of rock stars and fans of all clubs loved them for it. Their appeal went beyond club rivalries. They all featured frequently in *loaded* and they all feature frequently in the historic understanding of how football and music are intertwined.

Inspired by the 1998 Bridges to Babylon shirt, this release for the Rolling Stones coincided with their Hackney Diamonds album launch.

2000–

Replicating the classic tracksuit worn by Bob Marley.

This combination of looks and skills wasn't just confined to these shores — one of the best films I've ever seen about football is former Jesus & Mary Chain bassist-turned-film-director Douglas Hart who made a brilliant 15-minute short for the BBC called *Brazil 70; The Sexiest Kick Off*, which combined a sun-bleached collage of classic Brazil footage with a mixture of samba classics and Primal Scream.

Go anywhere in the world and you'll find devotees of flamboyant football, great music and classic football shirts all slipping easily from one to the other in conversation. *Loaded* was a big part of the legendary five-a-side tournaments at the Phoenix Festival — bands queued up to enter teams and *loaded* then-member and former Liverpool player Craig Johnston took the idea to Sky, who then created their music and football 'Soccer Sixes'.

The experiences enjoyed by fans of both football and music transcend the barriers erected by tourists around each form of entertainment. Certain bands very much in touch with their audience understood their fans would be as likely to buy a match ticket as a gig ticket, ideally both.

Behind many a studied band image, you'll find musicians who've grown up idolising footballers; nowadays it's easy to hear Ian Wright and Roy Keane talking about their love of Madness, The Specials and The Farm, but I've found myself talking to Chris Lowe of the Pet Shop Boys about how much he loved Arsenal and was surprised when I asked Bernard Sumner of New Order whether former Joy Division band mate, the late Ian Curtis, was as dark as the photos and footage have presented him and he replied: "No, he was just like us really, not into music and books, and he really loved Man City."

Alice Cooper relaxes in full English regalia — cigar, bowler hat, umbrella and England shirt.

2000–

Football and music provide a natural crossover and it's been this way for generations. The Who played at The Valley, Happy Mondays headlined Elland Road and Oasis played Maine Road. Go to a festival now and more people are wearing vintage nylon football shirts to drink and dance to music in than they did during the late '80s rave scene when round-necked cotton retro shirts were all the rage. Wearing a football shirt to a festival or gig or club is a badge of identity as much as going to a game in a band T-shirt.

Smart brands understand this crossover, which brings us to Admiral and their music and football collaborations. The label has worked with some of the greatest British bands, many already mentioned here. They've done it through a true collaboration and they've limited the numbers of shirts produced so they've become as collectible and desirable as limited-edition releases on Record Store Day.

Go back as far as 1976 and Neal Preston's iconic image of Led Zeppelin's Wolverhampton Wanderers fanatic Robert Plant, in his blue and white Admiral England tracksuit top, staring out from the Brooklyn Bridge, and you have a starting point to this relationship. Back then, Planty was just a fan wearing a very cool top and, as the lead singer of the biggest band of the 1970s, he could wear whatever he wanted. And he chose Admiral. Just over 20 years on and Admiral are maintaining the link between pitch and stage, sponsoring the Happy Mondays as they bring the century to a close headlining Brixton Academy.

Wearing a football shirt to a festival or gig or club is a badge of identity as much as going to a game in a band T-shirt.

Spin through another reel or archive music and football images and there's Pete Doherty hanging out of the Libertines van in Admiral's iconic red and blue chest bar England shirt from 1982.

Admiral has always been associated with the music and football crossover, because the bands love the brand or the brand supports the bands. It's this history that's allowed the label to confidently begin its retrospective classic collaborations with The Jam, Style Council, and Bob Marley, and reissue The Rolling Stones' Admiral shirt from their 'Bridges To Babylon' tour.

The likes of Paul Weller don't go willy nilly into any old garment deal and he was really impressed with the pale blue shades of the classic Admiral 1982 England shirt, with a Jam logo inside a vintage button badge which also features the arrows that appeared on much of their sleeve art. Likewise, the Style Council collaboration used the original black and orange colourway that Weller announced would be synonymous with the band from the off in 1983.

With the Stones releasing Hackney Diamonds, their first album of new material in 18 years, Admiral revisited the shirts they produced for the band in the late '90s, adding a Paint It Black 'away' sherif to the 'Little Red Rooster' original.

Iconic bands, iconic brand. ●

> "I love what Admiral has done with these shirts, very cool."
>
> – Paul Weller, The Jam

A shirt for Rotherham's finest, The Reytons (far left). Credit: The Reytons

The collaboration between Admiral and Australian rock band, DMA's (left). Credit: DMA's

Decking out The Jam, with a crest inspired by an original 1980s pin badge (right).

2000–

Walthamstow '23–'25

Credit: Jake Green/ Leyton of London

Words: Andi Thomas

"Have nothing in your houses that you do not know to be useful or believe to be beautiful." So said William Morris, to an audience in Birmingham in 1880, pre-empting Marie Kondo by more than a century.

A football kit cheats the system, of course. It has to be useful. It's there in the very nature of the thing. If one even threatens to be useless, if it seems that a shirt might not serve its purpose of distinguishing the beloved Us from the hated Them, then it gets put away and the change strip comes out. The FA insists on it. Remember Manchester United's grey kit: Sir Alex Ferguson, among others, stated the players couldn't pick each other out against the crowd, ergo, a bit useless, ergo again, disappeared.

But football kits aren't just football kits (United's grey number was meant to look good with a pair of blue jeans.) This kit right here, the William Morris x Walthamstow 23-25 shirt, does its work for the players as they try and pass to their comrades. But upon release, it instantly became a sensation, a coveted object, for fans of the club, for fans of other clubs, for fans of interesting kits; perhaps even for football-agnostic fans of unusual things.

2000–

It has been shipped out to all seven continents; to 21 states of the USA; to Japan, Australia, Mexico, Argentina, and all across mainland Europe. The V&A have picked one up, along with the National Football Museum and the Westminster Menswear Archive, neatly illustrating the spread of this kit's appeal. Walthamstow MP Stella Creasy even wore the walk-out jacket into Parliament. Hansard does not record if she subsequently clapped her hands together and shouted: "Come on boys, into these, they don't fancy it."

William Morris was a Walthamstow boy, and the William Morris Gallery is a Walthamstow endeavour. There can't have been many football shirts designed in collaboration with museums, but Admiral worked closely with the gallery for more than three years to get this kit into the world. London, like any big city, can often feel like a lot of different places that just happen to be layered on top of one another: you go to your bits and other people go to their bits and the most anybody sees of one another is a few uncomfortable minutes on the bus. This, then, is an attempt to stitch together two Walthamstow institutions through the work of perhaps the most famous Walthamstowian. (And that's saying something: Walthamstow has raised or hosted two Prime Ministers, Attlee and Disraeli, along with 'One Size' Fitz Hall, Ian Dury, Vivian Stanshall and all of East 17.)

The pattern is Yare. It's not actually a Morris, as it goes; it's a wallpaper designed by John Henry Dearle, one of Morris's trainees, who took over as art director of Morris & Co. when the main man died. But then arts and crafts is a team game, and Morris lived a life of enthusiastic, sometimes chaotic, collaboration. Here and now, it's emblematically Morrisish, naturalistic shapes braided together in intricate and thrillingly unnatural symmetry; repeated, repeated, endlessly repeated. It is available not just as a football shirt but as a bookmark, sketchbook, gift wrap, soap and, of course, a face mask.

Credit: Jake Green/ Leyton of London

2000–

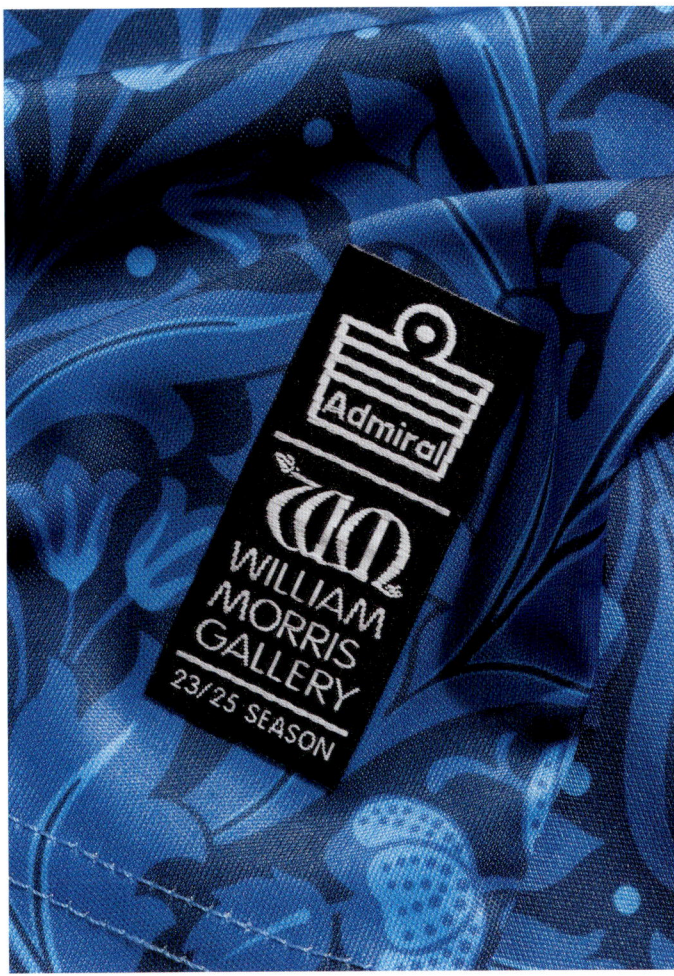

2000–

It's seeing the shirt in this company, among the other stuff, that really rams home what a delightful oddity it is. And reminds us what a delightful oddity he was. One of the great tensions of Morris's life and cultural afterlife was, and still is today, the tension between his socialist activism and his business practices: the class struggle on one hand, and on the other the successful operation of a firm making beautiful, exclusive, expensive objects. This isn't necessarily an intellectual contradiction; once you stop and think about it, champagne socialism sounds like a pretty decent way to organise society — bubbles for all! — and so does arts and crafts socialism. Arts and crafts capitalism, though: that can get pricey.

Football shirts can get pricey too, of course, particularly if you're just looking for a simple, useful t-shirt. But nevertheless, there is something excitingly inappropriate about seeing the print wrenched out of its context — down from the walls, out of the big art books — and slathered across something as defiantly quotidian as a football shirt. Culture? Here? Culture everywhere, why the hell not.

It's nice to think Morris might have approved, though his life seems to have been football-free; it was early in the game's organised history, and while he and his pre-Raphaelite associates were fond of a spot of medieval nostalgia, they preferred to focus on the lost age of chivalry, rather than two villages at war over a football somewhere nearby.

I asked a few people where on the pitch they thought William Morris might have played, had he swapped arts and crafts for mud and studs. It is testament to his polymath reputation that between all the answers, he's got most of the pitch covered: "enterprising" full-back; left of the two in the 2-3-5; fancy but inconsistent winger that "gets fouled a lot"; visionary playmaker; box-to-box no. 8, "hard in the tackle, linking up defence and attack while smashing in the occasional worldie." (Nobody, not a single person, thought he'd be a goalkeeper.) Personally, I lean towards the full-back theory, and not just because the beard and politics bring Paul Breitner to mind. There's something about the determined, busy, do-it-allness of Morris that seems to suit the job of getting up and down, up and down, creating and defending, defending and creating. Half Breitner, half Denis Irwin. Up and down like the shuttle of a loom.

Think of your most beloved football shirts, those that stir you when you see them. Think of why.

What do we mean, when we say a football shirt is beautiful? I'm going to say we often mean two things, muddled together, one to do with the shirt and one a question of something broader, bigger: the shirt and what happens with the shirt.

To illustrate: I support Wales. I own several Wales football shirts. There are those that I think are quite pretty in themselves, generally the ones that have a big splash of yellow and a natty collar. And then there is the one that I think is the most beautiful, and that has nothing to do with how it looks — it's a fairly plain white away shirt, almost totally unremarkable. It's because of what happened to me as I was wearing it. It's because of what the shirt did.

I was on a beach in Brazil during the 2014 World Cup, and a Brazilian man in a bright yellow Brazil shirt walked up to me, pointed, and said "Wales! Wales!" I said, "Yes!" It quickly became clear that he possessed little English and I had less Portuguese, so we lapsed into the common language of all roaming football fans: player names. I looked at the back of his shirt and said "Neymar!" Then again, in a sadder voice, "Neymar," as he was injured. I shook my head sympathetically. Then he pointed at the Wales badge on my chest, and opened his mouth to say, I was sure, "Gareth Bale." He'd moved for many millions to Real Madrid the summer before. He'd scored that goal against Barcelona in April. He'd scored in extra time against Atlético Madrid to win the Champions League just weeks before the World Cup began. Who else was he going to say?

As it turns out, "Craig Bellamy!"

The shirt did that. Or rather, the shirt was there while that happened. Football shirts are doing things, they are work clothes, and so their beauty is not just a question of form and style and colour, but of the work that they do, the work that is done in them. Think of your most beloved football shirts, those that stir you when you see them. Think of why. Some of them may just be lovely; some of them, I'm happy to bet, have been elevated by that goal, by that save, by that trophy or title challenge or chance meeting on Copacabana. They were bought for you by somebody you loved, now gone. They were bought for you by somebody you loved, still here, still loving you, wearing the same shirt each Saturday as you walk together to the same stadium. They might be ugly, shiny, disfigured by a sponsor that went bankrupt halfway through the season. Still beautiful.

Was Morris's Red House beautiful because of the proportions of the windows and the classical figures painted on the walls? Or was it beautiful because here he and his family and friends found, for a few short years, a new way of living and being and working together? Yes and yes.

For the rest of us, there's the gorgeous objects themselves. For some people, most likely Walthamstow FC fans and players, there will be work done with and in this kit that will make it the most gorgeous kit there ever was. Beautiful or useful? Why not both. ●

Credit: Jake Green/ Leyton of London

2000–

Shirt directory

Shirt
directory

England and Wales

Shirt directory

England and Wales

Charlton Athletic
1989–91

Third

Charlton Athletic
1991–92

Home

Charlton Athletic
1991–92

Away

Colchester United
2004–05

Home

Colchester United
2004–05

Away

Colchester United
2004–05

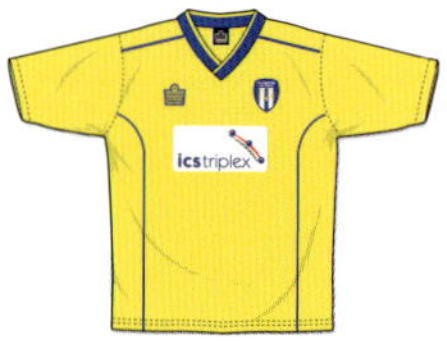

Third

Coventry City
1975–81

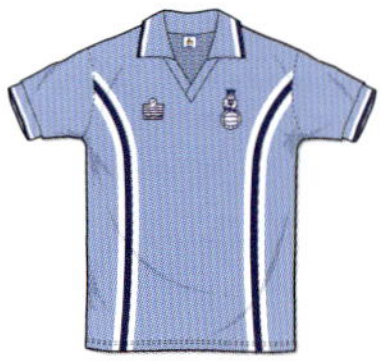

Home

Coventry City
1975–78

Away

Coventry City
1978–81

Away

Crystal Palace
1977–80

Home

Crystal Palace
1977–80

Away

Crystal Palace
1977–80

Third

Crystal Palace
1987–88

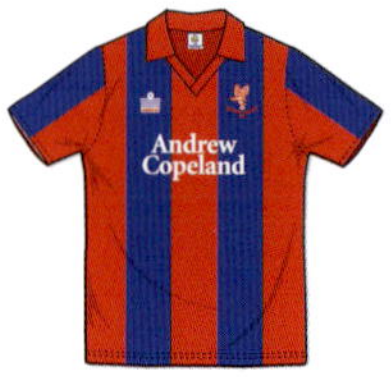

Home

Crystal Palace
1987–88

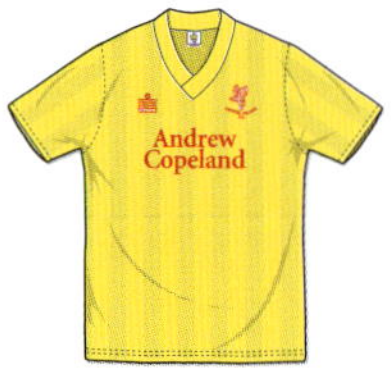

Away

Crystal Palace
1987–88

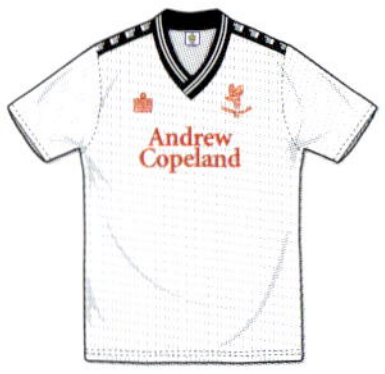

Third

Crystal Palace
1987–88

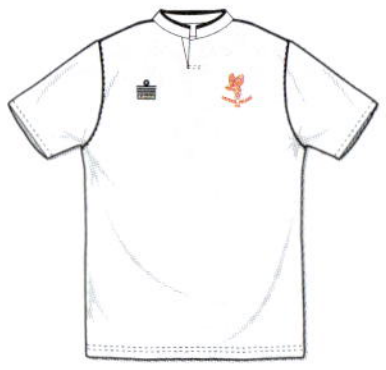

Fourth

Crystal Palace
2003–04

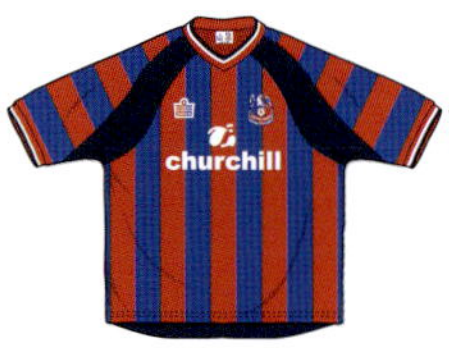

Home

Crystal Palace
2003–04

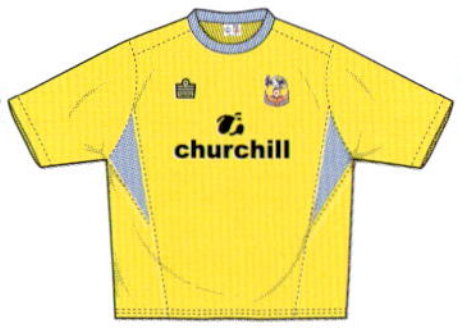

Away

Dagenham & Redbridge
2023-24

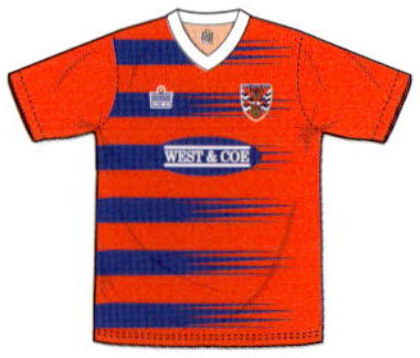

Home

Dagenham & Redbridge
2023-24

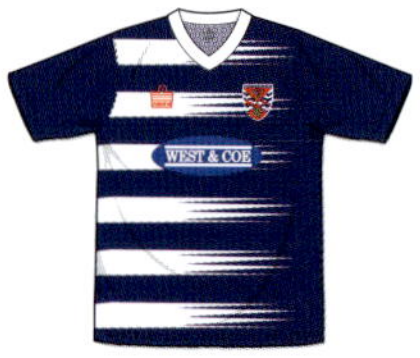

Away

Derby County
1984–85

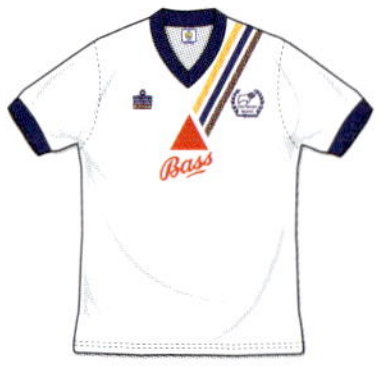

Home

Derby County
1984-85

Away

Exeter City
1975–77

Home

Exeter City
1975–77

Away

Grimsby Town
1977-80

Home

Grimsby Town
1977-81

Away

Grimsby Town
1980-81

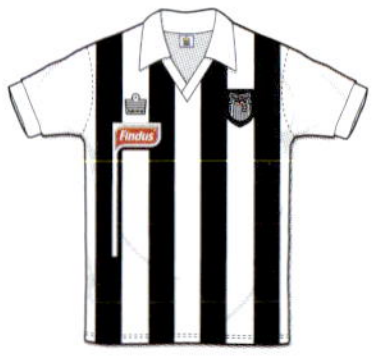

Home

Grimsby Town
1980-81

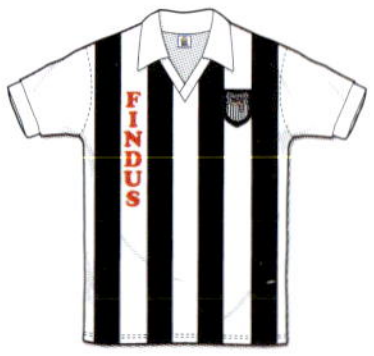

Home (Alternate)

Grimsby Town
1993-94

Home

Grimsby Town
1993-94

Away

Grimsby Town
1993-94

Third

Halifax Town
1983-84

Home

Halifax Town
1983-84

Away

Hartlepool United
1978-80

Home

Hartlepool United
1978-80

Away

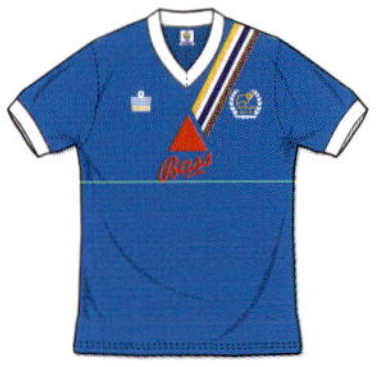

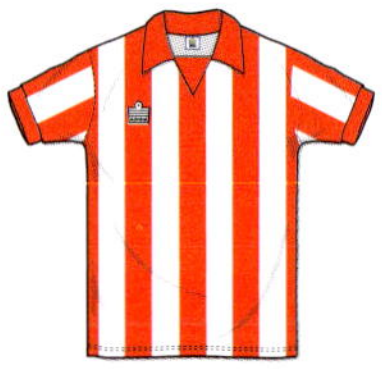

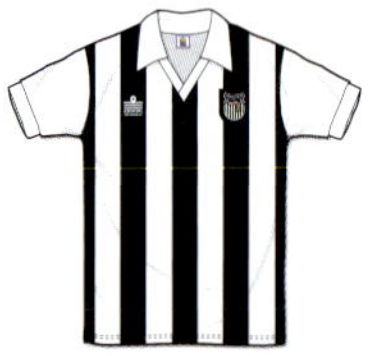

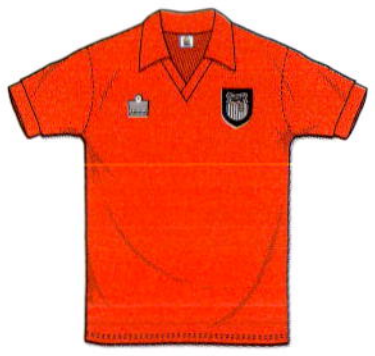

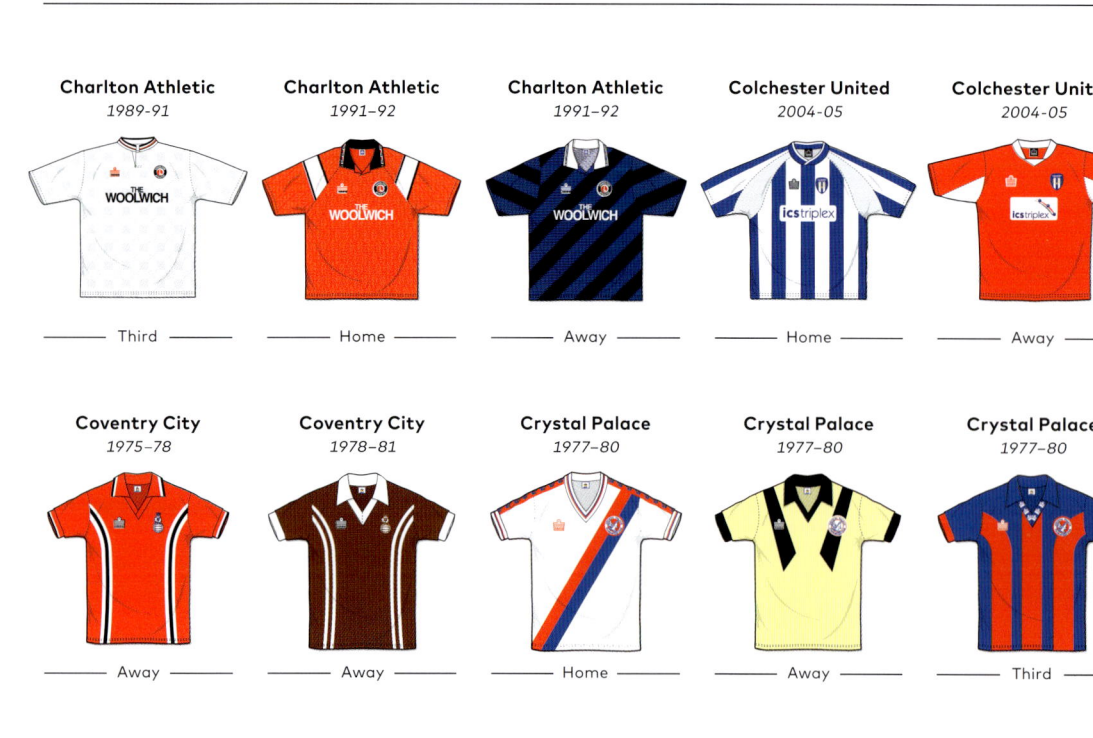

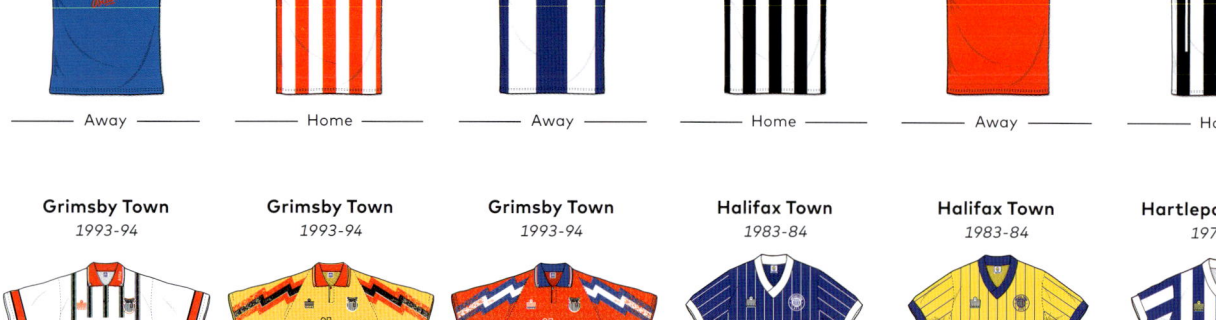

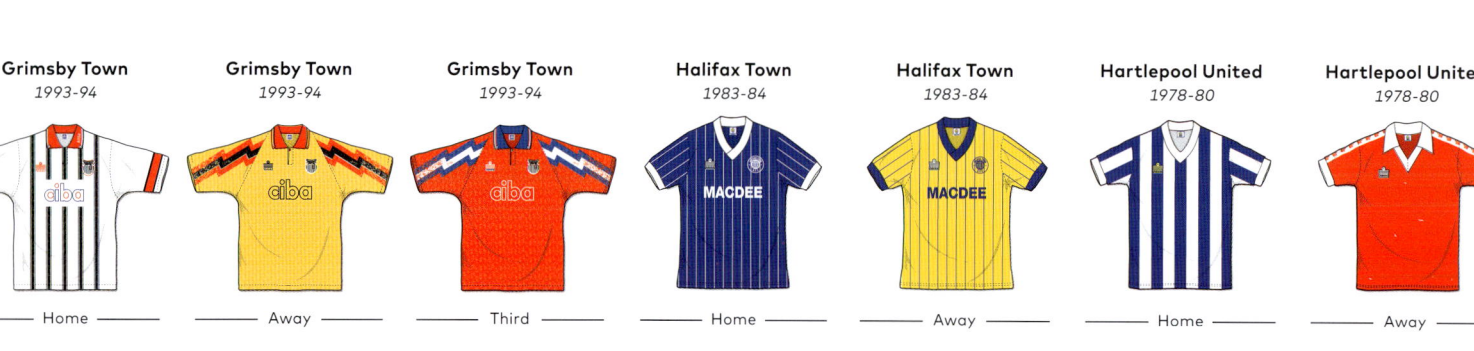

| Hartlepool United 1983-84 Home | Hartlepool United 1983-84 Away | Hartlepool United 1983-84 Third | Hereford United 1978-80 Home | Hereford United 1978-80 Away | Hereford United 1980-81 Home | Hereford United 1980-81 Away |

| Hereford United 1980-81 Third | Hereford United 1988-89 Home | Hereford United 1988-89 Away | Hereford United 2009-10 Home | Hereford United 2009-11 Away | Hereford United 2010-12 Home | Hereford United 2011-12 Away |

| Huddersfield Town 2003-05 Home | Huddersfield Town 2003-04 Away | Huddersfield Town 2004-05 Away | Huddersfield Town 2005-07 Home | Huddersfield Town 2005-07 Away/Third | Huddersfield Town 2006-07 Away | Hull City 1982-83 Home |

| Hull City 1982-83 Away | Hull City 1983-86 Home | Hull City 1983-86 Away | Hull City 1986-88 Home | Hull City 1986-88 Away | Kidderminster Harriers 2004-06 Home | Kidderminster Harriers 2004-06 Away |

| Leeds United 1973-76 Home | Leeds United 1973-74 Away | Leeds United 1974-81 Away | Leeds United 1975 European Cup Final | Leeds United 1976-81 Home | Leeds United 1992-93 Home | Leeds United 1992-93 Away |

Shirt directory

England and Wales

Newcastle United 1973–74 — Away	Newcastle United 1973–74 — Third	Norwich City 1976-81 — Home	Norwich City 1976-81 — Away	Notts County 1983-84 — Home	Notts County 1983-84 — Away	Notts County 1984-86 — Home
Notts County 1984-85 — Away	Notts County 1985-87 — Away	Notts County 1986-88 — Home	Notts County 1988-89 — Home	Notts County 1987-88 — Away	Notts County 1987-89 — Third/Away	Orient 1977-80 — Home
Orient 1977-80 — Away	Orient 1977-80 — Third	Orient 1977-80 — Fourth	Oxford United 1977-80 — Home	Oxford United 1977-80 — Away	Oxford United 1977-80 — Third	Peterborough United 2003-04 — Home
Peterborough United 2003-04 — Away	Peterborough United 2003-05 — Third/Away	Peterborough United 2004-05 — Home	Peterborough United 2005-06 — Home	Peterborough United 2005-06 — Away	Plymouth Argyle 1992-94 — Home	Plymouth Argyle 1992-94 — Away/Third
Plymouth Argyle 1992-93 — Third	Plymouth Argyle 1994-95 — Home	Plymouth Argyle 1993-96 — Away	Plymouth Argyle 1995-96 — Home	Port Vale 1974-76 — Home	Port Vale 1974-77 — Away	Port Vale 1976-77 — Home

Shirt directory

Whilst every effort has been made to ensure the completeness of the shirt directory, we appreciate there may be omissions and inaccuracies due to the historical data available at the time of print.

England and Wales

Port Vale 1978-79 Home	Port Vale 1978-79 Away	Portsmouth 1978-80 Home	Portsmouth 1978-80 Away	Portsmouth 1987-89 Home	Portsmouth 1987-89 Away	Portsmouth 1997-99 Home

Portsmouth 1997-98 Away	Portsmouth 1998-99 Away	Preston North End 2003-04 Home	Preston North End 2003-04 Away	Preston North End 2004-05 Home	Preston North End 2004-05 Away	Queens Park Rangers 1974-75 Home

Queens Park Rangers 1973-75 Away	Queens Park Rangers 1974-75 Away (Alternate)	Rotherham United 1977-80 Home	Rotherham United 1977-80 Away	Scarborough 1977-78 & 1979-82 Home	Scarborough 1977-78 & 1979-82 Away	Scunthorpe United 1975-76 Home

Scunthorpe United 1975-76 Away	Sheffield United 1975-77 Home	Sheffield United 1975-77 Away	Sheffield United 1977-79 Home	Sheffield United 1977-79 Away	Sheffield United 1977-79 Third	Shrewsbury Town 2019-20 Home

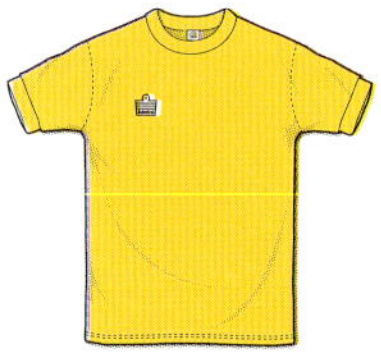

Shrewsbury Town 2019-20 Away	Shrewsbury Town 2019-20 Third	Shrewsbury Town 2020-21 Home	Shrewsbury Town 2020-21 Away	Southampton 1976-80 Home	Southampton 1976-80 Away	Southampton 1991-93 Home

Southampton 1991–93 Away	Southampton 1991–93 Third	Southend United 1975–76 Home	Southend United 1975–76 Away	Southend United 1976–78 Home	Southend United 1976–78 Away	Stevenage Borough 1982-83 & 1985-86 Home
Stoke City 1974-75 Home	Stoke City 1974-75 Away	Stoke City 1974-75 Third	Stoke City 1987-89 Home	Stoke City 1987-89 Away	Sutton United 1979 Alitalia Cup Final	Swansea City 1986-87 Home
Swansea City 1986-87 Away	Swansea City 1987-88 Home	Swansea City 1987-88 Away	Swansea City 1988-89 Home	Swansea City 1988-89 Away	Swindon Town 1977-78 Home	Swindon Town 1977-78 Away
Swindon Town 1978-80 Home	Swindon Town 1978-80 Away	Tottenham Hotspur 1977-80 Home	Tottenham Hotspur 1977-80 Away	Walsall 1982-83 Home	Walsall 1982-83 Away	Walsall 2009-10 Home
Walsall 2009-10 Away	Walsall 2010-11 Home	Walsall 2010-11 Away	Walsall 2011-12 Home	Walsall 2011-12 Away	Walthamstow 2023-24 Home	Walthamstow 2023-24 Away

Shirt directory

Whilst every effort has been made to ensure the completeness of the shirt directory, we appreciate there may be omissions and inaccuracies due to the historical data available at the time of print.

England and Wales

Scotland

Aberdeen 1976-79 Home	**Aberdeen** 1976-77 Away	**Aberdeen** 1977-78 Away	**Aberdeen** 1978-79 Away	**Albion Rovers** 1977-83 Home	**Albion Rovers** 1977-83 Away	**Alloa Athletic** 1976-77 Home
Arbroath 1977-80 Home	**Arbroath** 1977-80 Away	**Clyde** 1995-97 Home	**Clyde** 1995-97 Away	**Clyde** 1997-98 Home	**Clyde** 1997-98 Away	**Clydebank** 1975-77 Home
Clydebank 1975-77 Away	**Cowdenbeath** 1975-76 Home	**Cowdenbeath** 1975-76 Away	**Dumbarton** 1977-78 Home	**Dumbarton** 1978-79 Home	**Dundee** 1976-80 Home	**Dundee** 1976-80 Away
East Fife 1976-77 Home	**East Fife** 1976-77 Away	**East Fife** 1977-80 Home	**East Fife** 1977-80 Away	**East Fife** 1980-82 Home	**East Fife** 1980-82 Away	**Forfar Athletic** 1977-80 Home
Forfar Athletic 1977-80 Away	**Hamilton Academical** 1977-79 Home	**Heart of Midlothian** 1991-92 Home	**Heart of Midlothian** 1991-92 Away	**Heart of Midlothian** 1992-93 Home	**Heart of Midlothian** 1992-93 Away	**Kilmarnock** 1973-76 Home

Shirt directory

Whilst every effort has been made to ensure the completeness of the shirt directory, we appreciate there may be omissions and inaccuracies due to the historical data available at the time of print.

321

Scotland

Europe

Club	Season	Kit
Anagennisi Karditsa	2022-23	Home
Anagennisi Karditsa	2022-23	Away
Anagennisi Karditsa	2023-24	Home
Anagennisi Karditsa	2023-24	Away
Apollon Smyrnis	2022-23	Home
Apollon Smyrnis	2022-23	Away
Apollon Smyrnis	2022-23	Third
Aprilia	2013-14	Home
Aprilia	2013-14	Away
Ascoli	1994-95	Home
Ascoli	1994-95	Away
Astrea	1988-89	Home
Beitar Jerusalem	1983-84	Home
Beitar Jerusalem	1983-84	Away
Beitar Jerusalem	1983-84	Third
Beitar Jerusalem	1984-85	Home
Beitar Jerusalem	1984-85	Away
Beitar Jerusalem	1985-86	Home
Bologna	1978-79	Home
Bologna	1978-79	Away
Bologna	1978-79	Third
Citta di Sora	1998-00	Home
Citta di Sora	1998-00	Away
De Graafschap	1976-77	Home
De Graafschap	1976-77	Away
Dynamo Kyiv	1989-91	Home
Dynamo Kyiv	1989-91	Away
Dynamo Kyiv	1990-91	Third
Dynamo Kyiv	1991-92	Home
Dynamo Kyiv	1991-92	Away
Dynamo Kyiv	1991-92	Third
Egaleo	2023-24	Home
Egaleo	2023-24	Away
Egaleo	2023-24	Third
Eintracht Frankfurt	1976-78	Home

Shirt directory

Whilst every effort has been made to ensure the completeness of the shirt directory, we appreciate there may be omissions and inaccuracies due to the historical data available at the time of print.

Europe

Shirt directory

United States and Canada

United States and Canada

New York Cosmos *1979*  Home

New York Cosmos *1979*  Away

Oklahoma City Energy *2014-17*  Home

Oklahoma City Energy *2014-17*  Away

Philadelphia Fury *1978*  Home

Philadelphia Fury *1979-80*  Home

Portland Timbers *1976*  Home

Portland Timbers *1976*  Away

Portland Timbers *1978*  Home

Rochester Lancers *1980*  Home

Seattle Sounders *1979*  Home

Seattle Sounders *1979* Away

Seattle Sounders *1980-82* Home

Seattle Sounders *1980-82*  Away

Tampa Bay Rowdies *1978*  Home

Tampa Bay Rowdies *2013*  Home

Tampa Bay Rowdies *2013*  Away

Tampa Bay Rowdies *2013*  Third

Tampa Bay Rowdies *2014*  Home

Tampa Bay Rowdies *2014*  Away

Tampa Bay Rowdies *2014*  Third

Toronto Blizzard *1980*  Home

Tulsa Roughnecks *1978*  Home

Tulsa Roughnecks *1978*  Away

Vancouver Whitecaps *1978*  Home

Vancouver Whitecaps *1978*  Away

Vancouver Whitecaps *1979-80*  Home

Vancouver Whitecaps *1979-80*  Away

Rest of the World

Club	Year	Kit
Avispa Fukuoka	1994	Home
Avispa Fukuoka	1995	Home
Avispa Fukuoka	1995	Away
Bolivar	2011-12	Home
Bolivar	2011-12	Away
Bolivar	2012-13	Home
Bolivar	2012-13	Away
Bolivar	2012-13	Third
Bolivar	2013-14	Home
Bolivar	2013-14	Away
Gamba Osaka	1982	Home
Jubilo Iwata	2022-23	Home
Jubilo Iwata	2022-23	Away
Jubilo Iwata	2023-24	Home
Jubilo Iwata	2023-24	Away
Jubilo Iwata	2024-25	Home
Jubilo Iwata	2024-25	Away
Kerala Blasters	2017-18	Home
Kuala Lumpur City	1999–2000	Away
Pretoria Callies	1985-86	Home
Puerto Rico Islanders	2011-12	Home
Puerto Rico Islanders	2011-12	Away
Tacoma Stars	2011-12	Home
Tacoma Stars	2011-12	Away

Shirt directory

Whilst every effort has been made to ensure the completeness of the shirt directory, we appreciate there may be omissions and inaccuracies due to the historical data available at the time of print.

International

Shirt directory

Acknowledgements

Editorial team:

Writing, editing and commissioning – Halcyon Publishing (Adam Bushby and Rob MacDonald)
Design and art direction – Glory Studio (Lee Nash)

Additional contributors:

Shirt photography – James Hendley
Stock and retro photography – Graham Chadwick; Offside Sports Photography; Alamy; Colorsport; Mirrorpix; Jake Green/Leyton of London; James Pearson-Howes; Dordrecht FC; Malmö FF/Pierre Mens; Getty Images; Lee Brown
Shirt illustrations – John Devlin
Additional writing – Professor Andrew Groves; Professor Jean Williams; Jacqui McAssey; Rob Bagchi; Andi Thomas; Ian King; Ian Plenderleith; Jacob Steinberg; Mick Clifford; Andrew Lawn; Harry Pearson; Phil Lowe; Pete Jones; Alasdair McKillop; Daniel Gray; Grant Young; Paul and Mark Watson; James Bird; Maisie Adam; Daniel Chapman; James Brown

With thanks to:

Classic Football Shirts; Cult Kits; Rob Segal; Ian Adie; Mark Pritchard; Josh Chapman; Billy Pointer; Dan Warner; FourFourTwo magazine; Roger Wash; Nick Jones; Peris Hatton; Liam Ridley; Wouter Bos at Dordrecht FC; Paul Bowser at York City FC; Jordan Morcom at Swansea City FC; Linus Logren at Malmö FF; Barry Davies; Represent; Eddie Gray; Gerry Francis; Viv Anderson; Alan Curtis; Jonny Owen; Gary Lineker; Lou Macari; Gilbert Guyot; Tommy Hutchison; Roy Hodgson; Staffan Tapper; Alvin Martin; Martin O'Neill; Mark Hateley; Alan Shearer; Davide Gaultieri; Guy Mowbray; Andy McMillan; Sue Smith; Elis James; historicalkits.co.uk; footballkitarchive.co.uk; The DMA's; Gemma Thompson; Jim Brown; Atef Nahass; David Kilpatrick; Mundial; The Reytons; Bobby Bridgeman; Rich Mills; Peter Anderson; Frits Barend; Alan Smith; Alan Bennett; Lizzie Fee; Daniele Verri; Marc Jones; Scott Dawson; Paul O'Dowd; Michael Leckie; Mark Clack; Andy Wells; Lindsay Jelley, Daniel Visentini; Mike Walters; Phil Delves; Alyson Rudd; Charlie Eccleshare

©Admiral Sports. First published 2024. Printed in China.
ISBN (hardback): 978-1-9196-2409-9 / ISBN (paperback): 978-1-9196-2406-8

All rights reserved. No part of this publication may be reproduced, stored in a retrieval system or transmitted, in any form or by any means electronic, mechanical, photocopying, recording or otherwise, without the prior permission of Admiral Sports.